PROJECT SEASONS

PROJECT SEASONS

Hands-on activities for discovering
the wonders of the world.

written by Deborah Parrella

illustrated by Cat Bowman Smith

SHELBURNE FARMS

Shelburne, Vermont

Copyright © 1995 by Shelburne Farms.
All rights reserved. Revised Edition.
First printed in 1986 by Shelburne Farms.

3 5 7 9 10 8 6 4 2

Educators may photocopy these materials for the
non-commercial purpose of educational advancement.

Writer: Deb Parrella
Illustrator: Cat Bowman Smith
Book Designer: Elizabeth Nelson
Printer: Queen City Printers, Inc.
Editorial and Production Staff: Megan Camp, Margaret Boyle Campbell
Copy Editors: Peter B. Camp, Castle Freeman, Deidre Stapleton

PROJECT SEASONS ISBN # 0-9642163-0-2
Library of Congress CIP information is available.
Printed in Burlington, Vermont in the United States of America.
by Queen City Printers, Inc.
Printed on recycled paper.

The Stewardship Institute
Shelburne Farms
Shelburne, Vermont 05482
Phone: 802-985-8686
Fax: 802-985-8123

Acknowledgements

The Board of Directors of Shelburne Farms will always be deeply grateful to everyone who has helped create and nurture our education programs.

We thank all our supporters for providing the resources that have sustained our curriculum and staff development, annual operations and facility improvements over the years.

We extend special thanks to *The Burton G. Bettingen Corporation, The Freeman Foundation, NYNEX-Vermont, Queen City Printers, Inc., and The Vermont Community Foundation* for providing the financial support needed to publish this second edition of PROJECT SEASONS. Their incredible generosity, faith, and patience made this publication possible.

We want to express our gratitude to Johnson State College, the University of Vermont, and the Vermont Department of Education for their ongoing support and cooperation.

We also want to thank the volunteers, student interns, teachers, and advisors who so generously helped make PROJECT SEASONS a reality. Finally, our thanks to Megan Camp and Deb Parrella, who have collaborated since 1985 in the development of PROJECT SEASONS and profoundly touched so many teachers and students, and to their predecessors and to all their colleagues over the years: David Barash, Anne Campbell, Donald Campbell, Maggie Charpentier, Lissa Bogner, Judy Elson, Susan Gilmore, Eileen Growald, Suzy Kneeland, Lark Lieb, Mindy Liebert, Marilyn Neagley, Scout Proft, Julie Rickman, Stevie Spencer, Pat Straughan, Caroline Warner, Reina Warren, and Linda Wellings. Their collective dedication, tireless and careful work, wholehearted commitment to excellence in environmental education, great warmth, spirit, and sense of fun have inspired us all.

Thanks from the Writer

This book came about thanks to the curiosity, ideas, and enthusiasm of thousands of Vermont students and their teachers who encouraged all of us in the Education Program at Shelburne Farms to think of ways to make science and agriculture engaging and fun. They are the inspiration for these activities!

This book is really a collection of ideas gathered from the many talented and creative people with whom I have had the pleasure of working over the years. They have all added their own special touch to the activities in this book. Many thanks to Julie Rickman, Reina Warren, Scout Proft, Anne Campbell, Judy Elson, Linda Wellings, Susan Gilmore, Pat Straughan, Caroline Warner, Mindy Liebert, Sharon Behar, Heidi Palola, Lisa Pierce, Ginger Johnson, and especially to Megan Camp who taught me how to make science fun and was a source of creative inspiration for many of the activities.

In addition to wonderful staff, our programs and activities have been enriched over the years by the creativity and hard work of a dedicated group of volunteers and college interns. Thanks to the University of Vermont Environmental Studies Department and especially to Tom Hudspeth, who directs many outstanding interns our way.

Thanks to Alec Webb, President of Shelburne Farms, the Board of Directors and particularly the Education Committee and its Chair, Casey Murrow, for their support, encouragement, and enthusiasm for this and all the work of the Education Program.

This book was a pleasure to write thanks to: Cat Bowman Smith, whose illustrations make the activities come alive; Megan Camp, whose ongoing support and dedication to this project and all the educational work at Shelburne Farms kept me focused; Meg Boyle Campbell, whose careful editing makes directions clear, concise and consistent; and Elizabeth Nelson, graphic designer extraordinaire, whose keen eye and fine sense of design pulls it all together.

Finally special thanks and a big hug for my family, Everett, Nicholas, and Hannah, who gave me the space, time, and encouragement to complete this book. Come on Nicky and Hannah, let's go out and play!

Introduction

PROJECT SEASONS is a wonderful collection of creative teaching ideas and practical activities for educators who want to integrate science-based environmental education into their curriculum.

The Stewardship Institute of Shelburne Farms published the first edition of PROJECT SEASONS in 1986 as part of a professional development program designed to give kindergarten through sixth grade teachers the confidence, motivation and skills to become more effective science and environmental educators. The goal of the Institute is to empower students and teachers with the awareness, knowledge, skills and attitudes needed to become active stewards of the earth.

PROJECT SEASONS is rooted in the belief that direct contact with agriculture and the natural world at an early age has a powerful life-long impact — this is when a child first begins to develop a conservation ethic. Classroom, pre-school and after-school teachers, summer camp instructors, and parents will find PROJECT SEASONS helpful in cultivating an awareness and appreciation of agriculture and natural resources.

Increasing science and environmental literacy is a prerequisite for preparing future generations for the difficult natural resource choices that lie ahead. We have developed these hands-on activities to show children how all things are interconnected and to nurture their natural curiosity by helping them to question and seek answers. Through investigative activities, teachers will increase science literacy in a way which is meaningful and builds a fundamental ethic of stewardship.

For ten years, PROJECT SEASONS has served thousands of students and teachers from Vermont and around the world and we are very pleased to offer this updated and expanded second edition. We hope you enjoy using it and that you have a chance to participate in one of our programs or visit us in Shelburne. We'll look forward to hearing from you.

Megan Camp
Shelburne Farms Program Director

How To Use This Book

Project Seasons follows the school-year seasons of Fall, Winter, and Spring. Each season contains thematic groups of activities that reflect changes on the farm and in the natural world. Fall themes include Harvest, Farm Life and History, and Soil and Worms. Winter themes include Forests, Snow, Animals in Winter, and Tracks. Spring themes include Maple Sugaring, Green Plants, Birds, Insects, and Water.

The format of PROJECT SEASONS was designed by teachers to be clear, simple, and easy to use. Each activity is written to stand alone with its own introduction and conclusion. Often they are part of thematic series of activities. Where applicable, we present the activities in the order we teach them at Shelburne Farms. Most of the activities can be adapted for any season, different geographic locations and can be taught anytime throughout the school year.

For each activity, we list the learning objective, recommended grade level, groupings, materials, and approximate time. Most activities can be modified to accommodate different grade levels or time constraints. The directions include an introductory idea or question along with a sequence of steps for each activity. Recommendations for prior knowledge, experiences or activities appear in italics before the numbered steps in the directions. Extensions present additional related activities and teaching ideas. Many of these were developed by teachers who participated in our workshops over the years. We encourage you to create, record, and share your own.

Throughout the book additional background information is provided for some of the activities. This information provides a closer look at the topic addressed in the activity and enriches both the teacher and students understanding the topic. These "Close Ups " are marked by a magnifying glass and the appropriate seasonal symbol.

The Bibliography at the end of PROJECT SEASONS offer a selection of story books, children's information/ activity books and teacher resource/activity books on all the themes introduced in the book. Most of these are available at your local bookstore or library.

Table of Contents

FALL

W I N T E R

TREES

SNOW

ANIMALS and TRACKS

ANIMALS and TRACKS *(continued)*

S P R I N G

MAPLE SUGARING

WATER

WATER WIZARD LEARNING STATIONS

MORE WATER

FALL ACTIVITIES

Harvest Blanket

Objective:
Students will learn examination and description skills by identifying fruits and vegetables without using their sight.

Grade Level: K-5

Groupings: Entire class

Materials: A collection of different fruits and vegetables typically harvested in your area; paper grocery bag; large blanket.

Time Allotment: 30 minutes

Directions:
Before the activity, collect a variety of fruits, vegetables and seeds typically harvested in your area and store them in a paper grocery bag so the students can't see them.

1. Spread out the blanket and place under it one vegetable, fruit or seed from the collection you have assembled in the paper grocery bag. Make sure the students can't see what's under the blanket.

2. Ask five or six children to sit or lie on their stomachs around the blanket. The rest of the children should make a circle around the outside of this group.

3. Have the children put their hands under the blanket. Explain that they will be passing a fruit, vegetable or seed around the circle underneath the blanket. Each student will get a chance to handle the object. Remind the children not to peek or to mention what they think the object is.

4. Explain that each student will feel the object and give an adjective or clue to describe it. With younger students, ask specific questions to elicit adjectives. Is it hard or soft? Long or short? Big or little? After all the students have given an adjective or clue, have the rest of the class try to guess what fruit, vegetable or seed it is. Does the group who felt the object agree on the type of fruit, vegetable or seed it is? Why or why not?

Extensions:

a. *In place of fruits, vegetables and seeds, use a variety of objects related to a specific theme. For example, you many use items made from trees, objects found at the seashore, or things that can or can't be recycled. For objects of each variety, have the students guess their relationship to each other. This is a good introduction to a new topic or unit.*

b. *As the students around the blanket offer words describing the hidden object, have another student record their words on the blackboard. Have the students write a poem using the words.*

c. *For objects you are unable to pass around conveniently, have the students come up one at a time and feel the object under the blanket. Have the students return to their seats and draw what they felt. Remind the children to keep their guesses and drawings a secret. Have the students compare drawings and then reveal the object.*

Directions: *(continued)*

5. Reveal the fruit, vegetable or seed and let another group of five or six children take a turn feeling and describing a new object under the blanket.

6. Use the fruits, vegetables and seeds to make a snack.

Sort by Sound

Objective:
Students will increase observation skills by sorting a variety of seeds based on sound.

Grade Level: K-5

Groupings: Entire class and small groups

Materials: Coffee cans each filled 1/4 to 1/2 full with a different type of seed (be sure these cans have tight-fitting opaque lids); clear plastic bags filled with the same selection of seeds.

Time Allotment: 15-20 minutes

Directions:
Choose seeds for this activity that vary in size, shape, weight and hardness. For younger students, use seeds in which these characteristics contrast greatly. For older students, select seeds with more similar characteristics.

SEEDS TO USE

Large	Medium	Small
Walnuts in the shell	Corn	Grass seed
Almonds in the shell	Peas	Ground coffee
Lima beans	Whole coffee beans	Oatmeal
Chick peas	Sunflower seeds	Wheat berries

1. Pass out the coffee cans to several students in the class. Make sure they can't see the seeds in the cans. Explain that each can is filled with a different type of seed. One at a time, have each student shake his or her coffee can in two different ways (up and down, from side to side, rolling the can, etc.). Ask the class to listen carefully to the sounds the seeds make.

2. Break the class into small groups, each with a can of seeds. Have the students in the groups guess the characteristics of the seeds inside. Are they big? Small? Hard? Soft? Round? Smooth? With edges? Are there many seeds in the can, or just a few?

Extensions:

a. *Place the same type of seeds in two coffee cans. Make a collection of at least three different types of seeds and their matches (a total of six cans). Let the students pair the cans that sound alike.*

b. *After sorting the seeds by sound, graph the seeds by size. Students can glue the seeds onto a graph.*

Directions: (continued)

3. Show the students the selection of seeds in the clear plastic bags. Explain that the bags and the coffee cans contain the same types of seeds. Ask each group of students to match by sound the seeds in their coffee can with the seeds they see in one of the plastic bags.

4. Have the students discuss the choices in their small group.

5. Once everyone has made a decision, bring the class together and ask the groups, one at a time, to shake their coffee can and tell their choice of seeds. Have the rest of the class show with thumbs up or down whether they agree or disagree with each choice.

6. Open the cans one at a time to check the guesses.

Grocery Bag Botany

Objective:
Students will learn to identify and classify the parts of plants we eat.

Grade Level: 2-6

Groupings: Entire class and small groups

Materials: Several grocery bags filled with a selection of food items that come from plants (see *Grocery List* for possible ideas); six boxes labeled with the six different plant parts we eat (roots, stems, leaves, flowers, fruit, seeds).

Time Allotment: 30 minutes

GROCERY LIST

Roots: *carrots, beets, turnips, radishes, ginger, gingersnaps*

Stems: *asparagus, celery, cinnamon, onions, potatoes, potato chips*

Leaves: *lettuce, cabbage, sauerkraut, spinach, tea, oregano, basil, many other herbs*

Flowers: *broccoli, cauliflower, whole cloves, artichokes*

Fruits: *tomatoes, tomato sauce, salsa, cucumbers, oranges, orange juice, grapes, raisins, grape jelly, green peppers, zucchini, apples, applesauce, bananas, avocados*

Seeds: *corn, corn chips, wheat, bread, crackers, pasta, cereal, cookies, oats, oatmeal, granola bars, peas, peanut butter, chocolate bars, coffee, rice cakes*

Directions:
For this activity, use empty containers or packaging of various food items such as cereal boxes, potato chip bags, tomato sauce cans, etc. A few items of fresh produce can be added the day of the activity.

1. Begin the discussion by asking the students if they ate any plants for breakfast. List the foods they mention on the board. Tell the class that you had a delicious breakfast of plant parts, explaining that people rarely eat a whole plant. Brainstorm with the class the six different parts of a plant that people eat: roots, stems, leaves, flowers, fruits, and seeds. Tell the students you ate a bowl of oval, flattened seeds and dried, brown, shriveled fruit with fragrant, crushed bark sprinkled on top. You also drank a cup of dried leaves soaked in water with a spoonful of granulated stems and a slice of yellow fruit. Can they guess what you ate? (A bowl of oatmeal and raisins with cinnamon sprinkled on top, and a cup of tea with a spoonful of sugar and a slice of lemon.) Review the class' list and classify the foods by the part of the plant from which they came.

2. Explain to the class that they will be doing a sorting activity based on the different plant parts that people eat. In the center of the room set up six boxes labeled with the six different plant parts: roots, stems, leaves, flowers, fruits, and seeds.

Extensions:

a. *Write up a snack menu using some food items from the sorting activity. Can the students guess what you will be serving? Then serve the real thing and enjoy the roots, stems, leaves, flowers, fruits and/or seeds.*

b. *Share the song "Roots, Stems, Leaves" from the tape **Dirt Made My Lunch** by the Banana Slug String Band (available through **Let's Get Growing Catalog**, 1900 Commercial Way, Santa Cruz, CA 95065, 800-408-1868). Teach the class the chorus then divide them into six groups. Have each group learn one stanza of the song. Then perform the song together.*

Directions: (continued)

3. Divide the students into small groups. Bring out a grocery bag for each group, filled with a different selection of food items made from plants. Explain to the students that they will need to look over the food items in their bags and decide which plant parts they are made from. As a decision is made for each item, one person from that group should place that food item in the box labeled with the correct plant part.

4. When all the groups have finished sorting the contents of their grocery bags, have the class look at the items placed in each of the plant part boxes. Does everyone agree with the contents? Can the students think of any other examples of foods that might be included in each of the six categories?

5. Have each student write up a breakfast, lunch or dinner menu based on the plant parts he or she would eat, similar to the breakfast menu presented at the beginning of the activity. Students will then read their menus to their small groups, and the groups will try to guess what foods the menus describe.

Vegetable Twister

Objective:
Students will review the parts of plants we eat.

Grade Level: 1-4

Groupings: Small groups

Materials: Old bed sheet; waterproof fabric crayons, markers or paints; cardboard; poster board; metal fastener.

Time Allotment: 2 hours to make; 15 minutes to play.

Directions:

1. Make a *Vegetable Twister* board from an old top sheet. Divide the sheet into a grid of 16 equal spaces (four rows of four). Using waterproof fabric crayons, paints or markers, draw an assortment of common fruits and vegetables. You will need at least two representatives for each of the six basic plant parts: roots, stems, leaves, flowers, fruits and seeds. (See *Grocery List,* page 7, for examples.) Your students can help create the board by drawing an assigned fruit or vegetable in a grid space.

2. Construct a game spinner. Use a large piece of cardboard for the base and divide it into four quarters. Label the quarters respectively, from top to bottom, left hand, right hand, left foot, right foot. Cut a circle from poster board and divide it into six equal parts. Label each section with one of the six plant parts: roots, stems, leaves, flowers, fruits, seeds. Cut out an arrow from the poster board. Attach the plant parts circle and arrow to the cardboard base with a metal fastener. Now you and your students are ready to play.

3. Tell the students that *Vegetable Twister* will test their knowledge of the parts of plants that they commonly eat. Explain the rules of the game. Four students can play at a time. Each stands along one edge of the board. You will spin the inner

Extensions:

a. As a review to an Animal Tracking unit (see tracking activities pages 149-170), make a "Track Twister" by drawing different animal footprints on a sheet. Simply replace the plant part circle with a new poster board circle identifying the different animal tracks. Then try "Leaf Twister," "Winter Twig Twister," "Soil Twister," or even "Cow Twister"! The possibilities are endless. You can scale the game down for younger students by varying the information on the inner circle dial, making it a simple matching activity.

Directions: (continued)

circle and then the arrow. The arrow will indicate which limb must be placed on a particular plant part. When you announce the plant part and limb, the first player must locate the correct plant part and place the appropriate limb in that position.

4. This continues for each student for several rounds. At each turn, it becomes more difficult to maneuver around other players to place the appropriate limb in the correct spot. This is when the fun begins. Anyone who falls down or places their hand or foot in the wrong place is out of the game, until only one student remains "planted" on the board. That student is the winner and can challenge three more people to play.

A-Maize-ing Grain

Objective:
Students will learn about the historical and modern-day significance of corn as a food item.

Grade Level: K-3

Groupings: Individuals or pairs

Materials: Grocery bag full of food items that contain some form of corn (see *Corny Facts*, page 12); wooden bowls (one for every student or pair); large rocks that fit inside the wooden bowls (ask student to bring these from home); heavy canvas cut in circles big enough to cover the inside surface of the bowl (one for every student or pair); whole corn kernels (available from a health food store or food cooperative); ingredients and cookware for *Indian Corn Pancake* (see recipe, page 12); spoons.

Time Allotment: 30 minutes

Directions:
1. Explain to the students that the mainstay of the early New England settlers' diet was Indian corn or maize. They ate it 365 days a year. The Native Americans taught the settlers how to grow, grind and cook corn or maize in several dishes. In fact, corn first originated in the Americas. Columbus and other early European explorers were introduced to it upon their arrival by the Native Americans and shared this discovery with the rest of Europe. Popcorn was even served at the first Thanksgiving dinner the Pilgrims celebrated with the Native Americans. Do we still eat corn today? In what types of dishes? Is it still an important food source? How often in a week do we eat corn?

2. Pass around the bag of food items. Ask the students to take one item from the bag. Have the students quickly sort themselves into two groups based on whether or not their food item contains corn. Now ask them to look more carefully and read the label on their food item. Were they surprised? Discuss the various corn by-products that are used in everyday foods. (See *Corny Facts*, page 12)

3. Tell the students that they will get a chance to prepare and sample corn the way the Native Americans and early settlers enjoyed it. Have individual students (or pairs) take out their wooden bowls and rocks. Explain that these are similar to the tools the early settlers used to grind their corn. They placed the corn in three foot stumps which had been hollowed out slightly. Wooden clubs or **billets** suspended from thin saplings over the stump were used to grind the corn into meal. Let each student take a handful of corn kernels and place them in their bowl. Pass out circles of canvas cloth. Direct the students to cover their corn with the cloth before they begin to pound. This keeps the corn from flying out of the bowl.

4. Have the students (or pair, taking turns) pound the corn with their rocks until the kernels are completely crushed and it resembles coarse cornmeal. To pass the time, try pounding out a rhythmic pattern for the students to copy. Let them take turns creating new pounding patterns. You can also have the students make up chants to sing while pounding.

Extensions:

a. Ask the students to read the labels on the various foods they eat and drink for an entire day. Did anything contain some form of corn? Make a class list of all the foods that are made with corn products. Have each student keep a tally of how many days in a week they ate corn.

c. Read THE POPCORN BOOK by Tomie dePaola (Scholastic, 1978) and then enjoy a snack of popcorn. In a large open space, set a popcorn popper in the center of a large sheet. Add one teaspoon of oil and popcorn. Plug in the popper but don't put on the cover. Have the students stand a few feet from the edge of the sheet and watch the corn pop. Then cover the popper, unplug it and let the students gather and eat the popcorn.

INDIAN CORN PANCAKE RECIPE

Grind a handful of dried corn until all the kernels have been finely crushed. If the grain is fine, the pancake will have a better consistency and taste. Add enough water to cover the ground cornmeal and stir. This allows the tougher husks to rise and float on the water. Pour them off with the excess water. Mix the wet corn-meal with honey (approximately 1 tablespoon) until it holds together. Form a patty. Cook it on a hot griddle, turning once. The final product tastes a bit like crackerjacks or caramel corn as the honey caramelizes and holds the pancake together.

Directions: (continued)

5. When his or her corn is ground, have each student measure the remaining ingredients and mix an Indian Corn Pancake in his or her bowl. The teacher can then fry the pancakes in a skillet. Serve and enjoy them together.

CORNY FACTS

As American as Mom, apple pie, baseball and... corn?! Corn originated in the Americas. Just as in the time of the early settlers, corn is still the number one grain grown today. If all the corn fields in the United States were put together, they would cover an area the size of Colorado. Now that is a lot of corn! And just as the early settlers, we eat corn 365 times a year. Surprised? Aside from obvious foods like sweet corn, popcorn, and cornflakes, a surprising number of processed foods are made with two important corn by-products. Look at the list of foods below and see if you, too, eat corn everyday.

Products that contain corn starch, a common food additive derived from the starchy endosperm of the corn kernel: baked goods made with baking powder, puddings, gravies, candy, canned soups and vegetables, salad dressings, and mayonnaise.

Corn syrup, a sweet derivative of corn, is used in a variety of candy, chocolates, chewing gum, crackers, doughnuts, cakes, pies, breakfast cereals, catsup, ice cream, soft drinks, canned and frozen fruits and vegetables, frankfurters and luncheon meat, peanut butter and jelly, to name a few! A most a-maize-ing grain, wouldn't you say?

Lucky Harvest Dolls

Objective:
Students will make a good luck harvest figure from corn husks.

Grade Level: 1-3

Groupings: Entire class

Materials: Corn husks (available in autumn from local farmers or florists); yarn; glue; scissors; markers; fabric scraps; magnets (optional).

Time Allotment: 20 minutes

Directions:

1. Tell the students that throughout history, in many different cultures, good luck harvest figures were made to celebrate each harvest and insure a good one the following year. In many cultures, the last sheaf of grain cut was considered special. It was bundled and tied together and paraded through the village as part of a harvest festival. Stalks of grain were braided together, hung in homes as decorative good luck charms, and saved until the following year when new ones were made. Explain to the students that they will be making their own good luck harvest doll from an important American grain. It was given to the first settlers by the Native Americans. Can they guess what the grain is? (Corn.)

2. Explain that you will demonstrate how each step is done. Pass out two or three large pieces of corn husk to each student. Ask them to place them on top of one another and fold them in thirds lengthwise, making a long narrow piece. Have the students hold up their work after they have completed each step. This lets you monitor progress and correct mistakes.

3. Next ask them to fold this long piece in half. Remind them to keep the folds hidden on the inside. Explain that this piece will be the body of the doll.

4. Pass out two pieces of yarn to each student. Ask them to tie one piece of yarn a little below the top fold to create the head of the doll. Suggest they work in pairs to help each other secure the yarn. One person can hold the yarn tightly with a finger, while the other completes the knot.

a. *Visit a nearby farm and get permission to pick and husk corn for harvest doll supplies.*

b. *Get directions and supplies from a craft store to make simple wheat weavings — the traditional good luck harvest symbols.*

Directions: (continued)

5. Distribute a smaller piece of corn husk to each student. Explain that this will form the arms of the doll. Ask them make it narrow by folding it in half or in thirds lengthwise. Next have them fold it in half so it is half as long, with the folds to the inside. Have them slip this piece crossways below the head of the doll, between the main fold in the body.

6. Tie the second piece of yarn below the arms to form the waist of the doll. For a doll wearing pants, use scissors to split the section below the waist in two. Use two extra pieces of yarn to tie off the pants at the ankles. For a doll wearing a skirt, tuck extra pieces of corn husk under the waist band to form a full skirt.

7. Glue corn silk or yarn to the head for hair and make facial features using markers or seeds. Decorate the dolls with beads or buttons and use fabric scraps to make aprons, vests or other simple clothes.

8. Complete the doll by gluing a magnet or a loop of yarn on the back. Suggest they hang it in their homes, in their kitchens or on their refrigerators as good luck symbols of the harvest.

Magic Bread

Objective:
Students will learn about the importance of wheat in our diet and how it is processed to make bread.

Grade Level: K-4

Groupings: Small groups

Materials: Wheat berries (available from health food stores); wheat stalks (available from florists or local farmers); grain mill (optional); bleached and unbleached white flour; whole wheat flour; hand lenses; sifters; *Magic Bread* ingredients (see recipe, page 17); plastic measuring spoons and cups; grease pencils; towels; extra yeast and sugar; small plastic cups; margarine tubs or other container that plastic cups can fit inside.

Time Allotment: 30 minutes plus baking and eating time

Directions:

1. Tell the students there is an important seed most people eat everyday. Can they guess what it is? Ask them cup their hands in front of them, close their eyes and you will give them a clue. Place some wheat berries in each student's hands. Ask them to feel and smell them. Suggest they even taste them by grinding and crushing them with their back molars, releasing the flavor. Finally, hold up some wheat stalks and have them open their eyes for another clue. Can they guess its identity now? Explain that wheat is an important grain. Pass a stalk to every two or three students and ask them to find the wheat berries inside.

2. Explain that most people don't recognize wheat berries or seeds because we usually eat them after they have been ground and baked into a variety of foods. What are ground wheat seeds called? (Flour.) Ask the students to list things made from flour (bread, cereal, muffins, pasta, cookies, cakes, pizza, etc.). Have the students share what they had for breakfast. How many students have already eaten this seed today or will eat it for lunch?

3. Tell the students they will have a chance to make their own flour. Show the students the grain mill and explain how it works. Inside the mill are two flat stones, one on top of the other. The seeds fall between the two and are crushed. Let students take turns adding wheat berries to the mill and grinding them into flour. Set up bowls of different types of wheat flour for students to investigate while they are waiting their turn. Provide hand lenses and encourage them to use all of their senses. How does the flour they made compare to these? Have them sift their flour and compare again. (If you are unable to obtain a grain mill, grind small amounts of grain using a mortar and pestle, a rock in a wooden bowl or a food processor.) Stress the difference between whole wheat and white flour. Whole wheat flour is made from the entire seed — the endosperm, germ and bran — and contains natural B vitamins and protein. Unbleached white flour has the germ and bran removed.

4. Divide the class into groups of 5 to 10 students. Tell them they will be making their own loaves of *Magic Bread*. Provide each group with a recipe, mixing bowl, measuring cups and spoons. Lead all the groups through the recipe, having

Extensions:

a. *Have the students dramatize the bread baking process. Have them begin as wheat berries and lead them through the process from mill to mixing bowl, through kneading, rising, shaping and baking. Sampling bread is a good ending to this activity.*

b. *Get plenty of wheat stalks and let the students thresh and winnow it. Spread an old sheet or piece of plastic tarp on the ground outside and let the students stomp on the wheat stalks to remove the berries from the seed head. Next, have them winnow it to separate the wheat berries from the chaff. Ask the students to work in pairs and give them each a dish towel. Have them add a handful of the threshed wheat to the towel. Direct them to pull the towel tight between them and gently bounce the wheat up and down. Ask them stand so that the wind blows across the towel. The wheat chaff will blow away and the berries should collect in the bottom of the towel.*

c. *Grains are important in many cultures. Show the students bags of eight common grains (wheat, oats, corn, rye, rice, barley, millet, buckwheat). Have them match the bags to food made from these grains.*

Directions: (continued)

students take turns adding ingredients. Throughout the discussion, highlight what each ingredient does in the recipe (see **Flour Power**, page 17).

5. Have the students in each group take turns kneading the dough then set it aside. Ask them to make predictions as to how high it will rise. Have them mark the outside of their bowls with a grease pencil and initial their predictions. Then have them cover the bowls with a towel and set aside in a warm place to rise for 30 minutes to one hour.

6. While the dough is rising, have small groups of students try the following experiment to see the yeast in action. Fill a plastic cup 3/4 full of warm water. Set the cup inside an empty plastic margarine tub. Add 1 teaspoon of yeast and 1 teaspoon of sugar. As the yeast begins to 'eat' the sugar, it releases bubbles of carbon dioxide gas which form a head similar to a root beer float. This head will grow until it spills over the top of the glass. (Students can also try making a similar solution of warm water, yeast and sugar in a small soda bottle and cover the top with a balloon. As the yeast starts to feast, the carbon dioxide gas will expand the balloon.)

7. After the bread has risen, ask each group to punch down their dough and divide it evenly among themselves. Each individual can then form their dough into an imaginative shape. Have the students place their 'loaves' on a baking sheet, let them rise for a second time, then bake according to the recipe. Together enjoy fresh hot bread with homemade butter (see **Butter Making** page 49).

© 1995 PROJECT SEASONS, Shelburne Farms, Shelburne, VT.

MAGIC BREAD RECIPE

2 pkg. active dry yeast
1-1/4 cups warm water
4 to 4-1/2 cups flour (mix 1 part whole wheat and 3 parts unbleached white)
1 Tbs. sugar, honey or maple syrup
1 tsp. salt
1/4 cup olive oil or salad oil
Optional: 1 egg white beaten with 1 Tbs. of water and sesame or poppy seeds

Add warm water to a large mixing bowl and stir in yeast with a spoon until dissolved. Let sit for a 2-3 minutes. Stir in 1 cup flour, sugar, and salt . Gradually add oil and stir until well mixed. Set aside for 5-10 minutes. Add the remaining 3 to 3-1/2 cups of flour to make soft dough. Turn onto floured board and with floured hands knead for 10 minutes into smooth ball. Set aside in covered bowl to rise for 30 minutes to 1 hour. Gently push the dough down, cut it into pieces and shape into small loaves. Let these small loaves rise again for 15 minutes. If desired, brush the loaves with the egg white/water mixture and sprinkle with seeds. Bake at 375° F for about 15-20 minutes until lightly browned.

FLOUR POWER

Bread is called the 'staff of life' by people all over the world. The ingredients alone are simple — flour, water, sugar, salt and a bit of yeast. Yet their combination is magical, nutritious and delicious, with each ingredient playing an important role in formation of the final product. Here's how they work together:

Yeast is a tiny microscopic fungus. It may be small but it can double the size of your bread dough as it grows. Just give it a warm home, some liquid, a little sweet food and it starts to multiply, releasing carbon dioxide gas as a by-product. It is this gas that leavens the bread and helps it rise to the occasion, doubling in size.

Water provides a warm, moist home for the awakening yeast cells and helps mix and hold the ingredients together.

Flour is the foundation for the bread. It is ground from the seeds of grain plants. Wheat seeds are ground to form the flour used in our Magic Bread and most of the bread we eat. Whole wheat and white flour are high in gluten, a substance important in bread baking. When flour is mixed with the other ingredients, proteins clump together in a tangled mass. Kneading the dough helps unknot the tangles and the proteins combine to form gluten which has a unique elastic structure, similar to a cellulose sponge. The gluten's many elastic walls surround the yeast cells and then expand like hundreds of balloons to hold the carbon dioxide gas as it is released. When your dough is fully kneaded, try pulling it into a paper thin sheet. Then hold this sheet up to the light to see the webbing of the gluten.

Sugar is optional in bread because the flour is capable of providing the yeast with enough food. The addition of sweetener also speeds up the action of the yeast and the rising of the bread. There can be too much of a good thing, however, and too much sugar actually slows or stops yeast growth.

Salt contributes more than just flavor. Salt controls yeast growth and strengthens gluten. The gluten can then capture more carbon dioxide and the bread can rise to even higher heights.

Oil is optional but it enhances flavor making a richer tasting, tender bread which keeps longer. It also helps the bread rise higher while baking in the oven.

Any one of these ingredients alone is neither substantive or interesting enough to be eaten every day. Yet when combined together to form the final product, most people would agree that the whole loaf is tastier than the sum of its parts!

Plant Parts We Eat
• E X H I B I T •

Materials: One large salad bowl; pretend salad ingredients such as plastic or cloth vegetables (available from the craft section of department store), empty food containers or laminated pictures from magazines; six bowls labelled with the different plant parts — roots, stems, leaves, flowers, fruits and seeds; container labelled olive oil; container labelled cider vinegar; large background drawing of various vegetables as they would appear in the garden.

POSSIBLE SALAD INGREDIENTS

Roots: *Carrots, beets, radishes*
Stems: *Celery, asparagus spears, onions*
Leaves: *Lettuce, spinach*
Flowers: *Broccoli, cauliflower, artichoke hearts*
Fruits: *Tomatoes, cucumbers, avocados, olives and olive oil, cider vinegar*
Seeds: *Croutons (from wheat seeds), chick peas, peas, alfalfa sprouts*

Design:
1. Set up a small table with a large bowl in the center. Fill the bowl with an assortment of salad ingredients (see list below for ideas). Place the oil and vinegar containers next to this bowl. Place the six labelled bowls around the table. For each plant part bowl, create an index card answer key that lists the salad ingredients in the large bowl that are from that part of the plant. Attach to the bottom of the plant part bowls.

2. Make a large drawing of many of the salad ingredients as they would appear growing in the garden. Mount this drawing on the wall behind the table. This often helps the students to identify plant parts on vegetables they are not familiar with.

3. Write the following directions on or near the the exhibit:
   Peter Rabbit loves to munch on leaves and stems and roots. How about you? Sort the items in this salad bowl into the different plant parts you are eating when you enjoy a bowl of salad. And don't forget the dressing!

Activity:
1. Have the students work in pairs. Direct them to sort the salad ingredients in the large bowl into their proper plant part categories in the smaller bowls. Have them check their answers with the cards attached to the bottoms of the smaller bowls.

Travelling Lunch

Objective:
Students will learn what common foods are made of and how far they travel from the field where they are grown to the table where they are eaten.

Grade Level: 3-6

Groupings: Entire class

Materials: Large index cards; paper lunch bags (have students save their lunch bags over several days); paper cups; small paper plates; United States and World maps; atlas; encyclopedia or other general reference books.

Time Allotment: 30 minutes

Directions:
This activity is best done after lunch.

1. Ask the students to write down everything they had for lunch today. Explain that they will create a large graph on the floor to show the different types of lunches. Begin a vertical axis with an index card labelled *Hot lunch* of the day. Beneath it place a second card labelled *Peanut butter and jelly sandwich*. What other types of sandwiches did the students have in their lunches? Record these on index cards and add these to the column. Make one last card labelled *Other* for foods other than sandwiches and hot lunches to complete the column.

2. Pass out paper lunch bags to the students. Explain that one at a time they can come forward and place their lunch bags in a line next to the label describing what they had for lunch. What was the most popular food item for lunch today?

3. Create a second graph for lunch beverages with cards labelled *Milk, Juice,* and *Other*. Give each student a paper cup and have them place it in the proper column. What was the most popular beverage?

4. Make a third graph for dessert items including fruits and sweets. Pass out small paper plates and have them place the plates in a row next to their dessert item. What was the winning dessert?

5. Tell the class that they will now 'dissect' the most popular food item in each category into its main components. For example, a peanut butter and jelly sandwich is composed of

Extensions:

a. *Have a contest to find the 'lowest mileage' snack. Review the entries and encourage the students to bring these 'winners' in for snack the next day.*

b. *Do a survey to see how far the clothes we wear have travelled. Pair students and have them look at labels in the shirts, sweaters, coats and shoes they are wearing. Have the students share where their clothing is made, locate these countries on a map and approximate distances.*

c. *Most parts of the world can grow an amazing variety of foods. Research and compile a list of fifty local foods. Contact your State Department of Agriculture for listing of local farms and find out where their products are sold.*

d. *Read the book* HOW TO MAKE AN APPLE PIE AND SEE THE WORLD *by Marjorie Priceman (New York: Knopf, 1994) for a fanciful story of one girl's trip around the world to find the ingredients for an apple pie. Have the students calculate her mileage and discuss other places she might have gone to get the same ingredients. Let the students write about journeys they might make in search of ingredients for their favorite recipes.*

Directions: (continued)

bread which is made from wheat, peanut butter which is made from peanuts, and grape jelly which is made from grapes. Ask for a volunteer to record the basic ingredients on the board as they are determined.

6. Explain they will now look at how far their food travelled from the farmer's field to their tables in the cafeteria. Ask the students where various food items are commonly grown. For a peanut butter and jelly sandwich, what area of the country is known for growing wheat? Where are peanuts grown? Where are grapes grown? Have them refer to an atlas, encyclopedia or other general reference book to help determine this information. Ask for a second volunteer to mark the point of origin on the map and approximate the mileage travelled from field to table using the scale of miles given at the bottom of the map. Have him or her record these and keep a running tally of the lunch mileage.

7. Repeat this process for the most popular beverage and dessert. How far did the most popular lunch travel? Which ingredient travelled the farthest distance? Which ingredients travelled the shortest distance? Dissect some other lunch items to find other 'high and low mileage' foods.

WHERE FOOD COMES FROM

Chocolate: *Central America*

Sugar Cane: *Cuba, Puerto Rico, Santa Domingo, Brazil and tropical African countries*

Pineapple: *Hawaii (75% of the crop), Cuba, Florida, Puerto Rico, the Azores, and Thailand*

Banana: *Central America and the Canary Islands*

Tea: *China (50% the world's supply), India, Sri Lanka, Japan, Indonesia and Taiwan*

Coffee: *Central and South America with Brazil the leading producer, Africa, East Indies, Southeast Asia, and India*

Cranberries: *Northeast America with 60% from Massachusetts, the rest from Wisconsin and New Jersey*

Cashews: *India is the main exporter, Mozambique, Latin America with Brazil the leading producer*

Coconut: *Malaysia and Indonesia*

Sesame: *Africa, Asia and India*

Pecans: *Southern United States of Texas, Georgia, Oklahoma and Florida*

Peanuts: *India and China are the leading growers, and southern United States*

Source: L. P. Coyle, Jr., The World Encyclopedia of Food, Facts on File Inc., 1982.

Directions: (continued)

8. Discuss the implications of food travelling great distances to reach our tables. What are the hidden energy costs? Are there environmental costs, too? How does buying food from far away affect the local economy? Does it make more sense to buy locally?

FOOD *on the* MOVE

Is the apple in your lunch a globe trotter or a local yokel? Imagine this: a truck in Washington state is loaded with apples and drives east to the markets in New York City. At the same time, a truck in upstate New York is being loaded with apples which will head west to markets in Seattle. It sounds crazy but things like this happen daily in our food distribution system. Not only do foods that could be grown in our own backyards travel across the continent, some even travel across the ocean! Today getting food from the farm to your table uses almost as much energy as was used to grow it. Of course, since only 2% of the people in this country still live on farms, some travel is necessary. It is important to look for ways to reduce this distance, for the less food travels, the less energy consumed, and the less pollution produced.

Here are some tips to shorten the trips your food takes. All of them can save energy and money, improve the local economy, reduce pollution and help the environment.

• Visit your local farmers market and enjoy fresh seasonal foods. Buy extra to freeze, can, and store for winter. Or visit local "pick your own" farms and pick extra to 'put up' for winter.
• Shop at food cooperatives where local foods are often featured. Encourage your local grocery store to do the same.
• Look into local Community Supported Agriculture (CSA) projects and consider buying a yearly share in their farming operation. It entitles you to a generous portion of the food they harvest, be it vegetables, meat or poultry.

Harvest Herb Kitchen

•EXHIBIT•

Materials: Bunches of fresh herbs (a Farmers Market is a good source if you do not have access to a garden); string; spice rack with matching bottles of dried herbs (these can be purchased inexpensively in bulk at food cooperatives); sticky labels; basket with assortment of pictures of food items that commonly use the above herbs for flavorings.

Extensions:

a. *Try using herbs in simple recipes. Make some of the food pictured or try simple recipes such as herb butter as a flavoring for popcorn, chips with herb dips, herbal iced teas or even potpourri.*

b. *Make a similar matching activity with ground spices and their whole counterparts. (Suggested spices: cinnamon, cloves, allspice, nutmeg, star anise, ginger, peppercorns.) You can match them to the foods they are commonly used in and sample some recipes. Turn the exercise into a geography lesson as you map where different spices are commonly grown. Afterwards, soak the whole spices and using needles and elastic thread, string them to make fragrant spice necklaces.*

Design:

1. Collect small bunches of fresh herbs and tie them into bundles. Attach a small tag to each bundle and number it. Tie the herb bundles at intervals along a long piece of string. Hang this string across a bulletin board or wall. Set up a spice rack nearby with labelled bottles of matching dried herbs. Attach a sticky label to the inside of each lid with the corresponding number of the fresh herb.

2. Draw or cut out pictures of food items that commonly use these particular herbs in their recipes for flavoring. Write the name of the dried herb on the back. Place these pictures in a nearby basket.

3. Write the following directions on or near the exhibit: *Smell the fresh bundles of herbs, then smell the herbs in the jars. Can you match the fresh herb to its dried counterpart. Only the nose knows...*

Have you smelled these herbs somewhere before? Look through the food items in the basket and imagine how each smells. Which herb is responsible for each of those pleasant aromas? Make a guess, then look on the back of each picture to check your answers.

Activity:

1. Have the students work in pairs. Have them smell the fresh and dried herbs. Ask them to match the fresh herb to its dried version. Let them look inside the lid of each jar for the matching number.

2. Explain to the students that certain food dishes have strong aromas. Ask them to look through the assortment of food items in the basket and match them to one of the herbs. Have them look on the back to check their answers.

A Year in the Life of a Seed

Objective:
Students will learn about the life cycle of a seed.

Grade Level: K-3

Groupings: Entire class, in pairs

Materials: Egg cartons (one for each pair); old socks; pieces of material, old towels or baby blanket; cassette tape of lullaby or other quiet music and cassette player; plant mister; snack food in small bags.

Time Allotment: 30 minutes

Directions:

1. Tell the students that they are about to embark on a safari in search of one of nature's wonders — seeds. Explain that people on safari always bring special equipment. Divide the students in pairs and give each pair a specially designed seed collecting container (the egg carton). Explain that their mission while on safari is to fill each of the twelve compartments with a different type of seed. Pass each group another important piece of collecting equipment, specially designed to attract "hitch hiking" seeds (the old socks). Seeds that stick to clothing or animals are seeds that get a "free ride" and we call them "hitch hikers." Each partner can wear one over their shoes. Then head out to a field, garden or other well seeded area in search of seeds.

2. After they have collected seeds, gather the class together (outdoors or inside). Have the students share their largest seed, their smallest, and their favorite. Ask the students what all these seeds have in common. What is the purpose of a seed? What does it need to grow? Have the students put their collections aside, and tell the students that they are about to experience the life of a seed. Ask each student to plant themselves nearby in a comfortable spot.

3. Explain that in autumn, seeds are getting ready for a long winter rest. Have the students curl up tightly and pretend that they are little seeds just fallen to the ground. Ask the students what kind of seeds they are. Explain that each seed comes equipped with its own food to help it begin life in the spring. Give each student a small snack in a little bag. Stress that in order to survive and grow into healthy plants, the seeds must not eat their food until the spring rains begin to fall.

Extensions:

a. *Have the students look over their seed collection and sort them into groups. Have two groups trade collections and try to guess how the groups were determined. For younger students, give guidelines to help them sort their seeds — smooth vs. rough seeds, seeds that roll, seeds of a particular color, seeds that float or fly, etc.*

b. *Look at and compare the collection of "hitch hiking" seeds. Try sprouting these seeds by placing the toe of the sock in water. The sock wicks up water to allow the seeds to sprout and begin to grow. Transplant them and see if you can grow them to maturity under grow lights.*

c. *Do **Adapt a Seed** (page 25) to learn about other ways seeds travel. On a windy day have outdoor races with milkweed seeds and other seeds that float through the air.*

Directions: (continued)

4. Describe the coming of winter and snow and pretend to cover each student with a blanket of snow. Drape pieces of material or towels gently over the students' shoulders or use one baby blanket to pretend to cover each student, repeating this until all the students are "beneath the blanket" of snow. If indoors, this is a good time to turn out the lights. Have a brief period or silence or play a short quiet lullaby and have the students pretend to sleep through the winter.

5. Next comes spring. Explain that the ground is gradually starting to warm and the seeds slowly awaken. Encourage them to wiggle just a bit and yawn. Once they feel the warm spring rains of your plant mister, have them to pop out a root and begin to drink up water. Now the seeds uncurl and eat some of their stored food.

6. After they have enjoyed their snack, explain that they now have the energy to grow and sprout from underground. On the count of three have them throw off their "blanket" and stretch their arms upward. If indoors, turn on the lights at this time. Play some quiet music and have them slowly rise to a standing position while stretching out their leaves (arms) to gather sunlight. Have them sway in the breeze and enjoy the sunshine.

7. Describe the change to summer with plants now forming flowers. Have the students encircle their head with their arms and pretend to be flowers basking in the sun. The teacher should pretend to be a bee and buzz around, visiting each flower and collecting nectar and pollen. Briefly discuss pollination.

8. Summer is coming to and end and fall is in the air. Have the students flutter their arms to indicate petals falling to the ground. Explain that in every plant where there was a flower, a fruit has begun to grow. Have the students widen their arms to indicate the fruit growing bigger and bigger until it falls to the ground. When it falls to the ground, the fruit breaks open and something falls out to start the cycle anew. What is it? (Seeds!)

Adapt a Seed

Objective:
Students will learn about various seed dispersal mechanisms.

Grade Level: 2-6

Groupings: Small groups

Materials: Assortment of seeds that are dispersed in different ways (see *Traveling Seeds*, page 26, for examples); hand lenses, miscellaneous simple construction materials (clay, pipe cleaners, paper clips, rubber bands, string, aluminum foil, Popsicle sticks, cotton balls, etc.); *Traveling Seed* cards (a selection of cards each with a description of one way a seed may travel, see page 26).

Time Allotment: 30 minutes

Directions:
This activity works best if the class has gone on an outdoor seed hunt. In New England, September and October are the best months for student seed safaris. Use empty egg cartons to hold the seeds and challenge the students to find a dozen different seeds.

1. Tell the class that you need help solving a gardening mystery. Plants cannot move, yet some new weeds have recently appeared in your garden. Can the students help you discover how the weed seeds have gotten into your garden? Show a selection of two or three different types of weed seeds. Pass out one seed to every two students. Have them examine these seeds carefully, using hand lenses and looking specifically for features that help the seeds travel. Discuss the students' ideas about how these different seeds might have gotten into your garden.

2. Explain that even though plants do not move, seeds do travel. Challenge the students to invent or design their own seeds that travel in different ways. Explain that each group will be choosing a Traveling Seed card which will describe a particular seed's way of being dispersed. Ask them to use their imaginations and the materials provided to create a seed on the go that fits this description.

3. Divide the children into small groups and have a member of each group draw a *Traveling Seed* card (page 26). The students will create their seeds, and then test them to make sure they meet the dispersal requirements detailed on their cards. Each group should give their seed a name and think about the life history of the plant from which the seed came.

4. When everyone is finished, bring the students together and have them demonstrate how their invented seed travels. Have them tell their seeds name and parent plant's story. Compare their seeds to the real seeds they examined at the beginning of the activity. Do they see any similarities? Can they think of other seeds that travel?

Extension:

a. *Go on a seed hunt looking specifically for seeds that travel in different ways. Most of the seeds you find easily will be wind-blown, but some may be hitchhikers. Have the students wear large old socks over one shoe to see if they pick up any hitchhiking seeds. Can a particular seed travel in more than one way? Test some real seeds to find out.*

TRAVELING SEEDS

Helicopters: maple samaras, ash samaras

Air passengers: cherries, berries, grapes

Parachutes: milkweed, dandelions

Hitchhikers: burdock, bidens

Animal express: blueberries, raspberries, apples

Cannonballs: touch-me-nots

Boats: coconuts, cranberries

TRAVELING SEED CARDS

Make a seed like a helicopter, which can spin, twirl or fly through the air when dropped from a height of eight to ten feet and land at least one foot away.

Make a seed that is carried by the wind like a parachute for at least ten seconds.

Make a seed that can hitchhike on a person or animal by sticking to it and going wherever it goes.

Make a seed that looks good enough for a bear to eat. It travels by animal express.

Make a seed that a bird might eat. This seed travels as an air passenger.

Make a seed that is thrown through the air like a cannonball and lands at least two feet away.

Make a seed that can float like a boat for at least one minute.

Tomato Planet

Objective:
Students will learn about seed survival rates and what seeds need to grow.

Grade Level: 2-4

Groupings: Pairs

Materials: (per pair) Cherry tomato; plastic knife. paper plate; index cards (one per student).

Time Allotment: 30 minutes

Directions:
1. Ask the students what is inside the fruits of plants. (Seeds.) How many seeds are inside? Are there the same number of seeds inside similar fruits? (It can vary from plant to plant.) Explain that they will do an activity to find out about the number of seeds produced by a plant and how this relates to seed survival.

2. Group the students in pairs. Pass around a bowl of cherry tomatoes, the plastic knives and paper plates. Ask them to pick one of each. How many seeds do they think are inside? Have each of them record their guess. Review the class guesses.

3. Have the students cut their tomato in half and ask each partner to count the seeds inside one half of their tomato. Remind them that it helps to group the seed by tens to aid in counting. Ask them to add up the number of seeds in each half to get the total number inside. How did this compare with their prediction? Review and record the class totals.

4. Ask the students how many seeds it takes to grow one tomato plant? (Just one seed.) Write the word *seed* on one (or two) of the index cards. Ask the students what kinds of things will help this seed to germinate and grow into a healthy plant. (Plenty of sunshine, enough space, good soil, enough water, fertilizer, weeding, warm weather, etc.) Record each idea on a separate index card. When you have listed as many positive growth conditions as the class can generate, duplicate or triplicate some of the cards until you have used 2/3 of all the cards.

5. How many tomato plants could they potentially grow from their cherry tomato? (The same number of plants as seeds.) Challenge them with a little math. Explain that one cherry tomato plant can have as many as 50 cherry tomatoes. How many plants could they grow from the seeds of all those cherry tomatoes, assuming they all have the same number of seeds? (The number of seeds multiplied by fifty).

6. Ask the students why tomatoes aren't growing everywhere? Record possible hazards to the seed germination and growth on the remaining index cards. (Drought, too cold, too wet,

Extensions:

a. *Count and compare the number of seeds produced by different plants. Use a pumpkin at Halloween and enjoy a snack of roasted seeds. Look not only at the fruits we eat but also trees, wild flowers and common weeds.*

b. *Read and discuss* THE TINY SEED *by Eric Carle (Picture Book Studio Ltd., 1987). This could also be used as an introduction to the activity.*

Directions: (continued)

competition from other plants, disease, some are eaten or stepped on, etc.)

7. Explain that they will now be enacting the risky life of a little seed. Pass out the index cards to the students. Explain that one or two students are seeds and the rest are positive or negative growth conditions. Explain that they should look at their card but keep the information on it a secret. In a large indoor or outdoor space set up four bases equally spaced apart. Explain to the students that when you say 'Go!', they should run around the bases in a circle. When you say 'Stop!' they should run to the nearest base.

8. Ask the "seed" to reveal where it has landed. Ask the other students to reveal the conditions on their cards. Have the students determine whether or not the seed is able to survive and grow in this spot. Check the conditions on the other bases to see if the seed could have possibly germinated.

9. Collect the cards, reshuffle and distribute them again to play another round. Was the seed able to survive this time? Play the game a few more times and be sure to keep a tally of the seeds survival rate. As a conclusion, ask the students why high numbers of seeds are produced.

Starting from Scratch

Objective:
Students will learn about the origins of everyday items and foods.

Grade Level: 2-6

Groupings: Pairs

Materials: Four bins labeled "Store," "Factory," "Natural World" and "Farms"; magazines for students to cut up; scissors; crayons; paper.

Time: 30 minutes

Directions:

1. Ask the students what kinds of things they do and use everyday. Have them work in pairs to record their daily routines, noting specific activities, items used and foods eaten. Have them cut out pictures from magazines to illustrate these everyday items and foods or draw their own.

2. Have several pairs share their pictures and routines with the class. How many students recorded similar activities, items and foods? Did anyone list anything different? Have the students classify these into basic categories: food, clothing, health, shelter, transportation, education and recreation. Which things are necessary for life? Which make life more comfortable or enjoyable?

3. Explain they will trace these items back to their source. Collect all their pictures and remove duplicates. Show the student four bins labeled "Store," "Factory," "Natural World" and "Farms." Tell them they will sort the pictures based on their source and place them in the appropriate bins.

4. Divide the students into two groups and have them form two lines. Set the bins opposite these lines. Place the collection of pictures a few feet in front of their lines. Explain they will participate in a relay race to sort the pictures. One student from each team selects a picture, runs and places it in the appropriate bin, then returns to the end of his or her line. The next person in each line will repeat the process. This will continue until everyone has had a turn or all the pictures are sorted.

Extensions:

a. *Have the students compare the cycles in the natural world such as the soil cycle, water cycle, and life cycles with the cycles of agriculture such as composting (an accelerated version of the soil cycle), manure management (keeps nitrates and phosphates from entering the water cycle), animal reproduction, seed/planting cycles, and grazing cycles. Do the cycles in agriculture mimic those in nature? How dependent is agriculture on the cycles of nature?*

b. *Have the students work in small groups to set up their own food processing factory to produce simple products such as fresh squeezed orange juice, smoothie drinks or juice Popsicles. Have them determine the equipment, energy and raw materials needed and their costs. Ask them to determine a final price for the product based upon their costs and labor involved. How does the cost of their processed food compare to the cost of the food in its original form? Have the students research the actual costs involved in processing a particular food product from farmer to store. Contact your local agricultural extension agency for help in obtaining information and figures.*

Directions: (continued)

5. Review the items in each bin. The students can show their approval or disapproval for each item with a show of thumbs up or down. Begin with the bin labeled "Store." Review one or two items, asking if they can be traced back even further. Does anything actually originate in the store? (No, that is where most of us purchase the things we need and use daily.) Encourage the students to offer suggestions on where items should be placed. Continue onto the "Factory " bin. Where do the raw materials come from to make these items? Can these items be traced even further back to their source? (Yes, to the natural world or farms.)

6. Review the items in the bin labeled "Natural World." (It will include a wide array of items including wooden objects from trees, metal mined from minerals in the earth and plastics and synthetic materials made from petroleum products.) What categories do these objects fall into? (Clothing, health, shelter, transportation, education or recreation.) Point out that some of the objects are made with renewable resources and others with non-renewable resources. Ask the students for a definition of these terms. (Renewable resources are those which can be replenished over time, such as plants, trees, solar and wind energy; non-renewable resources are those which once used cannot be replaced in this geological age such as petroleum-based products like plastic.) Which of the items pictured are made from renewable resources? Non-renewable? Point out that some non-renewable resources are also recyclable. What are examples of these? (certain plastics, tin, aluminum.)

7. Last review the items in the "Farm" bin. What categories do they fall into? (Mostly food, both fresh and processed with some examples of natural fibers, such as wool, cotton and silk.) Could we live without these things? (No, because food is essential to life and therefore so are farms!) Discuss the idea of farming as a renewable resource with food being produced year after year.

STARTING *from* SCRATCH

Understanding how natural cycles work together is critical to the success of farms today. Many people have the misconception that agriculture is a straight line from farm to table and that the land will produce forever no matter how it is cared for. But if fertile topsoil is lost, and soil, air and water are poisoned with harmful chemicals, both productivity and profitability declines. The natural cycles keep going round, but not fast enough to undo the damage done. Most farmers know the long-term health of the land is connected to their economic viability, and that good stewardship practices are essential for maintaining healthy production for years to come. Advances in agriculture like manure holding areas are reducing the nitrate and phosphate pollution of water. Special rotational grazing systems prevent overgrazing and soil erosion. Good soil management practices reduce the need for synthetic fertilizers and insure healthy, disease-resistant vegetation, thereby reducing the need for pesticides. Organic methods of pest control and integrated pest management can further reduce pesticide use. When farmers work with nature, working with the natural cycles, and everyone profits!

Directions: (continued)

8. Complete this discussion by talking about the wise care or stewardship of our natural resources and farmlands. Stress that the stewardship of farmland goes hand-in-hand with that of the natural world to insure a high quality of life. Care needs to be given to the soil, water and air to insure adequate and continued food production Discuss farming practices that reflect this caring attitude towards the earth and environment.

In the Good Old Days Inventory Sheet

FIND SOMEONE WHO HAS:

1. Carded and/or spun wool _____
2. Carried firewood _____
3. Dyed yarn with plant dyes _____
4. Fed a pig _____
5. Gathered eggs _____
6. Gone barefoot for a week _____
7. Been hunting or fishing _____
8. Taken a sleigh ride _____
9. Knit a pair of mittens _____
10. Sewn a patchwork quilt _____
11. Pressed cider _____
12. Made jelly or jam _____
13. Churned butter _____
14. Milked a cow _____
15. Planted a garden _____
16. Plucked a chicken _____
17. Ridden a horse _____
18. Shucked corn _____
19. Split fire wood _____
20. Boiled sap to make maple syrup _____
21. Seen a hen lay an egg _____
22. Watched a horse being shod _____
23. Dipped candles _____
24. Baked Bread _____
25. Composted food scraps _____

In the Good Old Days

Objective:
Students will learn how the changes in daily household activities over generations reflect our society's changing relationship to food and fiber.

Grade Level: 2-6

Groupings: Entire class

Materials: Inventory sheets

Time Allotment: 15-20 minutes, additional time to review homework

Extensions:

a. *Have your class become pen pals with a farmer to learn about daily chores and activities done on modern farms. Consider a local farmer if no one in your class lives on a farm; otherwise, contact someone farming in another part of the country for comparison. (Contact your State Department of Agriculture and/or extension office for assistance.)*

b. *Try doing some of the activities on the survey sheet with your class, such as natural dyeing or making jam or butter.*

c. *Make up inventory sheets for other subjects or topic areas. It is a good way to see how much your students know about a particular subject before starting a unit.*

Directions:
1. Ask the students whether daily life chores have changed since their parents were children. Have them share their parents' or grandparents' childhood stories about things they did around the house that are no longer done today. Are there activities that the students do today that might some day seem dated to their children or grandchildren?

2. Explain to the students that you have prepared an inventory sheet to see the types of agricultural activities they have done. Tell the students some of the activities on the list may seem like novelties, but they were a way of life for their parents or grandparents. Pass out the inventory sheet and give them time to read it over. Explain that they may add two or three additional old-fashioned farm activities to the list.

3. Tell the students that they will now get a chance to survey their classmates to find out which activities they have done. When you say "Go," they will move around the room trying to talk to everyone in the class. When they find a student who has done a particular activity, they should write his or her name on the inventory sheet in the blank space after the name of that activity. For example, if Jane has milked a cow, her name would go in the blank space after 'milked a cow'. The object of the activity is to find as many different people who have done different things. Once they have added an individual's name to their inventory, they should move on and question another classmate. (Even though Jane may have done ten of the activities on the list, her name should appear in one place only.)

FARMER *for a* **DAY**
Old MacDonald's children would be surprised if they visited a family today. In the "good old days" a country kid would help milk the cows, collect fresh eggs, feed the pigs and pick some berries for breakfast. Today with only 2% of the population in the United States involved in agriculture, most children get milk from cartons, strawberries from a box in the freezer, and their morning routine involves nothing more than choosing their favorite box of cereal from the cupboard. Their connection to their food has been reduced to a visit to the grocery store. But things are changing. Farmers' markets are springing up everywhere, bringing fresh produce, meat, dairy products and baked goods even to city dwellers. Community supported agriculture programs involve people in growing and harvesting their own food. Everywhere plots of land are being set aside for community gardens with local libraries checking out tools along with books to get people started growing some of their own food. Many schools are developing innovative educational programs centered on school gardens. And throughout the country, farm bed and breakfasts have become popular. Some even offer family vacations where you can become Old MacDonald for a week. So even if you don't live in the country, take the opportunity to become part of agriculture today, and enjoy "the good new days"!

Directions: (continued)

4. Explain that you will set a time limit for this activity and that you, too, will participate. Your participation will enable you to gauge how quickly the students are working, determine how they are interacting, and decide when to stop the activity. When the time is up, gather everyone and ask them to count the number of spaces they filled with different names. Did anyone fill them all? Who had the highest number? Which student has performed what they consider the most unusual task on the list? Complete the inventory by reviewing each activity on the sheet. Read the list and ask students to raise their hands if they have done a particular activity.

5. Pass out a second inventory sheet which has been modified slightly to use as homework. Explain that the students will conduct a similar survey with their families. Point out that at the top of the sheet it will ask *Have you ever:* and then there will be a list of activities. At the end of each activity there will be three columns. The first column is for their response to the question, the second for their parents' and the third for their grandparents' or older neighbors' response.

For example:

Have you ever:	You	Parents	Grandparents
1. milked a cow			
2. gathered eggs			
3. etc.			

6. After the students have done their homework, review their families' responses. Keep a tally of the number of students who have done each activity compared to the number of parents and grandparents. Count the number of activities the students did compared to those their parents and grandparents did. What kind of differences do the students notice? How many students grow their own food? Make their own clothes? Where do these necessities come from today? Explain to the students that these differences indicate the changes that have taken place over time regarding our relationship to agriculture and our connection to food and fiber production.

Farm Barnyard

Objective:
Students will be introduced to the different products from farm animals.

Grade Level: K-3

Groupings: Pairs

Materials: Pictures of farm animals hung on large string loops (two or more pictures of each animal depending on class size); a collection of farm animal products, one for each of the animals pictured (see *Animals and Products*, page 26).

Directions:

1. Challenge the students to name as many animals as they can that might be raised on a farm. Record the names of these animals on the blackboard. As an animal is mentioned, show them a picture of that animal. Ask them to imitate the sounds and motions each animal makes.

2. Explain to the students that you will be passing each of them a farm animal picture to wear around his or her neck. Have the students wear their picture face down so that no one can see it.

3. Explain that there is more than one picture of each of the different farm animals. Students will need to find the classmate(s) who has the same animal. Explain that they will do this by imitating the sound and motion their animal makes and by listening carefully to find their mate(s). When you call out "Farm Barnyard," all the students should start making their animal's sound. Remind them to continue to repeat their sound until each student has found his or her partner(s).

4. Once they have found their partners, have the pairs/ groups choose a product that comes from their farm animal from the collection of animals products. (See *Animals and Products*, page 36.)

Extensions:

a. *Have each group research different breeds of their particular animal. What do the different breeds look like? What are the strong points and weak points? Where did the breed originate?*

b. *Have the students look into vanishing breeds of farm animals (see* OUR VANISHING FARM ANIMALS *by Catherine Paladino, Little Brown & Co., 1991). Contact The American Livestock Breeds Conservancy, P.O. Box 477, Pittsboro, NC 27312 (919-542-5704) to learn more about these disappearing breeds and to find out whether there are any still being raised in your area.*

Directions: (continued)

5. When all the groups have selected their animal's product, review their choices. Have each pair hold up their selection and have the other students guess their animal's identity. Each pair can confirm the class' guess by imitating their animal's sound. Discuss the services or other products each animal provides.

ANIMALS *and* PRODUCTS

DAIRY COWS: *Empty dairy product containers.*

BEEF CATTLE: *Leather belt, shoes, beef product package made by placing a plastic steak dog toy on a Styrofoam meat tray, wrapping it in plastic and labeling it as a particular cut of beef.*

SHEEP: *Wool sweater, hat, mittens, lamb or mutton product similar to beef product.*

PIGS: *Bristle brush, football, empty ham, bacon or sausage container, a pork product package similar to beef product.*

GOATS: *Kid leather gloves, empty goat cheese package.*

CHICKENS: *Empty egg cartons, empty chicken noodle soup can, a chicken product package similar to beef product.*

HORSES: *Glue, dog food.*

TURKEY: *Large aluminum roasting pan covered with foil and labeled as Thanksgiving dinner.*

DUCKS/GEESE: *Feather pillow, down jacket, sleeping bag or comforter.*

RABBITS: *Angora sweater, fur-lined mittens, a rabbit meat package similar to beef product.*

From Farm to You

Objective:
Students will discover the connection between agriculture and the food and fibers we depend upon.

Grade Level: 3-6

Groupings: Small groups

Materials: Selections of farm animal products, large paper grocery bags.

Time Allotment: 15-20 minutes

Directions:

1. Ask your class to brainstorm the different animals that are raised on farms for food and fiber. Explain that you will say a few adjectives and phrases that describe a particular farm animal. Challenge the students to add another word or phrase that describes the same animal. What animal are you describing? Invite them play this guessing game with several different farm animals. Compile a list of farm animals and their descriptive words and phrases.

2. Beforehand, ask students to bring in a farm animal product from home in a brown paper grocery bag, keeping its identity a secret. Bring in a few of the more unusual ones to insure diversity. (See **Animals and Products**, page 36.) For perishable products, ask them to bring the empty container or a representation. For example, an empty egg carton can represent eggs, or a plastic steak dog toy placed on a meat tray wrapped in cellophane can represent a beef steak.

3. Divide the class into small groups. Give each group a farm product in a paper grocery bag. Have them look at their product, but keep its identity a secret from other groups. Ask them to write down ten adjectives or short phrases describing the product.

4. Explain that they will read their list of descriptive words or phrases to the class and that the rest of the class will guess the identity of their product. Ask them to arrange their word or phrases in an order that makes the guessing the most challenging.

Extensions:

a. *Do a similar activity with the class using just dairy products, or things made with wheat, corn, or other farm animal products or crops.*

b. *Have the students sample some of the food products made from the various animals. Introduce the students to especially unusual or unfamiliar ones.*

c. *Get information from your state Department of Agriculture on local farms and processing plants and plan a field trip.*

d. *Have students compare specialized farms of today with diversified farms of the past.*

Directions: (continued)

5. When the product is identified, reveal the farm animal item and read any remaining adjectives. Can the class think of still others? Where does this product come from? How many students eat or commonly use this product? Record this information.

6. Repeat this process with the remaining products.

7. Have each group use their descriptive words or phrases to write short riddles about their product. Create an exhibit with the riddles, and post it in the hallway, encouraging other students to guess the identity of the farm products.

From Sheep to Sweater

Objective:
Students will learn how wool is processed to make knitted garments.

Grade Level: 2-6

Groupings: Groups of nine or more students

Materials: (*per group*) Cards or props that represent the processing steps from grass to butter (see step #2); toy sheep or puppet; scissors to represent sheep shears; bag of raw fleece; dog grooming brushes or wool carders; sample of carded wool; drop spindle; skein or ball of white yarn; enamel pot with package of dye or natural dye recipe inside (optional); skein of colored yarn (optional); knitting needles; knitted wool sweater.

Time Allotment: 20 minutes

Directions:

1. Explain to the students that on farms long ago there were usually several different animals. Each animal provided the farmer and his or her family with important products they could use for food and fiber. Ask the student to name some farm animals and the products they gave to farm families.

2. Point out that sometimes a product could be used directly, as in the case of milk or eggs to eat. Other times they would process the initial farm products—using tools, methods or recipes involving other ingredients—to make other needed products. For example, milk could be turned into a butter, ice cream, sour cream or other dairy foods. Show the students a few of the cards or props that represent the steps in the sequence from grass to butter. Ask them to put these in order. (Grass, milking bucket, milk, butter churn, butter.)

3. Challenge the students to put another common processing technique in the proper sequence. Explain that it involves another farm animal and was done in homes in the United States until the late 1800s (and is still done in homes in other parts of the world today). The whole family was involved in the process. Explain that you will pass out objects that represent the various steps in the process. Some people will be given the animal or one of the products (or a representation), and others will be given the tools used to change the original product from one form into another. Refer to the original example of cow to butter if necessary.

(The sequence has eleven steps in it. You can adjust the number of students in each group to match class size by deleting optional steps or adding completely unrelated props. Be sure to tell students if unrelated props are included.)

4. If you feel your students are up for an added challenge, tell them they will not be able to talk during the sequencing. Give them time to brainstorm other ways to communicate the sequence order without talking.

5. Pass out the objects in random order. Ask them to look closely at their object. If they have a tool, tell them to look for clues to its function. If they have a product, ask them to compare it with the others to see how it has changed. Allow time for students to compare items and determine the

Extensions:

a. *Have the students try their hand at carding and spinning wool. Find an experienced parent to help you or contact your local craft shops or sheep farmers extension office to learn of a contact person.*

b. *Have the students check the tags in each others' clothing to see what they are made of. Make a list of the materials and classify them into natural and synthetic products. Research where each comes from and how they are processed.*

c. *Have the students research other fibers that are spun into yarn.*

d. *Explain to your class that knitting is just one way wool yarn is processed to make clothing. Woolen coats and blankets are woven on looms. Have the students make their own simple looms by notching two opposite ends of a 5"x 5" piece of cardboard. Have them wind a piece of yarn between the notches to create a series of parallel strands and tie it off at the back. Then, using other pieces of yarn, have them weave over and under the alternating strands of yarn on the loom from one side to the other to create a piece of woven fabric.*

e. *Contact your local extension office for more information on sheep farmers and wool processing facilities. Plan a class trip to one of these farms or facilities.*

Directions: (continued)

sequence order. If necessary, tell them that the alternation of tools and products is another clue to the sequence order.

6. As a class, review the steps in the process. Starting at the beginning, let each student identify the object he or she is holding and discuss how it was used or made. The process begins with the sheep (*toy sheep or puppet*). Special breeds were raised for their wool. The wool is sheared off the sheep with shears (*scissors*). The fleece (*small piece of raw wool*) is thick, tangled and smells of lanolin. This lanolin feels greasy and acts as waterproof protection. The fleece is picked clean of sticks, twigs and bits of plant material and then untangled or carded using carders (*dog grooming brushes*). The untangled wool is called rolags or rolls (*sample of carded wool*). These rolls are twisted using a *drop spindle*. This forms yarn that is wound onto bobbins or into skeins (*ball or skein of white yarn*). When different colors of yarn were desired, the skeins were placed in a dye bath (*pot with dye packet*). The skein absorbed the dye, and the color was set in the yarn (*colored skein of yarn*). The colored yarn was then knitted into pieces with *knitting needles*. These pieces were sewn together to make a *sweater*.

Cow Relay

Objective:
Students will learn what cows eat and gain an awareness of the many cow by-products.

Grade Level: 2-6

Groupings: Two groups

Materials: Two headbands with ears and horns; two cow tails that can be attached to the students with string or Velcro; four large containers; an assortment of dairy cattle feed in plastic sandwich bags; cow by-products (see *From Moo to You*, page 42).

Time Allotment: 20 minutes

Directions:

1. Explain to the students that dairy farming is an important industry in New England and other areas of the United States. Ask students to brainstorm a list of products we get from dairy cattle. Point out that in addition to milk and meat products, other parts of the cow are used to produce important by-products. Some farmers say they use everything but the *Moo*! Ask the students to think of other parts of a cow that might be useful. As they mention parts, tell them about the general category of items that can be made from that by-product. For example, from the hide or skin, leather products are produced; from the hooves, bones and horns, products containing gelatin are produced. See *From Moo to You* (page 42) for additional examples.

2. Explain that they will be sorting a collection of items into three groups: things a cow eats, things made from cow by-products, and unrelated items. Divide the students into two groups and have them form two lines. Place a large container a few feet in front of their lines. Explain that it is filled with the items to be sorted. Several feet in front of this, set up three containers labeled "What Goes In, " "What Comes Back" and "Unrelated Items."

3. Explain that the students will participate in a relay race to sort these items. Two students, one from each group, will simultaneously have a turn. Instead of using a baton, which is passed from person to person in an official relay, they will

Extensions:

a. *Set up* **The Ins and Outs of a Cow** *exhibit (page 53) to show students the actual quantity of food eaten and milk produced. Compare a cow's intake to a human's daily and yearly intake.*

b. *Have a relay race outdoors using a scale and wheelbarrows to weigh and carry food to a cow at the finish line. Students will weigh out the actual amounts a cow eats daily and haul individual items to the finish line in a wheel barrow. This provides an accurate visual representation of the true amount of food a cow consumes daily and the work involved in caring for them.*

c. *Let student experience how milk proteins are transformed into a glue-like substance.*

STICKS LIKE GLUE RECIPE
2 cups skim milk
3 Tbsp vinegar
1/4 cup water
1 Tbsp baking soda

Add milk and vinegar to a saucepan and stir at low heat until the milk curdles (about 10 minutes). Remove from heat and continue stirring until all curdling stops. You now have curds and whey just like Little Miss Muffet did. Pour this mixture through a colander to separate the solid curds from the liquid whey. Dry off the curds and place them in a bowl with water and baking soda and beat until smooth. You now have milk glue! Store it in a covered container in the refrigerator to keep it from drying out.

Directions: (continued)

pass the cow headband and tail. These must be worn throughout each student's turn. One student from each team will put on his or her cow headband and tail, run up to the container of items, pull out the first thing they touch, place it into the appropriate labeled container, then return to the starting line. He or she will help attach the cow headband and tail to the next student who repeats the process.

4. When everyone has had a chance to participate or when all the items have been sorted, review the contents in the bins. Have the students vote with a show of thumbs up or thumbs down to show approval or disapproval of each of the selections. For items incorrectly placed, ask for ideas on proper placement or give additional clues to help sort them into the proper bin. Review the diversity of cow by-products.

FROM MOO *to* YOU

WHAT GOES IN: *Hay, fresh grass, haylage or silage, grain mixes, crushed corn, calf starter, water, minerals, salt licks.*

WHAT COMES BACK:
Meat: *steak, hamburger, hot dogs, roast beef.*

Milk: *ice cream, yogurt, butter, buttermilk, cheese, whipped cream.*

Milk proteins: *glues or adhesives used in Band-Aids, wallpaper paste and Elmers wood glue; and whey used in animal feed.*

Tanned hide: *leather products such as shoes, purses, belts, luggage.*

Fat trimmings scraped from the hide: *fatty acids or stearins added to pet food, margarine, crayons, soap, chewing gum, and floor wax.*

Cooked horns, hooves, and bone: *gelatin added to mayonnaise, candy, marshmallow, photographic film.*

Internal organs and blood: *rennet from calf's stomach used in baby formula and cheese; cow pancreas used to make insulin for diabetics; blood used in chicken feed and medicine.*

Animal waste: *manure and other manure blend fertilizers.*

From Grass to Milk

Objective:
Students will learn how a cow processes food and makes milk.

Grade Level: 4-6

Groupings: Nine groups

Materials:
Grass to Milk cards (p. 45-48.);

Answer cards *(Write the part's name on one side and its role in digestion on the other. This information is in italic beneath each of the Grass to Milk cards)*;

Nine packets of props:

MOUTH: tongs, mortar and pestle, Alka Seltzer;

RUMEN: egg beater, small plastic bag labeled "bacteria" filled with colored confetti, sponge;

RETICULUM: egg beater, small plastic bag labeled "bacteria" filled with colored confetti, sponge, ruler, tennis ball;

OMASUM: funnel, egg beater, sponge;

ABOMASUM: vinegar, sponge;

SMALL INTESTINE: sponge, small Slinky;

LARGE INTESTINE & CECUM: large Slinky, sponge, small plastic bag labeled "bacteria" filled with colored confetti, small bag of composted cow manure;

BLOODSTREAM: paper heart cut-out, toy train car;

UDDER: empty milk carton, blown up rubber glove with one finger missing.

Time Allotment: 30 minutes

Directions:
1. Ask the students for their impressions of the saying "You are what you eat." What happens to the food they eat once it is inside their bodies? Discuss the amazing transformation of food into the basic nutrients our body needs for growth and development. In the case of mammals, the food they eat can also be transformed into milk to feed to their babies.

2. Divide the class into nine groups. Explain that each group will represent a part of the cow involved in the transformation of green grass to the milk we drink. Using the cow diagram and background information on page 44 briefly describe digestion in the dairy cow.

3. Pass out a Grass to Milk card to each of the groups. Ask them to read their cards carefully. Point out that the words in italic provide valuable clues to the function(s) of their part.

4. Show the students the nine packets of props. Explain that they represent the various roles each of the nine parts plays in the milk-making process. Have groups select the bag of props that best matches the function of their part.

5. Now ask each group to select an answer card listing their identity. Before making their selection, encourage groups to share the information on their Grass to Milk cards with other groups. Point out that important clues may be found on cards held by their friends.

6. Now ask the groups to put their answer cards and props into the sequence of the grass to milk story. Remind the class that two end products are formed, so that at some point the sequence will branch.

7. Review the sequence giving each group a chance to describe and demonstrate their role in the milk-making process using the props. Then enjoy a glass of milk!

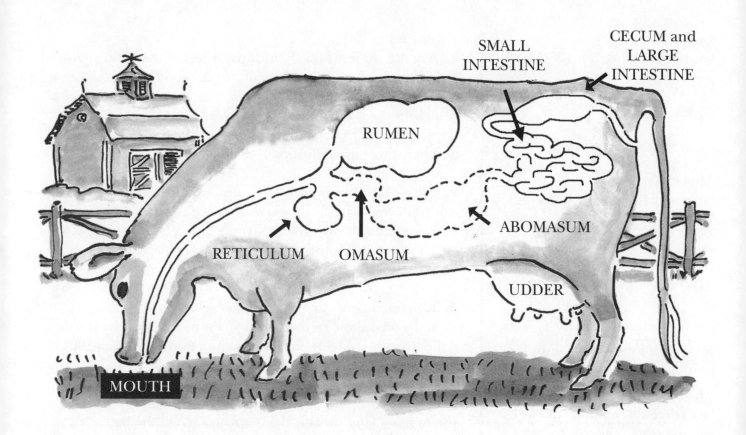

SMALL
INTESTINE

CECUM and
LARGE
INTESTINE

RUMEN

RETICULUM

OMASUM

ABOMASUM

UDDER

MOUTH

GRASS *to* MILK BACKGROUND

The secret to turning green grass into white milk lives in a cow's stomach. Make that stomachs*; a cow has four! Cows belong to a group of animals called ruminants. Thanks to microbes that live in a cow's first two stomachs — the rumen and reticulum — a cow can digest plant materials that many other animals cannot.*

*The **rumen** and **reticulum** are two separate organs connected by a large opening through which food passes constantly. Since the two organs serve a single function they are often referred to as the reticulo-rumen. The microbes in these organs break down plant material through fermentation, releasing nutrients important for milk production.*

*Only particles under a certain size can then pass through a small opening leading to the third stomach, the **omasum**. The omasum recycles water and minerals and passes the food to the fourth stomach, the **abomasum**. The abomasum works much like the human stomach, secreting strong acids and enzymes to break down any undigested food.*

*As food then passes through the **small and large intestines**, it is further broken down, nutrients are absorbed and waste consolidated. The small pouch off the large intestine, known as the **cecum**, contains microbes that ferment undigested food one last time to extract remaining nutrients.*

*The nutrients released by these organisms are carried through the cow's body by the **bloodstream**. Some are delivered to the **udder** where they are transformed, drop by drop, into milk.*

Unused material is passed from the cow in the form of manure. Rich in minerals and organic material, manure makes an excellent fertilizer for green grass. Not only does the cow provide us with nutritious milk, but it also can fertilize the grass that it eats to produce more milk!

Grass to Milk Cards

Grass to Milk Card

Cows are notorious for eating on the run. While out grazing in the field they use a strong muscle to *grab vegetation* and swallow it whole! Then they moo-ve on to the next clump. Now what would your parents say about such table manners? Tell them not to worry, the food gets chewed up eventually. Later the cow burps up a ball of food, called a bolus or cud, which it then chews and chews. Cows can spend up to eight hours a day chewing their cud or ruminating. The food is *ground up* and mixed with a white foamy froth. This froth acts like an antacid to keep the acidity level in the first stomach, the RUMEN just right for digestion.

What am I?
How do I begin the digestive process?

*Answer: I am the **MOUTH**. I grab food with my tongue (represented by the tongs), grind it up with my single set of bottom teeth (represented by the mortar and pestle), and buffer it with my saliva (represented by the Alka Seltzer).*

Grass to Milk Card

I am a very large organ and can hold up to 25 gallons of food. Most of the vegetation a cow eats comes to me looking much like it did when it was growing in the field. I work like a large fermentation vat along with my partner in digestion, the RETICULUM. We have a whole colony of microscopic organisms living inside of us that breaks down tough plant fibers without using oxygen! My muscles work to mix, moisten, *churn and blend* the food with these microbes. Important nutrients are then released and *absorbed* by the bloodstream. They are a major energy source for the cow and are important in milk production.

What am I?
What is my role in digestion?

*Answers: I am the **RUMEN**. I blend and churn food (represented by the egg beater), while bacteria inside me (represented by a plastic bag filled with colored confetti labeled "bacteria") breaks the food down through a process called fermentation. Important nutrients are then released and absorbed by the bloodstream (represented by the sponge).*

Grass to Milk Card

I am a team player in digestion. Food comes to me from my big buddy the RUMEN and I *mix it* with more microbes. We work together and pass food back and forth almost continuously. Important nutrients are also *absorbed* through my walls into the bloodstream. To keep moo-ving through the digestive tract food must *measure up*. If it can fit through the opening to the next organ in line, it is on its way. If not, lumps the *size of tennis balls* are formed and sent back, one at a time, to the mouth for more chewing and processing. Whenever you see a cow burp, a bolus or cud is on its way up to be re-chewed.

What am I?
What is my role in digestion?

Answer: I am the **RETICULUM**. *I also mix food (represented by the egg beater) with more bacteria (represented by the small plastic bag with colored confetti labeled "bacteria") and release important nutrients which are absorbed (represented by the sponge) into the bloodstream. Food must be below a certain size (represented by the ruler) before it can pass on to the next stomach in line. If it is too big, cuds (represented by the tennis ball) are formed and sent back to the mouth to be re-chewed.*

Grass to Milk Card

I have a *small opening* that lets me be selective about the size of food particles entering me. It's almost like the doorman at a fancy hotel. Once inside, the food is further *mixed* and softened. Water and minerals are *absorbed* from the food through my walls and pass into the bloodstream. The rest of the food moves to the true stomach or ABOMASUM.

What am I?
How do I function?

Answer: I am the **OMASUM**. *My small entrance (represented by the funnel) limits the size of food particles that can enter me. I further mix and blend the food (represented by the egg beater) and absorb water and minerals (represented by the sponge).*

Grass to Milk Card

I am often called the true stomach and I work much like your stomach does. I contain *special enzymes and acids* that completely break down the food that comes to me from the OMASUM. Here more nutrients are released, *absorbed* through my walls and passed into the bloodstream.

What am I?
What is my role in the digestive process?

*Answer: I am the **ABOMASUM**. With my special enzymes and acids (represented by the vinegar) I further break down the food, releasing more nutrients. The nutrients are then absorbed through my walls (represented by the sponge) into the bloodstream.*

Grass to Milk Card

The true stomach sends digested food and waste my way. More nutrients and water are released and *absorbed* through my walls into the bloodstream. I *expand and contract* to moo-ve the leftovers along my twisting path to my larger neighbors and relations, the CECUM and LARGE INTESTINE.

What am I?
How do I function?

*Answer: I am the **SMALL INTESTINE**. I absorb remaining nutrients (represented by the sponge) and pass them into the bloodstream. By expanding and contracting I move leftovers along my long twisting path (represented by the small Slinky).*

Grass to Milk Card

The SMALL INTESTINE passes its leftovers to me. These are *fermented by bacteria* in the CECUM and any remaining nutrients and water are *absorbed* through my walls into the bloodstream. I *expand and contract* to moo-ve the remaining unusable material to the end of the line. It comes out as *cow manure*, rich in minerals and organic matter. It fertilizes the green grass that can then be turned into more milk.

What am I?
What is my role in digestion?

*Answers: I am the **LARGE INTESTINE** and **CECUM**. I expand and contract to keep unusable food moving along (represented by the large Slinky). The CECUM, a small pouch like extension, with its associated bacteria, ferments the leftovers one last time (represented by the plastic bag of colored confetti labeled "bacteria") and any remaining nutrients and water are absorbed (represented by the sponge). The final product is manure (represented by the bag of composted cow manure), a rich fertilizer.*

Grass to Milk Card

I take all the nutrients absorbed from the RUMEN, RETICULUM, OMASUM and ABOMASUM and carry these throughout the cow's body. Think of me as a *mass transit system*, powered by a *strong muscular pump* that keeps nutrients moving continuously along. In a mother cow, I deliver important nutrients to the UDDER where they are used to make milk for her new calf.

What am I?
What is my main function?

*Answer: I am the **BLOODSTREAM**. My heart (represented by the red heart cut-out) pumps the blood, which carries important nutrients (represented by the toy train car) throughout the cow's body.*

Grass to Milk Card

When a cow has a calf I kick into action to feed the little tyke. The BLOODSTREAM delivers nutrients through tiny capillaries to each of my four chambers. Within these chambers, milk-making alveoli use the nutrients to *form milk*, drop by drop. It takes 50-70 hours for a cow to turn green grass into white milk. The milk is stored in me until it is needed. Then sensitive nerves within me trigger a series of responses making this milk available to whoever *squeezes my teats*, either the calf or the dairy farmer.

What am I?
What do I do?

*Answers: I am the **UDDER**. I make and store milk (represented by the empty milk carton) until the calf or farmer milks it out of my teats (represented by the rubber glove with one finger missing.)*

Butter Making

Objective:
Students will learn how to make butter.

Grade Level: K-3

Groupings: Two or three groups, 8-10 students per group

Materials: An old-fashioned butter churn or picture of one. Per group: whipping or heavy cream at room temperature, approximately one cup or a half pint; plastic peanut butter jar or other container that seals securely; two or three marbles; colander; bowl; wooden spoon; butter knife; crackers; small paper cups.

Time Allotment: 20 minutes

Directions:
An hour before beginning this activity, remove the cream from the refrigerator. Cream at room temperature will turn into butter more quickly than cold cream.

1. Tell the students that many food products are made from milk. Ask them to list as many as they can. Explain that you will be reading a few riddles and they need to guess which milk product you are describing.

Cold and creamy,
A frozen treat,
In a cone or a shake,
It can't be beat! (Ice cream)

A thick, tart, custard,
Fruit flavored or plain,
Curdled and cultured,
With a funny name. (Yogurt)

Rich, creamy, yellow,
Salted or sweet,
On toast or corn,
It's good to eat. (Butter)

2. Explain they will get a chance to make their own butter. Ask the students how they think butter is made. What ingredients are needed? Record their ideas. Show them an old fashioned butter churn or a picture of one. How was it used? What did it do?

3. Divide the class into two to three groups of eight to ten students each. Give each group a half-pint of cream, a plastic peanut butter jar and two to three clean marbles. Direct them to add the cream and marbles to the jar and fasten the lid securely. Ask the students why marbles are put in the container with the cream.

4. Now it is time to begin shaking. Have one student in each group shake their jar and ask everyone to

Extensions:

a. Do **From Farm to You** (page 37) using only dairy products. Have the students use their descriptive words and phrases to make short poems or riddles similar to those used at the beginning of this activity.

b. Make several flavored butters to sample. Honey butter is made by adding some honey to your butter. Try raspberry butter and add fresh or frozen raspberries and a bit of sugar. Chill them in small crocks and serve with homemade bread or rolls. You can even make bright red tomato butter that tastes great on corn on the cob by mixing 1 tablespoon of tomato paste to 1/4 lb. of butter.

c. Have the students chill their butter in old fashioned butter molds. Or have them decorate their butter with sprigs of fresh herbs, clover or edible flowers. Invite another class or parents in for a sample.

d. Try making yogurt or ice cream with your class.

Directions: (continued)

listen to the sound of the cream and marbles in the jar. What do they think will happen to the sound as the cream begins to thicken? Ask the students to predict how long it will take to make butter. Have each group record their predictions and starting time.

5. Since it can take 5-10 minutes to make a batch of butter, teach the class a traditional butter making song to sing while shaking (see **Butter Cake** page 51). Explain that as the butter was passed from child to child they sang this song, changing the name each time. When the next verse begins, the jar is passed to another student who continues the shaking. Or teach the class a more lively modern song, **Shake It!** (page 51), passing the jar after each chorus. Take breaks periodically to listen to the sound of the marbles in the jar. When do they notice a difference in sound? You can also turn the process into a competition to see which group can make butter first.

6. When the students see a lump of butter surrounded by a thin liquid, have them record the finish time. Ask whether they know the name of the liquid that is formed when making butter? (Buttermilk!) Direct the students to place a bowl beneath a colander and carefully pour the buttermilk off. Pour the buttermilk into another container and chill it for tasting later.

7. With the colander over the bowl, have the students wash the butter by pouring cold water over it to rinse off any traces of buttermilk. Direct them to gently press the butter against the side of the colander with a wooden spoon to be sure all the water is out. Then have them place their butter in a small bowl. A half-pint of cream will make approximately a quarter of a pound of butter.

8. Now it's time to enjoy the taste of fresh homemade butter. If the students will be eating the butter on salted crackers, they do not need to add salt. Otherwise, each group can add a pinch of salt and mix it into the butter.

ALL BUTTERED UP

How would you like a cluster of fat globules spread on your breakfast toast? Doesn't sound very appealing first thing in the morning, does it? Yet a piece of buttered toast is just that. Butter is made from cream which is liquid milk high in butterfat. The percentage of butterfat varies among the different types of milk and cream you buy. Whole milk has 4% butterfat, whereas heavy cream has at least 36% butterfat. That's why it's so thick and rich. Butter is made by shaking or churning cream. The butterfat particles in cream are wrapped in a coating or membrane. When you shake the cream, you break the coating around these fat particles, and they start to stick together. As you continue shaking, the particles completely separate from the liquid in the cream and form larger and larger fat clusters. When most of these fat particles are stuck together, you have a lump of butter floating in a sea of buttermilk. Just pour off the buttermilk (chill it to enjoy later), then dip your knife into some fresh creamy butter.

BUTTER CAKE
Come butter come
Come butter come
(Student's name) is at the garden gate
Waiting for a buttered cake
Come butter come

SHAKE IT!
(Sung to the tune of the "I Have Something in My Pocket" or the "Brownie Smile Song." Post the verses on the wall for the class to follow.)

We're going to make some butter,
Rich and creamy too,
With milk from a cow's udder
Before you can say moo.

Chorus:
So shake it, shake it, shake it,
Shake it if you can
Shake it like a milkshake,
And shake it once again.

Put some cream into a jar,
You can add a marble or two,
Make sure the lid is on tightly,
That's all you have to do.

Chorus

We're learning while we're churning,
Hey this is lots of fun!
It's easy to make butter,
Let's eat it when its done.

Chorus

Oh listen very carefully,
It's sounding different now,
Hooray it's finally butter!
Be sure to thank the cow.

Chorus

Say Cheese Please!

So who first discovered cheese? Everywhere around the world people make the claim. A common story is of a traveler carrying milk in a leather pouch made from a young animal's stomach or intestine. His trip is long, hot and bumpy. After several hours he stops to take a drink, and surprise! What was milk is now a tasty thickened substance — what we know now as cheese. Today the beginning steps of cheesemaking are similar to this tale. Milk is heated, stirred, and an enzyme called rennet, extracted from the lining of a calf's intestine, is used to coagulate the milk. The next steps vary depending on the type of cheese being made. Who would have thought that that bumpy ride long ago would have led to the gourmet section of your deli?

Silly Miss Muffet! She didn't have to sit around on her tuffet eating just curds and whey. She could have made delicious cottage cheese by following this simple recipe:

You will need:
- 2 cups of milk
- 3 Tbs. of vinegar or lemon juice
- a pinch of salt
- some whipping cream
- a sauce pan
- a wooden spoon
- a colander or sieve
- some cheesecloth
- 2 bowls

1. Put the milk in a sauce pan and add vinegar or lemon juice. Heat the milk for 8-10 minutes on low, stirring occasionally until it begins to curdle.

2. Remove the pan from the heat and continue stirring until all the milk has curdled. It has now separated into solid curds and liquid whey. Set this aside. (You might try tasting a bit now to see what Miss Muffet was eating.)

3. Now line your colander or sieve with a double thickness of cheesecloth. Set the colander over a large bowl and pour in the curds and whey.

4. Carefully gather the corners of the cheesecloth together and twist it to form a bag around the curds. Then continue twisting to squeeze out as much of the whey as possible. You can add the whey to the compost or dilute it with water and use it to water your plants.

5. Next put the curds in another bowl, add salt to taste, some cream to moisten and stir well. Then enjoy it alone or with your favorite fruit for a nutritious snack.

The Ins and Outs of a Cow

• EXHIBIT •

Materials:

Several pieces of poster board or cardboard; small blackboard listing daily foods eaten plus the milk and manure produced (see "What Goes In," page 54); bale of hay; a piece of a salt block; a bucket of grain; a bucket of haylage or silage; a bucket of water; plastic rake; small wheel barrow filled with composted cow manure; two milk crates filled with empty gallon milk jugs or cartons; bathroom scale.

Design:

1. Make a large cow from several pieces of poster board or cardboard. Attach it to a wall or bulletin board. Color it white with black spots like the common Holstein-Friesian cow or select a different breed of dairy cows. Brown Swiss are dark brown to silver-gray with black noses; Jerseys are brown or fawn colored; Guernseys are buff colored with white spots; and Ayrshire are white and reddish brown. Hang the small blackboard next to the cow (with the amounts missing).

2. On the front end of the cow, attach a sign that reads *What Goes In*. Beneath this sign assemble the following props: a hay bale, a bucket full of water, a bucket full of grain, a bucket full of haylage or silage and a salt block (or piece of one). To the rear end of the cow attach a sign that read *What Comes Out*. Beneath this set up a plastic rake on top of a small wheelbarrow filled with composted cow manure and two milk crates filled with empty gallon jugs. Attach envelopes to each of these props labeling the ins and outs. On scraps of paper, write the amount of food needed or the amount of milk or waste produced. Place the appropriate slip inside the appropriate envelope. (If you are unable to obtain props, draw a picture of each item and place it appropriately.)

Activity:

a. Pairs of students make predictions as to how much of each type of food a cow eats and how much milk and manure is produced daily. They then record these on a worksheet or in a journal.

b. Students check their answers by looking inside the envelopes attached to each of the buckets or containers.

c. Students weigh the actual buckets and containers and compare them to actual amounts eaten or produced daily. How many buckets of water would the cow need to meet its daily requirements? How much grain? How much hay?

Design: (continued)

3. Set up a bathroom scale nearby for students to use to weigh the various foods and products. Create a simple worksheet for the students to record their predictions of amounts consumed or produced, as compared to actual amounts, to record the weights of food and waste props and to calculate the quantities of each needed to meet daily requirements.

4. Write the following directions on or near the exhibit:

If you are what you eat, then cows are real heavyweights. In one year, a cow consumes literally tons of food. Talk about big appetites! On the blackboard is a list of foods a cow eats in one day and her daily by-products. Predict how much of each they eat or produce daily. Check your guesses by looking in the envelopes attached to each of the buckets or containers. Now use the scale to weigh the various foods and products displayed. Compare these weights to the actual amounts eaten or produced. How many buckets of each would they need to meet their daily food requirements?

DAILY INS *and* OUTS
of a **COW**

WHAT GOES IN:
water: 35 gallons
hay: 10 lbs.
salt or minerals: 5 oz.
grain: 20 lbs.
silage/corn or grass: 40 lbs.

WHAT COMES OUT:
manure: 60 lbs.
milk: 65 lbs. average
(8.6 lbs. per gallon)

SUSTAINABLE DAIRY FARMING

Most dairy farmers in this country still keep their cows confined in the barn all year and use tractors to bring them hay, silage and grain and to spread their manure.

At Shelburne Farms, and a growing number of other farms, all the cows have their calves in the spring, and their primary source of feed is pasture. The environmental benefits of this system include reduced soil erosion, elimination of herbicides and a decrease in fossil fuel use because the cows consume less grain, harvest their own feed and spread their own manure. At Shelburne Farms, each of our cows consume about 130 lbs. of grass and 10 lbs. of grain per day while on pasture.

Run for the Sun

Objective:
Students will demonstrate how energy flows through a food chain.

Grade Level: 2-6

Groupings: Entire class

Materials: Index cards with word and/or pictures depicting the different levels of the food chain (number of cards based on a class of 20): sun (10); producers (3 soybeans and 3 grain); primary consumers (1 vegetarian student and 2 herbivore cows); secondary consumer (1 omnivore student); seven buckets (2 labelled "sunlight energy," 2 labelled "producers," 2 labelled "primary consumers," and 1 labelled "secondary consumers"); ten containers with holes in the bottom; two 8 oz. cup containers without holes.

Time: 20-30 minutes

Directions:
This activity is best done outdoors on a warm day as the students will be running with water as part of the demonstration of energy flow.

1. Ask the students where all the energy on Earth ultimately comes from. (The sun.) Who can use this sunlight to make their own food? (Plants.) Explain that plants are the beginning or first level of a food chain. They are called the **producers** because they can make food from sunlight through the process called **photosynthesis**. Who gets their energy exclusively from plants? (Animals that eat only plants, called **herbivores** or in the case of people, **vegetarians**). Explain that they form the second level of the food chain and are called the **primary consumers**. Who is at the top of the food chain? (Animals that eat other animals exclusively, called **carnivores**, and animals that eat a mixture of plants and animals, called **omnivores**.) They are the **secondary consumers**.

2. Explain to the students they will represent members of the different levels of the food chain and demonstrate how energy flows through a food chain. Pass out a card to each student which will assign him or her to a role and level.

3. Ask the students what begins the food chain. Have all the sun students come forward and stand in a line. Who is in the first level? Have all the producers come forward and stand in a line in front of the sun line. Then have the primary consumers come forward and stand in front of the producers, followed by the secondary consumers. What do the students notice about the number of individuals at each level in the

Extensions:

a. *Try the activity with four different food chains. Place the last bucket in each of the four different chains at varying distances from the one below it based on the energy needed to produce the final product. Have the first chain end with a primary consumer (vegetarian). His or her bucket should be one foot away from the one below it. The second food chain will represent a secondary consumer who eats chicken. It takes twice as much grain to produce an equal amount of chicken, so the last bucket is placed two feet away from the one below it. The next secondary consumer eats pork, requiring four times as much grain, so the last bucket is placed four feet away from the one below it. The fourth food chain represents a secondary consumer who eats beef, requiring eight times the amount of energy to produce; his or her bucket is placed eight feet away.*

b. *Discuss new nutrition recommendations which suggest limiting the amount of red meat eaten and increasing the number of complementary vegetable protein combinations. Have the students look into these alternate sources of protein.*

Directions: (continued)

chain? (The number of individuals decreases as you go up the food chain.) Can they provide any explanations for this pattern? (Each level needs to support the one above it with adequate food so there must be more individuals in each previous level.) What would happen if this balance was destroyed? (A drop in numbers in one level is followed by a drop in numbers of each successive level; there is no longer food to support the original population.) Try building a pyramid from a similar number of blocks and removing some to demonstrate this concept.

4. Explain that the following outdoor demonstration will further illustrate the workings of a food chain. Head out to where you have set up two lines of buckets. Explain each line represents one food chain. The first line has three buckets equally spaced (5-6 feet apart). Label the first bucket "sunlight energy," the second "the producers" and the third "the primary consumers." The second line contains four buckets, similarly spaced, similarly labeled. Label the fourth bucket in this line "secondary consumers." Point out that the two buckets at the starting line are filled with water, which represent sunlight energy. Divide the sun students into two groups and have them form lines next to each bucket.

5. The next set of two buckets represents the producer level of the two food chains. Ask the soybean students to form their line next to the second bucket in the line of three, the grain students next to the second bucket in the line of four.

WHAT'S *for* DINNER?

Hamburgers, hot dogs, or pepperoni pizza? A large investment of food and energy is required to produce the meat people eat. A chicken has to eat twice its weight in grain for every pound of meat it yields. A pig eats four times its weight and a cow eight times its weight! Much of the grain produced in the U.S. to feed animals is grown in monocultures or large single crops. Monocultures can be hard on the soil, water and air, requiring the use of synthetic fertilizers and pesticides. Think of all the "people food" this grain could provide. Now we don't need to become vegetarians to change things. Meat is one of many foods that is a good source of protein. Doctors have found that eating leaner meat and combining vegetable proteins is better for our health. So try some bean and cheese burritos, add a peanut butter sandwich to your lunch, and eat more fish, turkey and chicken.

Directions: (continued)

6. The primary consumers are represented by the next set of buckets, Ask the vegetarian to stand next to the third and last bucket above the soybeans. The vegetarian eats hot dogs and burgers made from tofu derived from soybeans. Have the two cow students stand next to the third bucket in the line of four, as grain is one of their food sources.

7. Have the omnivore who enjoys all beef hot dogs and hamburgers stand next to the fourth and last bucket. He or she will represent a secondary consumer who gets their food energy from the meat of a cow. Pass out a cup to the omnivore and vegetarian. Explain that to make the hot dog and burger of their choice will take one full cup of energy or water.

8. Ask the students how the energy (water) from the sun will get into these hot dogs and burgers. (It will be passed up the food chain.) Review the sequence and rules for energy flow. The sun students will deliver energy (water) to the producers. Each sun team will take turns running with containers full of water and pouring them into the producers bucket. When the plants receive sunlight energy, they pass it onto the primary consumers. The plant students then also take turns running to deliver energy to the primary consumers' buckets. The primary consumers (cows) will in turn pass on their energy to the secondary consumer (omnivore). Explain that all the students should continue to take turns running and passing energy between levels until the person at the top of their food chain signals to stop, indicating their cup is full and their hot dog and burger are ready!

RUN *for the* SUN CARDS

PHOTOSYNTHESIS

PRODUCER

HERBIVORE

VEGETARIAN

PRIMARY

SECONDARY

Directions: (continued)

9. Casually pass out the containers with holes in them to the students while explaining that when you say "Go," both sun teams may begin the energy flow through their food chain. At this point someone will complain about the holes in the bottom of their containers. Explain that these holes represent the energy that is lost between levels. Not all the sun's energy is available to the plants and not all the food energy within the plants can be utilized by the primary consumers and so on. Remind the vegetarian and omnivore at the top of each line to signal a stop when their cup is full, then let the race begin.

10. When the vegetarian signals his or her cup is full, stop the activity. How much more energy is needed to fill the omnivore's cup? Discuss the results, being sure to point out it takes less energy to make and eat foods lower on the food chain. By eating foods lower on the food chain, there is more food available and more people can be fed. It is not necessary to become a strict vegetarian, but by eliminating some meat from our diets the land and feed used to raise those animals can then be used to feed more people. Discuss the implications with regards to food shortages and world hunger.

Soil Recipe

Objective:
Students will learn that soil is composed of many things, including living organisms, and will understand that time is important in the formation of soil.

Grade Level: K-3

Groupings: Pairs

Materials: Small paper bags (one per pair); chef's hat or apron; mixing bowl; wooden spoon; large index card; napkin large enough to cover the bowl; wristwatch; grocery bag containing a bottle of the herb thyme (real or pretend) and props or index cards to indicate water, nutrients, earthworms, sunshine, and bacteria.

Time Allotment: 30 minutes

Directions:

1. Invite the students into your garden test kitchen to make a special batch of soil. Explain that you have forgotten your recipe and you hope they can create a special class recipe for soil. Stress that you need soil and not dirt and ask if they know the difference. (Dirt is what is under your fingernails and gets washed off before meals. Soil is a living entity that grows the food we eat.)

2. Ask the students to raise their hands if they have ever cooked before using a recipe. Compare making soil to baking a batch of cookies. Explain that they are both a mixture of different ingredients in certain proportions. The final product is made by combining these ingredients according to a recipe.

3. Explain that a well organized cook has all the necessary ingredients on hand, so they simply add them as they are called for in the recipe. Tell the students that their first job is to gather the necessary soil ingredients to have on hand. Go outdoors and divide the class into pairs. Assign each pair the task of finding some soil ingredients (such as leaves, pinecones, grasses, small sticks, etc.). Give each pair a small paper bag in which to collect the materials and remind them to collect mostly non-living things.

4. At the end of the collecting time, gather the students together in a comfortable outdoor spot or back in the classroom. Ask for a volunteer who enjoys cooking to be the soil chef. Ask them about their favorite recipe while they are donning an apron or chef's hat. Give them the bowl and magic cooking spoon. Ask him or her to gather soil ingredients from the other students and mix them thoroughly. Record these ingredients on a giant recipe card.

Extensions:

b. *As a humorous ending or addition make a Dirt Cake. Consider dividing the students into small groups and making one small cake per group. Ask them to dissect this soil sample and pass out spoons and cups, inviting them to use their senses to determine this soil's recipe.*

DIRT CAKE RECIPE

1-1/4 lbs. Oreo cookies
12 oz. Extra Creamy Cool Whip
1/4 lb. (1 stick) margarine, softened at room temperature
2 small pkgs. of instant puddings (any flavor)
8 oz. cream cheese, softened with milk to remove lumps
3-1/2 cups milk
1 cup powdered sugar
Gummy worms (optional)
8" new plastic flower pot with saucer
Artificial flowers (optional)

1 Grind the Oreo cookies in a food processor. This is the "dirt".
2. In a large bowl, blend the remaining ingredients with an electric mixer.
3. Layer the "dirt" and filling in the plastic pot, starting and ending with "dirt."
4. Freeze overnight . Thaw 2 hours before serving.
5. Add the additional flowers if desired.

Serves 10 or more

Directions: (continued)

5. After all the items have been placed in the bowl, explain that there is a bit of magic in the science of making soil. Ask the soil chef to cover the bowl with the napkin and tap the bowl three times with the magic spoon. In unison, have the class whisper magic words (such as abracadabra, hocus-pocus or any other class favorites). Have the students give a drum roll by slapping their thighs, while the soil chef removes the cloth with a flourish. Since nothing has happened, exclaim to the soil chef that you thought he or she was a good cook. Ask the students what went wrong. Suggest that perhaps some ingredients were missing. Again compare making soil to baking, and make the analogy of baking chocolate chip cookies and leaving out the chips.

6. Pull out the shopping bag and tell the students you might have some of the missing ingredients inside. Give the students clues to the missing ingredients (sunlight, water, nutrients, earthworms, bacteria) and as they guess them, add the cards or props to the mixing bowl. Discuss the role of each item in the life of the soil.

7. Give additional clues so the students can guess the final, important missing soil ingredient — time. Pull out a bottle of the herb thyme as a joke when they guess. When the students protest, add a little more thyme and ask if that isn't enough. Point to your watch and ask the students if they mean that kind of time. Take off your watch and add it into the bowl. Is that enough time? Ask the students how much time they think is needed.

8. Compare their guesses to the actual figures. Explain that it takes 50 to 100 years to make an inch of topsoil. Using the their grandparent's age, give them a sense of the time span involved. Hold up a handful of soil and explain that when they are grandparents their soil ingredients will finally look like this. Finish by stressing the importance of soil in our lives and brainstorm ways to care for and save our soil.

Soil Trek

Objective:
Students will learn about the properties of soil through hands-on investigation.

Grade Level: 3-6

Groupings: Small groups

Materials: Introductory letter (see step # 1); cardboard box covered with aluminum foil; cassette tape with message from Tridians (see step #3); cassette player.
(*Per group, inside the aluminum foil covered 'space box*'): **Earth Investigation Worksheet** (see page 65 - 66); trowel; soil thermometer; pH kit; compaction stick (1/2 inch dowels that have been sharped at one end); coffee can with both ends removed; ruler; gallon jug for water; plastic zip-lock bag; aluminum pie pan; magnifying glass or hand lense.

Time Allotment: 20 minutes for opening activity, 30 minutes for Earth investigation, 30 minutes for skit development and 15 for presentation.

Directions:
This is a long, comprehensive activity designed to investigate the properties and importance of soil. It can easily be broken up and done over several days. It is a fantastic beginning to a subject that at first might not seem very exciting to your students.

1. Begin the activity with the following letter (or a similar one). Leave several copies around the classroom, in a manner atypical of your usual classroom protocol.

Greetings Earthling Students in Room # (list),
We are from the planet TRID. We have been watching you very closely and have seen you reading, writing, studying and asking questions. We have determined that you have all the scientific skills we've been looking for. Our planet is in deep danger, and we need your help. We are running out of all the things we need to live. We will be beaming down to your planet on (list date and time) in the Earth year (list). Please meet with us and help us solve the problem that is threatening our planet's future. May the forest be with you.

Ask the students to brainstorm a list of things they think the Tridians might be running out of. What might be the possible source(s) of their problems? Compare these to common problems on Earth and list some possible solutions.

2. On the designated day, ask the principal to bring the "Space Box" to your class. Ask him or her to play up its arrival in the school yard or office. Suggest that he or she carry it wearing fire gloves or potholders, explaining that it was glowing when it arrived. Have him or her point out that now that it has cooled, a message is visible on the top. Ask for a volunteer to read the message.

Due to strange and alien atmospheric conditions, we are unable to beam down to your planet. Instead, we are sending down this special space box. Please open it as soon as possible and listen to our story. Thank you for your help, and may the forest be with you.

3. Ask the volunteer to open the box and find a cassette tape, stressing that he or she not touch the contents until the class has listened to the Tridians' story. Then play the tape with the following recording (or something similar), recorded with a nasal Martian-like drone:

Extensions:

a. Follow up the outdoor percolation test with the indoor version presented in the activity **Soil Soakers** (page 67).

b. Use soil test kits to further evaluate and compare soil around the school.

c. As creative inspiration or a reminder of the importance of soil in our lives, play the song **Dirt Made My Lunch** from the album of the same name by the Banana Slug String Band (available from Music for Little People, P.O. Box 1460, Redway, CA 95560).

A MESSAGE *from the* TRIDIANS . . .

Greetings Earthlings! We are from the planet TRID. Our planet is in deep danger. It is so polluted we are no longer able to produce our own food, and our plants and animals are dying. We have detected life everywhere on your planet Earth. It appears to be lush, green, fertile and full of food. Our computers have been analyzing the reasons for this, and it appears that all food on your planet comes from a dead, brown grey substance we have heard you earthlings call soil or dirt. We find this hard to believe, but it is our last and only hope. If you will help us in our crisis, your mission is to find this substance called dirt, dissect it and record for our computers each and every ingredient. Then we will be able to manufacture dirt on our planet, and it can save us from the tragedy which is about to befall us.

We have sent down a special "Space Box" to help you with this mission. Please examine it carefully. Inside you will find the following:
*1. An **Earth Investigation Worksheet**. Please complete each and every section.*
2. Specially designed implements called trowels for digging up the soil.
3. Silver dissecting trays for sorting your soil samples.
4. Hand lenses for getting a closer look at the special ingredients.
5. Compact containers to transport your soil sample through space. They are rough, they are tough, they are zip-locked alligator space baggies. Please fill them to the brim with a sample of your rich Earthling soil.
6. Soil percolation kits in the form of a bottomless can with a ruler. Just add your abundant blue water!

Directions: (continued)

4. Have a few students sort the contents of the box into similar groups. Then review the ***Earth Investigation Worksheet*** and discuss how each of the tools will be used. Demonstrate how to set up the soil percolation test. Explain that the coffee can should be twisted or pushed into the ground to a depth of 1 inch. Then the can should be filled with water and the ruler, placed inside perpendicular to the ground, is used to measure the rate at which the water drains from the can. Explain that the compaction sticks will be pressed into the ground. What will this reveal about the soil? Determine how this will be tested so that all groups are using the same procedure and results are comparable. Demonstrate how to use the pH kit and discuss what pH measures. If you wish, do a pH test of a variety of common household items such as lemon juice, baking soda, and vinegar. Remind the students that the thermometer should be placed in the ground when they begin their testing and removed and recorded as they are leaving for an accurate reading. Suggest that all tests be done more than once to insure accurate results.

5. Divide the class into small groups. Ask each group to collect a complete set of "Space Box" materials plus a gallon jug full of water. Explain that each group should sample soil from a different area such as under trees, on the lawn, in a garden, or on the playground to get a good sampling of different soil types. Assign groups to a particular area and explain that they have 30 minutes to run their tests on site and complete the worksheet.

6. Bring the class together to share and compare test results. Create a chart and have the students list their results based on their sampling area. In which soil did water drain the quickest? The slowest? Which soil absorbed the most water? The least? Which soil was the most compact? The least compact? Compare the amount of air spaces in these soil. Plants need a combination of air and water in the soil to encourage healthy root growth. Which soils meet both these needs? Compare soil pHs. Most garden plants do best at a pH between 6.5 and 7. Which sites would make a good garden? To review soil ingredients, try using a giant recipe card and ask the students to list the important ingredients found in their samples. (This is a good time to do the activity ***Soil Recipe*** (page 59) or refer to it, stressing the critical ingredient of time.)

OLD FARMER'S TASTE TEST

Want to test the pH of your garden soil without using fancy equipment? Try the "Old Farmer's Taste Test." Just put a bit of soil on the tip of your tongue and try to determine the flavor. Do not taste soil if any chemicals have ever been applied. Is it bitter? Then your soil is too alkaline. Is it sour like a lemon? Then it's too acidic. Does it taste sweet? Hurray, then it is probably just right for growing most plants! pH is a measure of the soil's acidity. The pH scale ranges from 1-14 , the lower numbers indicating acidic conditions, 7 being neutral and higher numbers indicating alkalinity. Here's where some common household items fall on the pH scale: lemons, vinegar, and apple juice are acidic; baking soda, ammonia, and laundry bleach are alkaline; and water, cow's milk, and blood are neutral. A soil's pH is determined in part by the chemical nature of the rocks that made it, and the type of plants that live and die in it. pH effects the solubility, hence availability of nutrients important to plant growth. Most vegetables do best in the pH range 6.5 to 7. Various materials can be added to the soil to either raise or lower the pH to this desired level. So before you plant those seeds, dig in and taste your soil!

Directions: (continued)

7. Provide time for the students to work on their creative soil presentations. Encourage them to write scripts and to gather and make props to enhance their message. Then let them perform them for the class. Be sure to record their presentations on tape or with a video camera to be sent along to the planet TRID. (Incidentally, "trid" is "dirt" spelled backwards.)

Inspired by the activity Space Travelers in THE GROWING CLASSROOM *by R.Jaffe and G.Appel*

Earth Investigation Worksheet

Names of scientists: _____

Location of soil sample: _____

1. TAKE THE TEMPERATURE OF THE SOIL. Place the thermometer in the ground and perform all the following experiments. When you are finished with the experiments, record the temperature.

_____

2. DIG UP A SOIL SAMPLE and fill the zip-lock baggie.Keep digging and add another soil sample to the collecting tray. Now using your senses, write down at least two words to describe how the soil:

feels: _____

smells: _____

sounds: _____

looks: _____

tastes: _____

3. We need to make soil to save our planet. **DISSECT YOUR SOIL SAMPLE** and list the ingredients on the card below. Use the hand lense to get a close look.

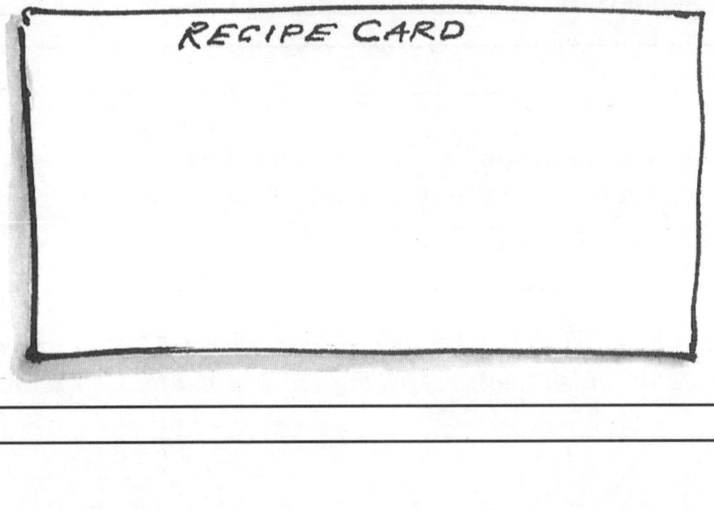

RECIPE CARD

4. Perform a **SOIL COMPACTION TEST**. Using your compaction stick, measure how deep you can press it into the soil. For accuracy, try this test more than once.

How many inches into the soil can you press the stick? _____

5. Perform a **SOIL PERCOLATION TEST**. Press the can into the soil to a depth of 1 inch. Stand the ruler inside the can. Fill the can with water to the brim and time how long it takes for all the water to be absorbed into the soil. Get ready, set, pour! (Make sure the water goes into the soil and does not spill out around the edges). Try this experiment again, both in the same spot and in a new location.

How long did it take? _____
How long did it take the second time in the same spot?_____
How long did it take in the new location?_____

6. Please take the **pH** of your soil sample (follow the instructions for your kit). What is the pH? _____

7. Now that you have finished all the experiments, please remove the thermometer from the soil. What is the temperature of the soil?

_____

Thank you for your hard work. Please remember to create a message that can be shown and/or broadcast on our planet to tell our people about the importance of soil. May the forest be with you!

Soil Soakers

Objective:
Students will observe and measure the relationship between water holding and drainage capacities of soils.

Grade Level: 3-6

Groupings: Small groups

Materials: (*per group*) Dry, diverse soil samples such as sand, clay, compost, garden soil, and peat moss; metal pie plate; glass lamp chimney or clear plastic soda bottles with bottom cut off; plastic window screening; rubber bands; 1-2 quart wide-mouth jar; masking tape; clear 8 oz. plastic cup; water.

Time Allotment: 30 minutes

Directions:

1. Challenge the students to collect unique soil samples from in and around their homes and gardens. Suggest they talk to gardeners to obtain special mixes or soil types. Have them bring their sample to class in a brown paper lunch bag. Ask them to keep their soil composition a secret. You might want to bring a selection of soils yourself to insure a diverse mix. Possibilities include: potting soil, compost or composted cow manure, sand, peat moss, and clay.

2. Collect and observe the students' soil samples. Select four to six distinct samples to be used in the activity. Divide the students into small groups and assign a soil sample to each. Have each group empty their sample into a metal pie plate. Ask each member of the group to use their senses to observe the soil and record an adjectives that describe their sample. Do not taste any soil if chemicals have been applied. Have the group use the words generated to create a short poem, verse or song about their sample.

3. Collect the samples and number each one. Display them in a central location. Ask the students to visit each of the samples and observe them carefully. Have each group then read their poem, descriptive verse or song and let the rest of the class try to guess which soil sample it describes.

4. Discuss the variety of soils, their basic characteristics and how each type might affect plant growth. Sand is composed of fairly large particles with rough edges, has a gritty texture, and a lot of air spaces between the particles. Clay is made of very fine particles with smooth edges. It is sticky and slippery when wet and can become hard and packed when dry. It is often hard to work. Loam is a mixture of particles sizes and has a crumbly texture and moderate air spaces. Soil rich in organic material tends to act like a sponge and hold water. Explain that the groups will be performing an experiment to investigate the water holding and drainage capacities of these various soil samples.

5. Pass out a glass lamp chimney (or plastic soda bottles or funnel), plastic screening, and rubber bands to each group. Ask them to attach the screening to the narrow end of the chimney with the rubber band. Provide masking tape and have each group label their soil sample with an identifying

Extensions:

a. *Make squirt bottles for younger students by punching holes in the lids of plastic soda bottles. Fill these bottles with water and explain they will be using them to test absorption rates of different soil areas in the school yard. Divide the class into pairs and give each pair a bottle. Outside, have them squirt an area of soil with water. Is the water quickly absorbed or does it pool up? Have the pairs share and discuss their results.*

b. *Have students repeat outdoor percolation tests as done in **Soil Trek** (page 61) throughout the school yard. Be sure to choose areas where the soil is compacted from heavy use, where it is covered by grass and where it is open and loose. Collect soil samples from these areas for comparisons. Discuss results.*

Directions: (continued)

name. Ask them to add their soil to the chimney to the predetermined line (each group should have the same amount of soil in their chimney). Pass out wide-mouth jars and have each group place their chimney into the jar, screen side down.

6. Have the groups place their setup in a central location with their original soil sample in the metal pie pan for observation. Explain that they will pour water into the wide end of the chimney (about 1/3 to 1/2 full) and observe and record how quickly water passes through the sample and into the wide-mouthed jar. This is called a ***percolation test***. They will also note how much water is absorbed by comparing the volume of water before it is poured into the sample to the volume of water after it has passed through the sample. What factors do they think will affect the percolation rate? Which sample will perc the fastest? The slowest? Suggest that they look closely and feel the samples in the metal pie plates for helpful information.

7. Ask each group to designate one student to pour water through their sample and another to monitor and record the times. Explain that when you say, "Go!" students will simultaneously pour water into the chimneys. In addition to observing and recording, the timers will announce when the first drop passes through the sample and when the water finally stops dripping steadily.

Extensions: (continued)

c. *Have the students conduct an experiment to look at particle size, pore sizes and water-holding capacity of some common materials. Give each group a cup full of marbles and one filled with the same amount of sand. Which cup has the most empty spaces or pores, the marbles or the sand? To check their guesses, give them cups containing the same amount of water. Tell them to add water until the water level is even with the top of the marbles or sand. Direct them to remove any excess water with an eyedropper and add it back to the original cup. Which holds the greatest amount of water? (The sand can hold more water than the marbles as there are more air spaces in the cup of sand.) Were they surprised? Suggest they try filling the empty spaces in a second cup of marbles with sand. How much sand can they add? Will they be able to add any water to this mixture? Record their predictions, then test by pouring in water.*

Directions: (continued)

8. Discuss the results from the samples. Were there any surprises? Compare the volume of water that passed through each sample. Have the students pour the percolated water back into the plastic cups. How does it compare to the original volume? Be sure to note any differences in color and clarity.

9. Wet the soil samples in the metal pie plates. Have the students feel and describe the wet soil. Explain that they will repeat the percolation test through the wet soil samples. Explain that when evaluating soils at a building site percolation tests are done in wet soil. Do they think the results will change?

10. Compare results from wet and dry samples. What can you determine about each sample's porosity and drainage abilities versus water retention? How would these factors influence plant growth?

SOIL SPONGES

What do a sponge and good garden soil have in common? They are both full of holes and absorb and hold water. Good garden soil is a mix of different particle sizes and rich in organic matter, with a crumbly texture and a range of air spaces. These characteristics allow for the free flow of oxygen and water through the soil, making it easier for plant roots and soil animals to work their way through. Organic materials in the soil improve absorption and water holding capacity, encouraging healthy and vigorous root growth. These materials also help to control erosion, as surface water is quickly and completely absorbed, leaving little damaging run off. Good garden soil maintains a balance between how quickly water drains through the soil and how much water is retained; hence, the soil is never too wet or too dry.

The Soil Chef
• E X H I B I T •

Materials:

Old clothes (preferably white) including two or three aprons and a chef hat; newspapers for stuffing a three-dimensional chef; small table and chair; binder labelled as soil cookbook; mixing bowl; measuring spoon and cups; mixing spoons and other kitchen utensils; shopping bag filled with soil ingredients (see list below); index cards or paper designed for use as recipe cards.

Activity:

1. Have students work in pairs. Have them sort through the ingredients in the shopping bag and place those chosen into the mixing bowls. Have extra aprons on hand for the budding soil chefs to wear while concocting their new recipes. Then have them refer to the sample recipe card in the binder to write up their own recipe complete with directions.

Design:

1. Have the students help create a three-dimensional soil chef. Ask them to bring in old clothes and use newspaper to stuff the chef. Seat the chef on chair behind table and be sure to add a chef's hat and apron to complete the look.

2. Set mixing bowls, measuring cups, spoons, and utensils on the table. Label a binder as the class soil cookbook, insert a sample soil recipe in the front and place it on the table.

3. On one corner of the table set a large sturdy shopping bag filled with a selection of possible soil ingredients (see list) plus a few tricks and surprises.

4. Write the following directions on or near the exhibit:

Welcome to Shelburne Farms Restaurant (substitute your own name). Today we are featuring a smorgasbord of soil dishes for your plant's dining pleasure. Tie on an apron, sort through the ingredients in the bag and mix together your own special recipe in the mixing bowl provided. Then name your recipe, write down the ingredients and list important directions on the recipe cards provided. Then add it to the class collection. Bon Appetit!

POSSIBLE
SOIL INGREDIENTS
(sealed in plastic sandwich bags)

stones	dried orange peels
twigs	bag filled with
dried leaves	colorful paper dots,
grass clippings	labelled bacteria
pieces of bark	blown-up bag labelled
various types of	air
soil	and a clear plastic
compost	jar filled with water.
peat moss	
gummy worms to	Other items to trick
represent earth	them might include
worms	an old tin can,
selection of plastic	old sock, Styrofoam
insects	cup or other non-
plastic mushrooms	biodegradable waste.

Soil Shakes

Objective:
Students will learn that soil is composed of different sized particles and how these particles influence water drainage and retention.

Grade Level: 3-6

Groupings: Pairs

Materials: Student soil samples; sample bags of sand, silt and clay (contact your local Soil Conservation Service for help in obtaining these); paper bags; large piece of paper for particle size chart; paper cut-outs the size and shape of basketballs, baseballs and small confetti dots (one each per student); clear quart jars with tight fitting lids; coffee filters; funnels.

Time Allotment: 30 minutes for initial activity, 15 minutes for later observation

Directions:

1. Ask students to bring in soil samples (approximately 2 cups) from home. Have students compare and discuss differences in appearance and texture. Explain to the class that soil is a composition of organic materials and mineral soils of three main particle sizes.

2. Set up the sample bags of sand, silt and clay in a central location in the room, with an empty paper bag next to each sample. Explain to the students that in three of the bags are soil samples of the three main particle sizes. Show the students a chart listing only the particle sizes (you will add more information as the activity progresses). Pass out one of each circular paper cut-out to each student. Explain that these represent the three particle sizes and show the relative difference in sizes between the particles. Ask the students to feel the soil samples without looking in the bags and place the cut out that matches its relative size in the paper bag next to that sample.

3. Review the cut-outs placed in each bag, then reveal the sample, from largest to smallest. Ask students to identify the first sample with the largest particles by name. (Sand.) Review the particle size chart and add the name next to the size listing. Discuss the basic features of each soil type and its quality with respect to gardening and growing food. Use the paper cutouts as a visual aid to show how the different particles would fit together. Note the amount of large air space between the sand particles indicating rapid drainage and the inability to hold much water or nutrients. How do the silt particles differ? (They have medium air spaces, moderate to poor drainage and can hold some water). Last, look at the clay and note its poor drainage. The particles are so fine that often water is unable to penetrate into the clay. Hard packed clay soils in the garden can be very difficult to work.

4. Explain that most soils are a combination of these particle sizes. Different types of soil are classified based on their percentages of these three particle size components (see **Particle Size Chart**, page 73). Some soils are better than others for gardening. Over time, the texture and composition of all soils can be altered by adding differing amounts of sand, silt or clay, plus compost and other organic materials.

Extensions:

a. *Have the students do a "soil snake test" to determine the particle size composition of the soil. This is a simple test which uses soil texture to determine the particle sizes in the soil sample. Ask the students to select a soil sample and pick up 2 teaspoon in their hand. Have them use a mister to gently spray the sample until it is moist, like putty. Try adding more water if it seems too dry or a bit more soil if it feels too wet. Now have them roll the soil into a ball. Can it stay in this shape or does it crumble apart? If it can't hold its shape and it feels gritty, there is probably a high percentage of sand in that sample. If it holds it shape, next try rolling it between your hands to form a soil snake. How long a snake are you able to make? Measure the snake before it breaks apart. If you are able to roll your snake to great lengths, this indicates a high percentage of clay, which binds well to itself as we know from the art of pottery. Shorter snakes indicate lower percentages of clay mixed with the other particles.*

b. *Obtain a soil sieve set (available for purchase from Forestry Supplier, Inc., P.O. Box 8397, Jackson, MS 39284 (800) 647-5368) and have the students use them to sort various soil samples. The screen openings are graded by size and run from large open mesh to very fine. Pass the screens around and have the students examine the different size screen mesh. Often the sizes are marked on the screen, and older students can compare these to the actual soil particle sizes (see chart on page 73). A soil sample is placed inside the screen with the largest holes and is then attached to the other screens in descending order. Have the students take turns shaking the soil sample. As they shake the sample,*

Directions: (continued)

5. Explain that they will determine the composition of their soil sample by using the "soil shake" method. Soil is added to a container of water, then the mixture is shaken to disperse the particles. How would they predict the three particles to settle? (The particles separate by size and weight, and distinct layers can be observed when the soil completely settles). Which particle type would settle first? Second? Last? (Sand settles first, then silt and lastly clay.)

6. Divide the class into pairs and have each pair fill a quart jar 2/3 full with water. Have them add their soil to the jar until it is almost full and screw the lid on tightly. Now they shake it for 1-2 minutes until the soil is well dispersed and the solution looks like a rich chocolate soil shake. Have them set the jar in a level place and not disturb it for 24 hours. Ask the students to predict which component will make up the greatest percentage of their soil sample.

7. After 24 hours, have the students observe and measure the layers. Can they determine which layer is sand, which layer is silt, and which layer is clay? Which layer is largest? Older students can calculate percentages using the simple formula: the height of a layer divided by the height of entire sample equals the decimal fraction of layer. Multiply by 100 to get a percentage. If the water is still cloudy, direct them to carefully pour it through a funnel lined *particles fall through the successive screen layers until they reach one whose mesh openings are too small to fit through. In the end the sample is divided into its component parts. Unscrew the screens and pass around for the students to observe and feel the individual components. Repeat this activity with a variety of soil samples.*

c. *Based on soil composition, make predictions on how various soil samples will percolate, then test them. See **Soil Soakers**, (page 67.)*

SOIL PARTICLE SIZE CHART
in millimeters diameter

clay	<.002
sand	.05-2.0
silt	.005-.05
gravel	≥2.0

Source: U.S. Department of Agriculture, 1984

with a coffee filter to collect the residue. Have them examine the residue after it dries. Have the students name their soil type using the soil type chart. Would their soil be good for gardening? Why or why not? How could they improve its quality for gardening?

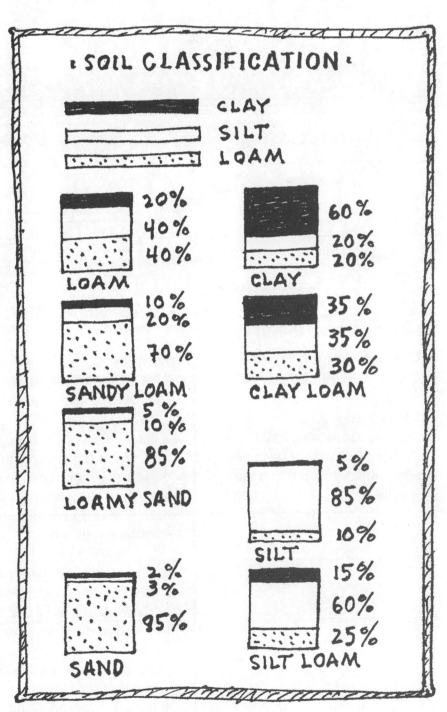

The World Beneath Your Feet
·EXHIBIT·

Materials:

Four sheets of poster board; markers; white glue; ground coffee; leaves and twigs; potting soil; sand; gravel; old sponges; spray paint or tempera paint; writing paper and pencils.

Design:

1. Attach four sheets of poster board together to form a large square. Use this entire space to create a soil profile. Near the top of the paper, draw a pair of feet standing on the soil surface. Consider attaching a pair of old, soft rubber boots to the exhibit for a three-dimensional effect. Draw or fashion grass and other plants along the soil surface to create a lush, green, growing layer. Attach thick yellow, white, and/or orange yarn in root-like designs beneath the surface, reaching to different depths.

2. The rest of the paper will be divided into four unequal layers. The first layer beneath the surface is called the "O horizon" and is very narrow, only one to two inches in depth. It is rich in organic matter, dark in color and includes fallen leaves and twigs. To represent this layer paint a narrow layer of white glue thinned with water just below the surface and sprinkle it with ground coffee. Add dried leaves, twigs, small stones and various other objects commonly found on the soil surface.

Activity:

1. Students work in pairs. Ask them to pull tabs to learn about the various horizons, read the riddles and guess the identity of the creature hidden in the world beneath their feet.

2. Students create their own riddles about soil creatures. Have them make soil horizons similar to those in the original exhibit. Direct them to cut a flap in the soil layer under which a soil creature will be placed. Ask them to draw a soil creature and glue their drawing beneath the flap. Next have them write a riddle about their soil animal and attach it to their soil horizon. Attach the students' soil horizons around the outside of the large exhibit with their accompanying riddles. Encourage students to read and guess the identity of the new soil animals on display.

Design: (continued)

3. The next layer, often about ten inches thick, is called the "A horizon." It is also dark rich soil and can be represented by gluing potting soil to poster board.

4. Next is the "B horizon" or the subsoil. It is a often two to three times as thick as the A horizon. It is lighter in color and rich in minerals. Glue sand and gravel in a wider band to form this layer.

5. The last last layer is the "C horizon." It is composed primarily of the parent material — larger rocks and particles that make up the soil type and reach down to the bedrock. Cut old sponges into uneven rock-like shapes. Color them with black, white and grey spray or tempera paint to create a mottled rock-like appearance. Glue the sponges interspersed with gravel to the lower portion of the exhibit.

6. Next to each of the four layers make a pull out tab listing the name and some information about that particular layer. To create these pull out tabs, staple thin strips of poster board to the back of the exhibit behind each layer, into which long strips of poster board can slide easily in and out. Write horizon information on these strips. Push them into the slots behind the exhibit so that the information is hidden and only a small part of the strip protrudes. Add a wider tab of poster board to both ends of these strips so that they can not be pushed or pulled too far in or out.

7. Next cut out four to six flaps in the O, A and upper B layers. Draw pictures of various creatures that might be found living in the soil and place them under the opening so they are visible when the flap is lifted. Number these flaps and display matching riddles near the exhibit for the students to read and guess the identity of the creature hidden beneath. See *Creature Features* (page 76) and *Soil Critter Chart* (page 82) for possible soil creatures.

8. Set up thick paper, glue and soil samples for students to make their own soil profiles with soil critters hidden beneath lift-up flaps. They will write their own riddles to attach to their soil horizon and add to the exhibit.

Design: (continued)

9. Write the following directions on or near the exhibit:

Welcome to the world beneath your feet. If you dig deep enough, you will find it is divided into four uneven layers. Pull the tabs to learn their names. Hidden in these layers are thousands of creatures of all shapes and sizes. Read the riddles and see if you can guess who a few of them are. Then lift the matching flaps to check your guesses.

Try creating your own soil creature riddles. Use the paper and materials provided to make a soil horizon complete with a soil animal beneath. Write and attach your creature riddle to your soil horizon and add it to the exhibit.

Soil on the Run

Objective:
Students will learn about soil erosion and how to control it.

Grade Level: 2-6

Groupings: Small groups

Materials: Old paint roller trays or 9 x 13 baking pans; soil; 2 to 4 bricks; watering cans; buckets filled with compost; a variety of mulch materials such as dried leaves, grass clippings, straw, Popsicle sticks, twigs, and toothpicks; selection of quick germinating seeds such as grass seed, wheat, buckwheat, or beans.

Time: 15 minutes for initial demonstration, variable time for research and soil tray preparation, 20 minutes for final experiment and discussion.

Extensions:

a. *Try this activity outdoors on a sloping plot of lawn. Remove sod from several plots and test various options: mulch, terracing , addition of organic matter etc.*

b. *Make splash sticks to show how raindrops can loosen and move soil. Have small groups of students make their own splash sticks by attaching paper to three foot lengths of lumber with thumb tacks. Explain they will be holding these sticks vertically over*

Directions:

1. Gather the students together for a demonstration. Explain that you are a New England hill farmer and you just finished harvesting and tilling up your fields. Show the students a tray full of soil which is propped up on one side with bricks, creating a slope. Place beneath the tray a collecting basin which runs the width of the tray. Tell the students it has been a rainy fall and another storm is brewing. Ask them what will happen to the soil in this field during a rainstorm. Record their predictions. Then using a watering can held one foot above the tray let it rain for 1-2 minutes.

2. Have the students examine the soil in the tray and observe the runoff collected in the basin. Pour it into a clear jar for closer inspection. (They should see gullies formed in the tray, and perhaps large areas where the soil was washed away. The water in the collecting basin will be muddy and full of sediment.) Have them test the soil at various depths to see how much water was actually absorbed. Discuss the results and what this means with regard to soil and plant health.

3. Explain to the students that soil erosion is a serious problem facing farmers throughout the world. Every year 3 billion tons of topsoil is lost, and it is the topsoil that is responsible for the soil fertility. Remind them it takes 100 years to make an inch of new topsoil Challenge the students to reduce the amount of erosion that occurs on sloping farm fields.

4. Divide the students into small groups and give each two trays to be filled with soil. They will need to research and discuss possible options for controlling erosion in these field. Possible options should include mulch covers, contour plowing, cover cropping, terracing, and addition of organic materials to soil to improve water absorption.

5. Provide materials for students to use on their fields including compost, various forms of mulch, twigs, Popsicle sticks and toothpicks (for creating terraces, water bars and roots), and seeds. Decide with the students a time limit for research and preparation. It can vary greatly depending on the students' desires to experiment with cover crops and planting patterns.

Extensions: (continued)

bare soil with the paper touching the ground and using a watering can to simulate rain. How high will the raindrops carry bits of soil? Ask them to record and initial their predictions along one edge of the paper. Then pouring water from a predetermined height (knee high, waist high, shoulder high) onto the bare ground, test their predictions. Note any dirt spots and measure their height. Try the experiment on soil covered with vegetation, with with mulch, etc. Compare results. Discuss the effect of splash erosion. Look for examples in the school yard.

c. *Go on a erosion walk around the school yard to identify where erosion is occurring. Have the students suggest solutions to these problems and try to implement their ideas.*

d. *Study the Dust Bowl era and how the health of the soil affected people's lives.* CHILDREN OF THE DUST BOWL *by Jerry Stanley (Crown Books for Young Readers, 1993) gives insight into this tragic era in history.*

e. *Let students experiment with cover crops and planting patterns as a follow-up to the original experiments.*

Directions: (continued)

6. On the day of the experiment set up the trays and have the students present their methods for erosion control. Have all groups pour the same amount from a set height onto the sloping field. Examine the runoff of each field, noting clarity, color and amount collected. Which methods were most effective at controlling erosion?

TREATING SOIL LIKE DIRT

Erosion, the wearing away of soil by water, wind, and ice is a major problem threatening our survival. How can that be, since soil is underfoot everywhere? The problem lies in our nutrient-rich topsoil and our use of this precious resource. Imagine the Earth as an apple with the skin representing all the soil. Only the topsoil, the first few inches of soil, is good for growing crops. Yet, every year over 3 billion tons of soil are lost. And replacing it takes 100-200 years or more per inch of topsoil! At this rate it won't be long before our topsoil is depleted. But people are taking erosion seriously and time, energy, and money are being devoted to solving this problem. Governments are spending billions of dollars teaching farmers everything from organic matter enhancement to improve soil quality and infiltration, to effective vegetation cover cropping to modern conservation tillage methods. Before long we hope to be in the black, black rich soil that is!

The Rotten Truth

Objective:
Students will learn about the decomposition process.

Grade Level: 3-6

Groupings: Pairs

Materials: Lunch leftovers; scissors; plastic zip-locked sandwich bags; paper and pencil; soil; plant mister; rubber gloves.

Time Allotment: 30 minutes for initial set up, short observation time throughout and 20 minutes for final analysis.

Directions:

1. Ask the students to name some of the things they have thrown away over the past two days. What happens to these things? Do they disappear? Decompose? Remain in the same form forever? Record the students' ideas on the blackboard. Explain that they will conduct an experiment with the leftovers from their lunches to learn the fate of some common throw-away items.

2. Give each student a plastic zip-locked lunch bag. Explain that they will place one small piece of each item in their lunch into the bag. This includes food, peelings, a corner of the lunch bag, paper napkins, plastic bags, waxed paper, plastic utensils, paper cups, milk cartons, and straws. Have them use scissors to cut items up, if necessary. Stress that they not add any meat to their bag as potentially harmful bacteria could grow.

3. Divide the class into pairs. While one student adds items to his or her compost bag, have the other student record the exact contents. The recorder should also note his or her partner's predictions as to what will happen to each item over time. Will it rot? Smell yucky? Remain the same? Have the students switch roles and create a second compost bag with a list of contents and predictions.

4. Ask the students to add a sprinkling of soil to their bags and to lightly mist the contents with a plant mister. Have the students breathe air into the bags and carefully seal them.

Extensions:

a. *Have the students conduct a similar experiment burying selected lunch items in clay or plastic plant pots. After 2-8 week, empty the pots and sort through the contents. Compare and contrast decomposition times between the pots and the plastic sandwich bags.*

b. *Read the book MOUSEKIN'S GOLDEN HOUSE by Edna Miller (Prentice-Hall, 1964) and discuss what happens to Mousekin's pumpkin. After Halloween, set up an old jack o' lantern inside an empty aquarium in the classroom. Cover the aquarium with Plexiglas and observe the changes that occur over time.*

c. *Start an outdoor compost pile with lunch leftovers (see **Compost Cake**, page 87). Have students weigh the amount of food added to the pile each day. Challenge them to reduce the amount of waste generated. Add finished compost to school gardens.*

Directions: *(continued)*

Explain that they will leave the bags for 2-8 weeks. You may decide to keep all the bags together, or place them in various locations with differing conditions (hanging in a sunny window, hidden inside a dark closet, in a cool entry way, etc.). Ask the students if these varying conditions might have a different effect on what occurs in the bags. (If you let the students choose their compost bag's location, be sure to have everyone register their location on a class master list or you may be unpleasantly surprised when a missing bag finally makes its presence known.)

5. Have students create compost bag journals. Ask them to observe their bags periodically and record what they see happening inside. Remind the students that they are not to open the bags until the designated time is up.

6. On the selected date, have the students bring their compost bags outdoors. Caution students with asthma or allergies to avoid contact with composted materials. Distribute rubber gloves for the students to wear while sorting through the contents of their bags with their partner. Record any items still identifiable and their present state. Are any items missing? Provide plant misters so items can be cleaned off for closer observation and identification. How did the results compare to the predictions?

WASTE WORDS

biodegradable - *capable of being broken down by living microorganisms into simpler compounds*

compost - *well-rotted plant and animal waste prepared by people to be used as a soil conditioner or fertilizer in gardens*

decomposer - *an organism that digests organic waste and dead organisms by breaking them down into simpler compounds and absorbing soluble nutrients*

decomposition - *the process of breaking down dead plants, animals and animal waste into simpler nutrients*

humus - *dark organic matter found in topsoil that consists of decayed vegetable matter; humus increases water retention of soil and provides nutrients important for plant growth*

non-degradable - *material that can not be broken down by natural processes*

nutrient - *any element an organism needs to live, grow and reproduce*

photodegradable - *material capable of being broken down by exposure to sunlight*

recycling - *the process of collecting and reprocessing matter from garbage or the waste stream so that it can be made into new products*

reusable - *a product that can be used over and over again in the same form*

Directions: (continued)

7. Define and discuss the process of decomposition or decay. Explain how certain materials are broken down by microorganisms, mainly bacteria and fungi, into basic nutrients and recycled back into soil. Talk about composting as an alternative to the garbage dump for certain items. Introduce the terms biodegradable, non-biodegradable, recyclable, and reusable (see ***Waste Words***, left). Have the students sort the items in their compost bags into these categories.

THE DIRT *on* DECOMPOSITION

Decomposition is a fundamental process on which all life depends. We'd all be knee deep in garbage without it. Bacteria, fungi and other microscopic organisms that live in the soil, air, and water are responsible for turning once living plants and animals into nutrients that can be used again and again. Think of them as nature's recyclers. They have the ability to produce special enzymes which allow them to break down these dead plants and animals and use them as food. No job is too big as they enlist the help of friends and family. As they eat, they grow and multiply at an amazing rate. In just four hours, one bacteria can grow into a colony of 5096! And at day's end, there are millions and billions of them working together. Why, in one spoonful of soil there are more bacteria and fungi than all the people on Earth! Despite their microscopic size you've probably seen evidence of them right in your own homes. Remember that orange with the blue-green mold in the back of the refrigerator? Or that black fuzzy slice of bread hidden in the bread box? Or those damp old gym socks, newly spotted with black and pink that you left in a plastic bag? These are colonies of our microbial friends hard at work at the fine art of decomposition.

Soil Critter Chart

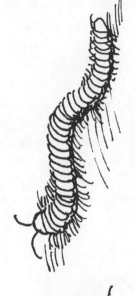

MILLIPEDE

Long, rounded soil critters that have hard segmented bodies with many legs. Each body segment has two pairs of legs. As vegetarians, millipedes eat holes in fallen leaves (among other things), thus enabling smaller decomposers to continue the decay process.

ISOPOD

These soil critters are covered with flattened plates of armor, resembling tiny armadillos. They are brown or gray in color. Isopods eat decaying leaves and wood and are often found in damp leaf litter and rotting wood. They are commonly called sowbugs or, if they roll into balls when disturbed, pillbugs.

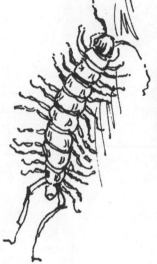

CENTIPEDE

Predatory soil critters that move about quickly on many legs. Their bodies are flattened and each body segment has only one set of legs. Gloves should be worn when handling these critters as they have a poisonous bite.

MITE

These very small soil critters look like minute dots moving about in the soil. There are thousands of species and they range in color from white to bright red. Mites are related to spiders and have eight legs and a round body. They eat fungi, other molds, and decaying wood and leaves.

EARTHWORM

Segmented soil critters without legs that move by expanding and contracting their bodies like an accordion. As earthworms eat, they break down plant materials into smaller pieces, aerate the soil, and add nutrients in the form of castings.

SPRINGTAILS

These soil critters literally spring to life when approached. A pointed projection folded inward at the tip of their abdomens can be quickly extended, acting like a spring to propel them into the air, hence their name. Springtails feed on fungi and other molds, bacteria and decaying matter. They are important producers of humus.

Buried Treasure

Objective:
Students will learn about the role soil micro- and macroorgansims play in the decomposition proccess.

Grade Level: 3-6

Groupings: Small groups

Materials: Soil sample; wire mesh screen with 1/2 inch holes; funnel; empty coffee cans; light source; shallow plastic containers; cottage cheese; spoons; plastic wrap; rubber bands; stakes or markers; plastic bags without holes; bags with large holes such as net onion bags; bags with very small holes such as nylon net or pantyhose; selection of vegetable scraps and other trash; scales; trowels or shovels; rubber gloves.

Time Allotment: 30 minutes for setup of introductory experiments, 30 minutes for buried treasure bags, 20 minutes at various intervals for observations

Directions:

1. Explain that soil is full of macro and microorganisms that are important in the decomposition process. Divide the class into small groups and have them set up two simple introductory experiments to learn more about these organisms.

2. Have each group collect a soil sample and accompanying leaf litter from a depth of 4-6 inches. Ask them to be certain that the sample is moist as there isn't much life in dry soil and leaves. Have them place a piece of wire mesh (1/2-inch holes) inside a funnel and rest the funnel inside an empty coffee can. Direct them to place their soil sample on top of the wire mesh then hang a light bulb over the whole setup, shining it directly on the soil. Explain that heat from the lamp will drive soil critters deeper as they look for moisture. The critters will land in the bottom of the can where the students can observe them. Have them try to identify the critters and speculate on their role in the decomposition process. (See *Soil Critter Chart,* page 82.)

3. In addition to these macroorganisms, the soil is teaming with microorganisms. The following experiment will allow students to see some of these microorganisms. Give each group two shallow plastic containers. Have them add 1-2 tablespoons of cottage cheese to each. Ask them to lightly sprinkle some soil over the cottage cheese in one of the containers. Have them seal both containers with plastic wrap, secure tightly with a rubber band and set aside. After two or three days, have them observe the containers. Caution students not to remove the plastic wrap. Can they see anything growing? Is there a difference between the two containers? (There should be more growth in the container with the soil. Under good conditions, whole colonies of microorganisms can flourish, making them visible to the naked eye. Fuzzy looking colonies are often types of mold. Soft, slimy, yellow, orange or white colonies are yeast. Tiny cream, yellow or red colonies that look moist and shiny might be bacteria.)

4. Distribute one of each of the three types of bags to each group. Explain to the students that they will be burying decomposable materials in these bags in the school yard. In light of the results of the introductory experiments, ask what effect they think the holes or lack of them will have on the decomposition of the materials in the bags.

Extensions:

a. *Conduct a similar experiment varying the soil depth at which each group of three bags is buried. For example, have one group of students leave their three bags above the ground, a second group buries their bag six inches below the surface, and a third group buries their bag one foot deep.*

b. *Read* DEEP DOWN UNDER-GROUND *by Olivier Dunrea (Macmillan, 1993). Count and identify the soil critters. Have the students create their own counting books about critters in their garden soils.*

Directions: (continued)

5. Have the students select an assortment of trash to add to each of the bags. They will need to gather three of each item selected, as the contents of each bag must be the same.

6. Ask the students to list the items to be placed in the bags and make prediction as to what they will look like after being buried for two weeks, four weeks, six weeks and eight weeks. Will the objects look different in the three bags over time? Why or why not? Have them weigh the bags and record their weights.

7. Have each group dig a hole large enough to hold all three bags. Direct them to place the bags in the hole at the same depth. Remind them to cover the bags completely with soil and mark them with a stake.

8. At the biweekly intervals, have the students dig up the bags. Outdoors, have them put on rubber gloves, weigh the bags and examine the contents, noting any physical changes in the selected items. Did the weight of the bags change? Did decomposition rates differ among the bags? How did the actual results compare with the predictions?

A ROTTING LIFE

It's a rotting life down under the soil. A whole web of decomposers is hard at work turning dead organic matter back into nutrients that help plants grow. First come the bacteria and fungi. They grow on and into the leaves, secreting enzymes that break them down. Next come small soil critters such as springtails and mites. The fungal or bacterial coating makes these decaying leaves more appealing than fresh ones, a bit like toast with the addition of butter and jam! Then larger soil critters, like earthworms, millipedes, and isopods get into the act, and they too consume these decaying plants. Before you know it, dead matter is reduced to rich brown humus, and the nutrients released enter growing plants, starting the cycle all over again. So the next time you bite into a juicy apple or drink a glass of orange juice, remember you are eating the goodness of the rotting life beneath the soil!

Directions: (continued)

9. Have the groups compare and discuss their results. What conclusions can the students draw about the role of oxygen and the presence of macro and microorganisms on decomposition?

Goldilocks and the Three Beans
• EXHIBIT •

Materials:

Large cardboard box; magic markers; scraps of material; several buckets; three small plastic rectangular plant pots; measuring cups; large containers of different types of soil such as sand, peat moss, composted cow manure, potting soil, and clay; dish basins; assortment of plant pots; index cards; water.

Activity:

1. Encourage the students to visit the doll house. Direct them to feel and describe the soil in each of the beds in the house. If they were a seed would they choose to grow in one of those beds?

2. After they feel the soil in the buckets, have them use the measuring spoons and cups to mix up their own special blend of soil in a dish basin. When they create a blend that feels just right, have them record their recipe on an index card, fill a plant pot with their special soil mix, plant a seed and give it some water.

Design:

1. Construct a miniature doll house from a large cardboard box. Cut out a door and windows. Be creative and decorate the interior to give it a homey appearance (use scraps of material as curtains for the windows and rugs for the floors, paste pictures on the walls, etc.). Turn three rectangular plastic plant pots into beds and set them in the house. Fill each bed with a distinctly different type of soil such as sand, peat moss and hard packed clay. Place mini pillows at the head and folded down blankets at the foot of each bed.

2. To one side of the doll house, set up several buckets filled with different soil types. Have measuring spoons, cups, and several dish basins available for mixing soil. Have a stack of index cards on hand to use to record soil mix recipes.

3. Write the following directions on or near the exhibit:

Remember Goldilocks and the three beans? Each bean had their own bed but none were just right for Goldilocks' purposes. Perhaps you didn't know it, but Goldilocks was a gardener, and she was searching for the perfect soil bed to start her bean seeds in. Feel and describe the soil in each bed. If you were a bean, would you want to grow in one of these beds? Now see if you can help make a soil bed that is just right for a bean seed. Using the measuring cups and spoons provided, make up your own special blend of soil from the different types of soil in each of the buckets. Record your special recipe on a index card. Fill a bed to the brim, plant a bean seed, give it a drink, and watch it grow!

Compost Cake

Directions:

Students will learn about the decomposition process by simulating what happens within a compost pile.

Grade Level: 3-6

Groupings: Entire Class

Materials: Compost Ingredient Cards (page 88); long rope (16 feet or more); plastic spray bottle; thermometer (real or pretend).

Time Allotment: 30 minutes

Extensions:

a. *Sing "Take Me Out to the Compost" to the tune of "Take Me Out to the Ball Game."*

> *Take me out to the compost*
> *Take me out to the pile.*
> *Add some soil and a few good worms*
> *I don't care if I'm turned and I'm churned*
> *'Cause it's root root root for the microbes;*
> *If they don't live it's a shame.*
> *For in two, four, six weeks, I'm out in the old garden.*

Teacher Credit: Pam Ahearn, Waits River School, East Corinth, VT.

b. *Take and record the temperature at different areas in an active compost pile (center, edges, top, bottom).*

Directions:

This activity works best if done just before or after students have built a compost pile.

1. Explain to the students that the basis of a good garden is the soil. One way to replenish soil and build up a good foundation is through the natural recycling process called *decomposition.* People speed up the decomposition process by *composting.* How many students have a compost pile or are familiar with what goes into compost? To illustrate what can go into a compost pile, sort a lunch bag of leftovers after lunch.

2. Tell the students they will get a chance to experience life in a compost pile. Pass out compost ingredient cards to the students. Ask them to hang them around their necks and explain that they will represent the ingredient on their card. Explain that the ingredients are divided into three categories: dried plant matter which is a source of carbon; fresh green plant matter and animal waste which provide nitrogen; and soil which contains a wide variety of macro and microorganisms important in decomposition. Ask the students to sort themselves into these three groups. (You might want to code the cards to make this sorting easier. A simple border around the edges of the cards with identifying letters C, N, and S or words can help younger students).

3. Outline the perimeter of your imaginary compost pile by placing a long piece of rope on the floor in a circle or square. Pretend to loosen the soil inside the rope and add an initial drainage layer. Explain that similar to a layer cake, compost is built in a series of repeating layers. The first layer is carbon materials, the second layer is nitrogen materials, and finally a layer of soil microbe 'frosting.' This pattern is repeated until the compost 'cake' is at least three feet high.

4. Ask the students how to begin. (Add carbon materials.) Pretend to use your shovel to choose and lift four to five carbon students into the compost. Line them up in a row inside the pile. What comes next? Do the same with the four to five nitrogen students, placing them in a row above the carbon students.

CARBON MATERIALS

Dried leaves, straw, dried grass, small dead branches, dead pine needles or anything dried. [Make enough cards for 1/4 of the class.]

NITROGEN MATERIALS

Kitchen scraps, manure, green lawn clippings, newly fallen leaves, weeds or anything fresh. [Make enough cards for 1/4 of the class.]

SOIL MATERIALS

Soil macroorganisms: *worms, mites, grubs and insects.*

Psychrophiles: *soil microorganisms (bacteria and fungi) that work best at 55 degrees, but can work in the 30-60 degree temperature range.*

Mesophiles: *soil microorganisms (bacteria and fungi) that work best between 70-90 degrees, but can work in 60-105 degree range.*

Thermophiles: *soil microorganisms (bacteria and fungi) that work best at 160 degrees, but can work in the 105 -180+ range.*

Anaerobes: *can work with little to no oxygen.*

[Make enough cards so the remainder of the class is distributed equally among the soil materials.]

Directions: (continued)

5. Ask the soil microbes to sit around the perimeter of the compost. Explain that the various organisms in the soil are active at different times and temperatures during the decomposition process. Those active at a particular time and temperature will move to the center of the compost circle when their optimum conditions are indicated. As conditions change, they will move back out to the edges and be replaced by other organisms who work best in the new conditions.

6. Explain that the decomposition process is speeded up when carbon and nitrogen materials are first broken down into smaller pieces. Ask the soil macroorganisms to introduce themselves and pretend to sprinkle them as a frosting layer on top of the nitrogen layer. Squirt the pile with a plant mister and explain that this provides the organisms with moisture and gets the pile cooking. Ask the macroorganisms to move around and begin to break down and mix up the other ingredients.

BAKE *a* COMPOST CAKE

The soil chef is back again with a new recipe for the garden that is heaps of fun. It's a rich compost cake and it is easy to make. Prepare the pan by loosening an area of soil at least 3 feet by 3 feet with a spading fork. Line the bottom of this "pan" with drainage materials such as corn stalks or thin branches. Now begin layering the cake. First add some materials high in carbon. Try any dead and dried plant matter including dried leaves, straw, sawdust, hay, small thin dead branches, or dead pine needles. Follow this with a layer of nitrogen rich materials such as kitchen scraps, manure, or fresh grass clippings. Then frost with a layer of soil or old compost. Any combination of carbon and nitrogen materials will work, but it is best to have a 3:1 carbon to nitrogen ratio. Continue these layers until the cake is at least three feet high, then moisten with a liberal dose of water from the garden hose. Now as the decomposers start working, the temperature rises and the cake starts to bake. Mix it up every three to four days and continue baking for four to six weeks until you have rich, dark soil. Then add a generous portion to your old garden. It's sure to improve its sense of humus.

Directions: (continued)

7. Tell the students that as decomposition progresses, the pile starts to heat up. Make the analogy of how we get warmer when we work hard or exercise. Pretend to use a thermometer to take the temperature of the pile, announcing a reading of 55 degrees. Have the soil organisms whose cards indicate that they work best at these lower temperatures (psychrophiles) enter the pile and begin to work as the macroorganisms move to the edges.

8. Continue checking and announcing new temperatures at 1 minute intervals, letting the mid-temperature range organisms (mesophiles) move in at 75 degrees, followed by the high temperature range organisms (thermophiles) at 110 degrees.

9. Explain that at this point the oxygen level of the pile is dropping. This usually happens within two to three days in an active compost pile. The thermophiles then move to the edges and the temperature drops again bringing back the mesophiles. Finally the oxygen supply is exhausted and the pile begins to smell. The mesophiles leave and the anaerobes enter. Anaerobes do not need oxygen but they work very slowly. The decomposition activity in the compost is reduced by 90%.

10. Ask the students how the decomposition process could be activated again. (Add more oxygen by stirring up the pile.) Use your imaginary shovel to mix up the pile. Add more moisture (a few squirts from the plant mister) and the decomposition process continues. Explain that after four to six weeks of such activity, decomposition will be complete and you can add rich compost to your garden.

Worm Observation Worksheet

Observe your worm closely. Notice anything special?

Record your observations.

_____

_____

_____

What would you like to know about your worm?

_____

_____

_____

How will you find out?

_____

_____

_____

What did you find out? Record your results.

_____

_____

Wiggle Worms

Objective:
Students will learn about earthworms through self-designed experiments and observation.

Grade Level: K-6

Groupings: Pairs

Materials: The materials for this activitiy vary depending on the kind of experiments the students choose to perform. You might want to have on hand: shoe boxes; containers of various sizes; plant misters and water; paper towels; flashlights; colored cellophane paper; hand lenses; different kinds of soil; thermometer; pieces of Plexiglas; alarm clock; musical instruments; assortment of food scraps; different kinds of paper; pencils.

Time Allotment: 30 minutes minimum.

Directions:
1. Have students collect and observe earthworms for homework. Ask them to bring them to school in a container filled with moist soil. Discuss where they found their worms and share ideas about where worms like to live. Ask the students to share one thing they learned about worms while observing them. Brainstorm a list of things they would like to discover about worms.

2. Divide the class into pairs. Have them design an experiment to discover something new about their worms. Pass out a *Worm Observation Sheet* (page 90) to guide them. Younger students may need help brainstorming and designing experiments.

3. Before they begin, ask each pair to review their experiment design with you. Help your students gather the necessary supplies.

4. Have the students perform their experiments and record the results. Bring the class together to share and discuss experiments, methods and results.

POSSIBLE WORM EXPERIMENTS

Do worms like it wet or dry?
Set up wet versus dry conditions on opposite ends of an otherwise similar container. Place worms in the middle and record which way they go. Do they stay in one place? After 5-10 minutes, where are most of the worms? Repeat this experiment several times with different worms.

Do worms prefer darkness or light?
Set up dark and light conditions in an otherwise similar container. Place worms in the middle and record where they go. After 5-10 minutes where are most of the worms? Repeat this experiment several times with different worms.

Extensions:

a. *Have the students make their own worm puppets from socks and use these to share the results of their experiments. Use the puppets later to create informative worm puppet shows.*

b. *Share the Shelburne Farms "Worm Rap" with your students. Have them incorporate their new found knowledge about worms into their own raps, songs or poetry.*

Directions: (continued)

Can worms see or sense different colors?

Examine the worm carefully with a hand lens to locate eyes. Can you find any? Shine a bright light on a the worm. What is the reaction? Cover the light with red cellophane and try again. Any reaction? Use different colored pieces of cellophane and record reactions. Can worms sense colored light?

Is there a top and a bottom to a worm?

Examine a worm carefully with a hand lens. Note any differences in color, anatomy, and shape between present upper and lower sides. Turn the worm over. What happens? Record reaction. Repeat several times with this worm and others.

SHELBURNE FARMS WORM RAP

Student's verse
No bones, no bones, no bones, no bones,
A worm ain't got no bones, no bones.
(Have students point to particular body part indicated while singing and shake head to the rhythm or beat.)

Teacher
A worm doesn't have any bones inside,
But that doesn't stop it from taking a ride.
Through the soil it pushes and tunnels all day,
Making channels for water and air on the way.

Students
No eyes, no eyes, no eyes, no eyes,
A worm ain't got no eyes, no eyes.

Teacher
A worm doesn't have any eyes to see
But that doesn't mean it will bump into a tree.
It feels vibrations deep in the ground,
And then it knows its time to wiggle around.

Students
No feet, no feet, no feet, no feet,
A worm ain't got no feet, no feet.

Teacher
A worm doesn't have any feet on the ground,
But that doesn't stop it from moving around.
Sets of muscles can flatten it long and thin,
Then squeeze it shut like an accordion.

Students
No teeth, no teeth, no teeth, no teeth,
A worm ain't got no teeth, no teeth.

Teacher
A worm doesn't have any teeth to chew
But that doesn't stop them from eating food.
They take little bits of dirt in their mouth,
And when it's digested rich castings come out.

Students
No bones, no eyes, no feet, no teeth
A worm ain't got none of these, that's neat!

Everyone
They make the soil better in many ways
So add a bunch to your garden today
Add worms, add worms, add worms, add worms,
They do a great job, add worms add worms.

As the Worm Turns

Objective:
Students will learn how earthworms mix and till soil.

Grade Level: K-6

Groupings: Pairs or small groups

Materials: Clear narrow jars (pickle or olive jars work well); variety of different colored soils, leaves and/or grass clippings; thick canvas or felt for jar coverings; worm foods (see *Invite a Worm to Lunch*, page 95); worms; plant mister; *Worm Stewardship Certificate* (see page 96); craft supplies such as colored paper, tissue paper, glitter, sequins, googly eyes, etc. (optional); plastic window screening; rubber bands; worm journals.

Time: 30 minutes to construct, additional observation time over several weeks.

Directions:
This activity works best if students have observed earthworms closely and/or designed and conducted some of their own **Wiggle Worm** *(see page 91) experiments.*

1. Tell the students that earthworms are prized in the garden and have been compared to plows working the soil. Solicit and record students' ideas on how worms till the soil. Explain that they will perform an experiment to test this unique ability of earth worms.

2. Divide the class into pairs or small groups. Beforehand, ask the students to bring in worms, soil samples and tall narrow jars for homework. Each pair will need two jars. Explain they will create distinct soil layers by filling the jars with differently colored soils. They will add two to three worms to one of the jars and monitor it over time to see the effect the worms have on the soil layers. What might be the purpose of the other jar? (It acts as a control.)

3. Remind the students that they will be responsible for the well being of their worms over the next few weeks. What kinds of things will they need to provide for the worms? (Food, water, air and a comfortable, cool, home.) Explain that to make their home comfortable, each pair needs to provide an air supply for their worm. Have them secure pieces of plastic screening with rubber bands to the tops of their jars. The jars also need light proof covers to protect the worms from the harmful rays of the sun. Pass out thick, dark paper or heavy material such as felt. Provide colored paper, tissue paper, glitter, sequins, googly eyes and various other odds and ends for the students to decorate their jar covers. In addition, the temperature of a worm's environment is also important. The best temperature for worms is around 50-60 degrees.

Extensions:

a. Before letting the worms go, have a day at the races. Provide several plant misters and have several students place their worms in the center of a large circle of moistened paper. Then it's on their mark, get set, go! Let the worms crawl their way out of the circle. Have the students mist them as needed. The first worm out of the circle is the winner.

b. Construct a worm farm with Plexiglas sides similar to an ant farm. You can purchase a dozen or so worms from a bait and tackle shop to add to the farm and then watch them till and tunnel through the soil.

c. Construct a large worm box and do some vermicomposting—that's the fine art of letting worms eat your kitchen scraps. Refer to WORMS EAT MY GARBAGE by Mary Appeldorf (Flower Press, 1982) for worm box plans and background information. Consider raising worms during the winter to sell at a spring garden festival or on Earth Day.

Directions: (continued)

4. Worms also need food. Ask the students what kinds of things worms eat. Record their predictions. Show the students a short list of traditional worm foods, such as grass clippings, lettuce bits, carrot scrapings and cornmeal. How could they determine which foods worms prefer? Suggest they add a small portion of different food items to their worm jar everyday, noting if it has disappeared or been pulled down into the soil the following day. If so, they can conclude worms like that type of food. Keep an ongoing class list of foods worms like versus foods they don't like. If a food item remains untouched, remove it promptly to prevent mold from growing in the jar.

5. Water is also very important to the life and environment of a worm. Worms need water to live but caution the students that too much water will flood their homes and tunnels, causing them to drown. Provide a plant mister for the students use and explain that they should mist their soil jar at least once every three days. If they see water pooling in the bottom of their jar, have them drain off the excess water by putting the jar on its side with paper towel beneath it.

6. Reiterate the importance of the job they are undertaking and ask them to take the "Worm Stewardship Pledge" (see page 96). With an air of solemnity, have them raise their right hands and repeat the promises printed on the worm stewardship certificate. Pass out the certificates to be filled out and signed by each of the new caretakers.

7. Ask the students to construct a special worm journal to record their observations over several weeks. Tell the students it is said that worms eat their own weight in soil everyday. Ask them to look for evidence of this in their jars. What do the students think will happen to the layers in the jar? How long will it take for the worms to till up all the layers? Record predictions.

8. Throughout the course of the experiment, you might want to plan class visits from the "Worm Doctor." He or she can visit the worms in the evening and leave notes to the students in the form of advice on care, comments on the menu they are offering (including possible food

Here are some serving suggestions. Bury the food just below the surface of the soil and check periodically to see whether it is being consumed. Keep track of those foods that disappear quickly and create a list of your worms' favorite foods. Experiment with some of your own menu ideas, but hold the meat!

Try apple and pear cores and peels, banana peels, outer leaves of lettuce and cabbage, celery leaves and stalks, a variety of cheeses including cream and cottage, carrot and cucumber scrapings, leftover breakfast cereal, oatmeal, cream of wheat and pancakes, pizza and bread crust, coffee grounds and tea leaves, potato peels, macaroni, grapefruit and orange rinds, or a variety of leftovers and plate scrapings, but remember no meat!

Directions: (continued)

suggestions), various worm trivia or simply congratulations on a job well done. When the experiment is complete, explain that they will let their worms go. Have the students count the number of worms in their jar. Did the population increase or decrease? A final visit from the Worm Doctor with a gift of gummy worms is a sweet ending.

GARDENER'S BEST FRIEND

You've heard of man's best friend, but do you know who a gardener's best friend is? Why, the earthworm of course! Even while you sleep, worms are burrowing through your garden, swallowing soil as they go. Inside the soil are tiny bits of plants and animals which they then grind up as they eat. Through the process of digestion, nutrients that are locked up and unavailable are released in their waste called castings. Worm castings are characteristic lumps and bumps of soil. Rich in nutrients such as nitrogen, potassium, and phosphorus, worm castings are vital to healthy plant growth. Not only do castings add nutrients to the soil, but they also improve the soil's ability to hold water, another bonus for plants. By tunneling through the soil, worms aerate the soil, providing a looser structure and openings for roots to grow. These tunnels provide channels for water to enter the soil and improve drainage. So forget the rototiller and bags of fertilizers, let a worm, a gardener's best friend, help you till and fertilize your garden.

Worm Stewardshop Certificate

Number of worms: _____

Lengths: _____

Names: _____

I hereby swear the following to be my sole intention for worm stewardship:

1. I will give these worms a comfortable, cool, moist, home, complete with a fresh air supply and curtains to keep out any harmful light rays.

2. I will feed my worms a varied diet of healthy foods and will remove any uneaten foods promptly.

3. I will assist any stranded fellow worms I see in my daily outings, and I will be on the worm rescue patrol, especially after rainstorms.

Signed by worm caretaker _____

Signed by official worm stewardship witness _____

The Wonderful Worm
· EXHIBIT ·

Materials:

Pink poster board or pink canvas cloth to create a diagram of the inner and outer parts of a large worm; markers; student copies of internal and external worm features (see pages 99 - 100); worm reference books.

Design:

1. Use the attached internal worm template to draw the innards of a worm onto several sheets of poster board. Or trace the worm innards onto canvas cloth and consider making your worm three-dimensional by stuffing it with cotton batting. An easy copying method involves projecting the worm's internal image on the wall using an overhead projector. Hang poster board or canvas on the wall and trace the image with markers.

2. Draw the external features of the worm on four pieces of poster board or canvas which fit together to completely cover the innards of the worm. These four pieces are flaps for students to lift up and learn about the inner workings of the worm. Reinforce the flaps at their points of attachment.

3. Write information on the underside of each of the flaps which corresponds to the internal features that are being revealed. Use the following text or make up your own:

Activity:

1. Students lift up the flaps of the diagram to learn about the inner workings of the earth worm.

2. Students make lift-the-flap worm cards. Give them a copy of both the internal and external features of the worm. Have them color these and attach them on top of one another. Have them research other amazing facts about worms in the books provided and write their favorite on the inside of the card. Then have them phrase a question to their fact and write it on the outside. Students hang these together to create a worm trivia board.

Design: *(continued)*

Flap # 1 In a worm, it is definitely what's up front that counts. It is here that you'll find the small but important brain, along with not one but five hearts! These pairs of enlarged blood vessels work to pump blood through out the worm. And considering they eat their weight in soil each day, the gut of a worm is quite simple. Soil enters the mouth, passes into a bag-like crop then into the gizzard, where the combination of strong muscle and bits of soil act like teeth to grind up food hidden in the soil. Everything then passes on and on through the intestines. Here digested food is absorbed by the bloodstream and the waste travels to the end of the line.

Flap #2. This ring around the worm is called **clitellum**. After two worms mate, the clitellum produces a slimy collar which rolls off the head of the worm forming a little cocoon around the worm eggs. There is no fuss in deciding upon a name for the new wormlets — they are both male and female so any name will do!

Flap #3. Make no bones about it, a worm is like a waterbed when it comes to anatomy. Not bones but a water skeleton gives them shape. Two sets of muscles work to alternately elongate and flatten, and contract and constrict the worm as it moves along. Just watch one as it squirms and turns its way along.

Flap #4. Not only do worms till the soil, they fertilize it too. Once soil passes through a worm, nutrients important in plant growth are released. The castings they deposit are five times richer in nitrogen, seven times richer in potassium and eleven times richer in phosphorus. No wonder worms are called plants' best friends!

4. Write the following directions on the exhibit:
You don't have to dissect a worm to see what is inside. Just lift up the flaps and take a peek at the inner workings of our hardworking friend, the worm. Then make your own lift-up flap worm cards with the materials provided.

The Outside of a Worm

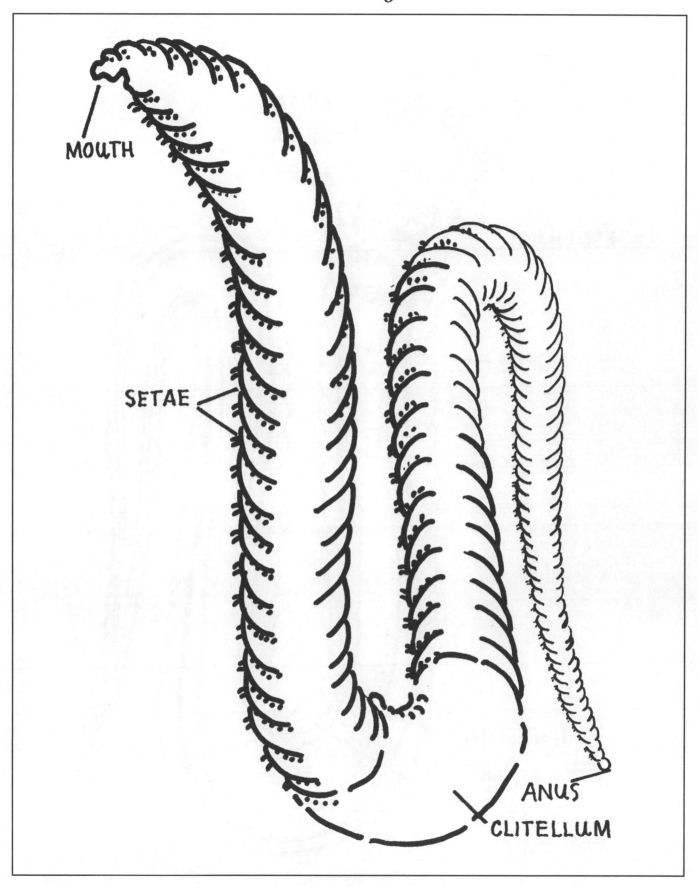

MOUTH

SETAE

ANUS

CLITELLUM

The Inside of a Worm

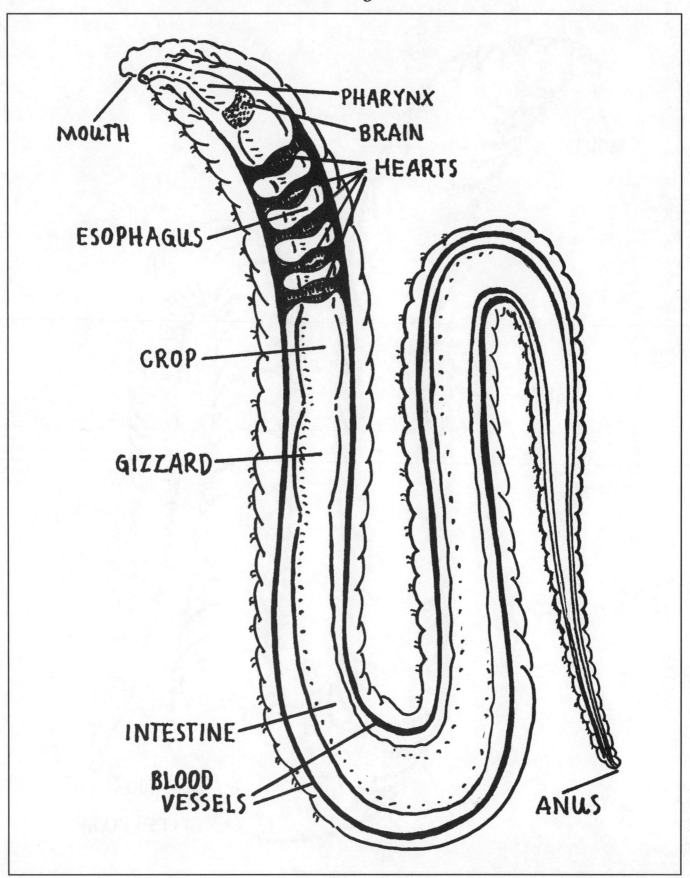

MOUTH

PHARYNX

BRAIN

HEARTS

ESOPHAGUS

CROP

GIZZARD

INTESTINE

BLOOD VESSELS

ANUS

Leaf it to Me Designs

Objective:
Students will create leaf impression artwork using a variety of media.

Grade Level: K-6

Groupings: Entire class

Directions:
Explain to the students that trees and their leaves have been an inspiration to artists and crafts people over time. Consider showing a selection of paintings and crafts that show this influence. Point out the variety of designs in leaves in particular: their interesting shapes, dazzling fall colors, varying textures, and intricate vein patterns. Tell them they will be using leaves to create a variety of artwork.

Have each student collect several different types leaves of various sizes for the activities. Stress careful collection and limit the number they can collected. Remind them not to damage the tree. Autumn is the best time to collect leaves for these activities. Freshly collected leaves work best.

Fall Leaf Crowns

LEAF IT TO ME DESIGNS

Materials:
Freshly collected leaves; toothpicks; tape.

Time Allotment: 15-20 minutes

Directions:
Use fresh or newly fallen leaves for this activity.

1. Ask the students to poke holes in the middle of each of their leaves with a toothpick. Explain that they will be connecting their leaves together to form a chain. Have them push the stem of one leaf through the hole on the top surface of the next. They can use tape to secure the stem to the under surface of this leaf. They then continue adding leaves by placing the stem of a new leaf through the hole of the uppermost leaf in the chain. It is not necessary to tape every leaf. They continue adding leaves until the crown is large enough to fit securely around their head. Attach the last leaf to the first in the same fashion to complete the circle.

Crayon Leaf Rubbings

LEAF IT TO ME DESIGNS

Materials:
Leaves; paper; crayons, tape; large index cards.

Time Allotment: 5-10 minutes

Extension: *Have students work in small groups to create a deck of leaf rubbing cards. Supply them with large index cards and explain that each student should make four rubbings of his or her leaf with the same color crayon. They will need 13 sets of these groups of 4 plus some creative "joker" cards to make a complete deck of cards.*

Directions:
1. Have the students place their favorite leaf, vein side up, on their desks. Next, have them place a piece of paper over the leaf and secure the edges of the paper with tape (optional). Using the side of a crayon, have them color over the surface of the paper. As they rub their crayon, a leaf impression magically appears!

Leaf Spatter Prints

LEAF IT TO ME DESIGNS

Materials: Smocks; newspaper; leaves; large pieces of white paper; cardboard or wooden drawing board; straight pins; paper; old toothbrushes; Popsicle sticks; paint.

Time Allotment: 10 minutes

Directions:
Students should wear smocks and cover the surrounding work area with newspaper for this activity.

1. Have the students tape a sheet of white paper to a board or large piece of cardboard. Next they pin a leaf or leaves securely to the paper. They then dip an old toothbrush in paint and with the bristles pointing downwards, use a Popsicle stick to scrape across the bristles to spatter the paint. Using this technique they work around the edges of their leaf and over the surface of the paper. Encourage them to experiment with different colors of paint (have one toothbrush for each color). When the paint has dried completely, they may remove their leaf. Make spatter prints on cloth to create banners.

Cloth Leaf Poundings

LEAF IT TO ME DESIGNS

Materials:

Pieces of cotton or muslin fabric (one per student); freshly collected leaves; hammer or hard wooden mallet; nonreactive (enamel) container; pickling alum (available from pharmacy or grocery store); washing or sal soda (available in grocery store, optional), clothes iron (optional).

Time Allotment: 20-30 minutes

Extension:

Use these fabric squares to create placemats, napkins, potholders or sew them together for a class quilt.

Directions:

Leaves must be freshly collected for this activity.

1. Give each student a large piece of paper to work on. Have them arrange their leaf (or leaves) vein side up and then place their piece of cotton or muslin on top. Have them hold the fabric in place and pound the leaf all over with a wooden mallet until its complete impression comes through the cloth.

2. Next they peel or flake off any bits of leaf that remain on the cloth and immerse the cloth in a solution of pickling alum and water (3 Tbs./gallon). They should let it sit for a few minutes in the solution. The longer they leave the cloth in the solution the darker their leaf image will be, but just a few seconds will still produce a permanent imprint.

3. They should then rinse the fabric thoroughly under running water. (Optional: They can then immerse their fabric in a washing soda afterbath (1 cup soda/gallon water) for a minute or two. It will further darken the colors. Rinse again under running water). Their images are fixed, and their fabric is ready to dry and press.

Leaf Print T-shirts

LEAF IT TO ME DESIGNS

Materials:
Smocks; newspaper; T-shirts(ask students to bring in his or her own from home); pieces of cardboard; brushes; fabric paint; fabric markers (optional).

Time Allotment: 20-30 minutes

Directions:
The students will need smocks and should cover their working area with newspaper.

1. Ask each student to place a piece of cardboard inside his or her T-shirt to prevent paint from seeping through to the opposite side. Have them center the cardboard beneath the area they will be printing and smooth out any wrinkles.

2. Encourage students to think about their T-shirt design, suggesting they arrange real leaves on the surface until they find a configuration they like. Point out they should also consider color combinations and any writing (spacing, size) they might include.

3. When they have a final design, they should carefully paint the vein side of the leaves with fabric paint. If they want to use more than one color on a leaf ask them to clean brushes between colors. Caution them not to paint the stems of the leaves as they can use them to arrange and remove the leaves. Have them place the painted leaves on the T-shirt and gently press them to create crisp images. Set the T-shirts aside to dry completely. Most fabric paint needs some kind of heat treatment to set the colors. Be sure to send home directions or complete the project in class using a clothes dryer or iron.

WINTER ACTIVITIES

Meet a Tree

Objective:
Students will learn about trees by using senses other than sight.

Grade Level: 1-6

Groupings: Pairs

Materials: Paper bags or winter hats (to be used as blindfolds).

Time Allotment: 30-45 minutes

Directions:
1. Discuss trees and their importance in our everyday lives. Make a list of all the things trees give us. Go outside and explain to the students that they will be meeting a new friend—a tree.

2. Use a volunteer to show the students how they will be performing the activity. The class will divide into pairs. One student will be blindfolded, and the partner will carefully lead him or her to a tree. Explain that each blindfolded student will depend on his or her partner to keep them safe and out of danger. Stress the importance of being careful and responsible while guiding someone who is wearing a blindfold and when wearing a blindfold.

3. Place a paper bag over your volunteer's head or pull a winter hat over his or her eyes. Demonstrate how you would like the students to guide their partners in this activity by having the blindfolded volunteer grasp your arm securely above the elbow. Walk just in front of the volunteer so you can safely lead them along. If he or she feels uncomfortable or would like to slow down, have him or her simply let go of your arm.

4. Slowly and carefully lead the volunteer to a nearby tree, giving guidance along the way such as "duck down," "step over," or "we're going uphill."

Extensions:

a. *Give your students paper to record observations about their tree. You might have them draw their tree, give it a name, describe how it might look in different seasons, make a bark rubbing or collect a leaf. You may also want to have the students keep track of their trees throughout the school year, make a class map of the trees, record how it changes from season to season, or who lives in, under or around it.*

b. *Play tree charades. Whisper to two students an important use for a tree and have them act it out for the group. Let the rest of the class guess what they are imitating. Once they have guessed correctly, ask for volunteers to do another charade. Have the class brainstorm their own tree-use charades. Make a list of the different charades and the ways people and animals use trees. Try sorting them into categories.*

Directions: (continued)

5. At the tree, have the volunteer feel the tree up and down, and the area all around it. Have him or her note the texture of the bark, any distinct smells, if and where any branches are, landmarks around the base, or any nearby trees or bushes. When the volunteer is familiar with the tree, lead him or her back to the starting place, preferably by an alternate route.

6. Remove the blindfold and have the volunteer try to find the tree. If the volunteer is having trouble, give clues as needed. When the volunteer reaches the tree, ask what clues helped him or her find it.

7. Have the students divide into pairs. Pass out paper bags or have them use their hats, pulled down over their eyes. Caution them once again about blindfolds and safety. Let the whole group begin.

8. Once a student has found his or her tree, have the partner wear the blindfold and repeat the activity.

The Giving Tree

Objective:
Students will discover how all of the parts of a tree are used to make a wide variety of common products.

Grade Level: 2-6

Groupings: Entire class

Materials: Tree Product Cards (page 110) placed in a brown bag with a few Non-Tree Product Cards; Tree Part Props (right); nine containers, brown bags or small boxes.

Time Allotment: 30 minutes

Extensions:

a. *Have the students brainstorm what people could do for trees to thank them for all that they give us.*

b. *Have the students conduct a tree product inventory in their homes by surveying each room for products made from trees.*

c. *Try some unusual edible tree treats such as mangos, pomegranates, dried figs, whole coconuts, kiwi fruit, or papaya.*

Directions:

1. Ask the students to brainstorm a list of all the things that trees give us. Explain that many things are made from wood but other parts of the tree are also used to make many important and useful items.

2. Have the students list the eight different parts of the tree: roots, wood, bark, leaves, flowers, fruits, seeds and sap. As each part is named, have one student come to the front of the room and give him or her a Tree Part Prop to represent that particular part. Ask the students to match one item from their list of tree products to each part of the tree they identify.

TREE PART PROPS

Leaves - *an umbrella with paper leaves attached*
Wood - *a small piece of wood with a long string attached to wear as a necklace*
Bark - *a vest made from a paper grocery bag, decorated with squiggly lines to resemble patterned bark*
Roots - *a straw in a paper cup with long pieces of streamers or yarn hanging from the bottom*
Flowers - *a headband decorated with small yellow, green, or white flowers made from pipe cleaners*
Fruits - *fruit shapes cut out of construction paper and hung on loops of string to hang over a student's outstretched arms*
Seeds - *large paper maple seeds attached to the end of a paint stirring stick*
Sap - *two jugs of water to shake*

TREE PRODUCT CARDS

This list of examples is only partial and is meant to show the more unusual products. Be sure to include familiar objects on your tree product cards.

To make each card, draw or cut out pictures of the items from magazines and glue them to an index card.

Leaves: *tea, oxygen, mulch, shade*
Sap: *maple syrup, rubber gloves, rubber hoses, rubber tires, rubber balls, rubber bands, chewing gum, paint, turpentine, varnish/lacquer, soap, rosin, asphalt/cement*
Bark: *cinnamon, cork bulletin boards*
Roots: *sassafras tea*
Fruit: *avocados, chocolate, carnauba or Brazil wax, furniture polish, spices: allspice, nutmeg, mace, figs, olives*
Seeds: *many edible nuts: pistachios, macadamia, almonds, coconuts*
Flowers: *cloves, herbal teas with hibiscus flowers, linden flowers, orange blossoms, perfume*
Wood: *many wooden objects and paper products*
Cellulose from Wood: *cellophane, cellulose sponges, eyeglass frames, carpets, photographic film, toothbrushes handles, combs, rayon clothing, rocket fuel*

Directions: (continued)

3. Label eight of the containers with each of the tree parts and one of the containers as "Items Not Made From Trees." Set up them up at one end of the room. Split the class into two groups and have them form lines for a relay race.

4. Explain that inside the paper bag are Tree Product Cards illustrating items made from the different parts of trees. When you say "Go," the first person in each line selects a card from the bag. They need to decide whether it is a tree product or not, then run and place their card in the appropriately labelled container. When they return, the next person begins his or her turn. The relay continues until each team member has had a turn.

5. As a class, review the contents of each container. Ask the students to show their approval or disapproval of each match by a show of thumbs up or thumbs down. Make any necessary changes and discuss any surprises.

THE CELLULOSE SECRET

You may never have heard of cellulose, but you encounter it every-day. Cellulose is the main structural component of the cell walls in trees. It is extracted from wood and processed to form a variety of common household items. Paper products, from grocery bags to cereal boxes, are made from wood pulp containing cellulose. The cellulose in wood pulp can also be dissolved with chemicals and forced through tiny sieves to form fibers. This regenerated cellulose fiber is used to make rayon clothing, curtains, upholstery, carpets, drive belts for automobiles and electrical insulation. Dissolved cellulose forced through narrow slots forms sheets of cellophane used in packaging. Regenerated cellulose can be mixed with various substances and molded into a variety of plastic items such as combs, eyeglass frames, buttons or toothbrush handles. From your kitchen sponge to rocket fuel to the clothes on your back, cellulose is all around you.

Are You Barking Up the Right Tree?

Objective:
Students will study textures of familiar objects and the bark of different tree species, and learn how to use bark texture in tree identification.

Grade Level: 3-6

Groupings: Small groups

Materials: For each group, a selection of objects with distinct textures (individually placed in labelled brown bags) such as a piece of window screen, sandpaper, canvas, burlap, corduroy, wood with a distinct grain, bark, sponge, or paper lace doilies; numbered rubbings to match the bagged items; randomly numbered rubbings from five or six trees in the school yard; brightly colored ribbon or string; paper and crayons.

Time Allotment: 1 hour

Directions:
This is a long activity and can be done over two days.

1. Ask the class for a definition of texture. What senses are used to gain information about the texture of an object? What are some things with distinct textures? How would texture be important in tree identification? (Each type of tree has its own unique bark pattern and characteristic texture.) Explain that the differences in bark texture are often very subtle to the untrained eye. A ***Twigger of America*** (see page 118) begins by studying the textures of familiar objects before heading outside to look at trees.

2. Show the class a rubbing and explain that it is the image of the texture of an object. Demonstrate how it is made by placing paper over an item and rubbing the side of a crayon over the paper to create the image.

3. Divide the class into small groups. Give each group a set of numbered rubbings. Ask them to describe their textures. Do they see any distinct patterns? What do they think the object will feel and look like? Have them record their observations.

4. When they have completed recording their observations, give the students the group of brown bags containing the objects that match their rubbings. Have them feel each object and describe its texture. Ask them to match each object, without looking, to one of the rubbings.

5. When they have made a guess for all the objects, have them remove each object from the bag to see whether they matched it correctly.

6. Now give each group a set of bark rubbings. Explain that these rubbings were made from trees around the school yard. Ask each group to observe their rubbings carefully. Have them record how they think the bark will look and feel, and note any distinct patterns or other observations.

7. Explain that each tree from which a rubbing was made is labelled with a letter and has a brightly colored string or ribbon around it. The groups will visit each of these trees and carefully observe the bark, noting any particular patterns and

Extensions:

a. *Identify the species of the flagged trees in the school yard using a tree identification guide. Ask the students to find other trees of this type in the area.*

b. *Have each group make clay impressions of the bark of different trees. They can create a similar matching game by marking the trees they used and exchanging clay impressions with another group.*

c. *Have the students make their own textures by applying glue designs on index cards. Encourage them to create random free flowing designs and to experiment with repetitive designs. Let the designs sit for several hours until the glue has hardened, then make rubbings. Exchange designs with a partner and try to match the rubbing to the glue pattern. Textures can also be created by gluing sand, seeds, glitter, soil, or other substances to the card.*

d. *Listen to the song "This Bark on Me" on the tape **Billy B. Sings About Trees** (available from Acorn Naturalists, 17300 E. 17th Street, #J - 236, Tustin, CA 92780, (800)-422-8886). Learn the words and make up accompanying motions.*

Directions: (continued)

textures. Be sure to stress any important boundaries, and if the school yard is large, provide a map to the marked trees. Have the students match each rubbing to one of the trees and record their guesses.

8. When a group finishes matching their rubbings to the marked trees, ask them to find another group that has finished and compare notes. As a class, review each rubbing and record each group's observations and guesses.

9. The groups can then check their answers by making their own rubbings of each of the tagged trees and matching them to the original rubbings.

People Key

Objective:
Students will be introduced to the skills of observation, identification and orderly classification according to simple characteristics.

Grade Level: 2-6

Groupings: Entire class

Materials: Blackboard or large sheet of paper and markers to diagram identification key.

Time Allotment: 25-30 minutes

Directions:

1. Explain that the class will be doing a sorting activity similar to one that scientists do when creating an identification key. For example, when identifying trees by their leaves, scientists observe leaf specimens, looking for a single characteristic that separates them into two distinct groups. They may put leaves with toothed margins (edges) in one group and those with smooth margins in another. They then continue to divide each of these two groups into two smaller groups, and so on into smaller groups, based on differing characteristics. The sorting process continues until each group has only one member. At this point, the identification is complete. Scientists record the characteristics defining each group in this process to create a **dichotomous identification key**.

2. Explain to the class that you will be the scientist and they will be your specimens. Secretly choose one characteristic that will divide the class into two groups. For example, you might put all the students who have straight hair in one group and those who have curly hair in another.

3. Explain to the students that you will be asking them to stand together in two groups based on this secret characteristic. Ask them to look closely at the members of each group to determine the characteristic you used to sort them into the groups. Stress that they not mention what trait they think you used. After you have sorted a few students, you might ask the next one to point to the group he or she expects to join.

4. Once all the students have been sorted, ask them what characteristic you used to divide them. Diagram on the blackboard how a scientist would begin to record this sorting

Extension:

a. *Have small groups of students collect an assortment of 8-12 different types of leaves. Ask them to use the sorting and recording technique they learned in **People Key** to create a dichotomous key to their leaf collection. Provide field guides so leaves can be identified. Have two groups exchange their leaf collections and keys. Ask them to identify a few leaves from this new collection using the accompanying dichotomous key. Have the groups share their results.*

Directions: (continued)

process to form a dichotomous identification key. For example:

5. If the children seem to have grasped this sorting process, let them make the next division. Ask each group to decide one trait that will further divide their group into two smaller groups. Then have each group physically separate themselves into two distinct groups.

6. Now you have four groups. Can the students determine the characteristics that were used by other groups to make the last division? Continue to record the sorting process on the board. For example:

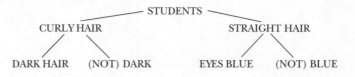

7. Each of these four groups then works to divide again, for a total of eight groups. Once again have the students determine the traits that were used to further subdivide the groups. Explain to the class that they will continue this sorting process until everyone has been singled out by a unique set of characteristics. Be sure to record the characteristic for each division. For example, for a small group of six, the key would continue as follows:

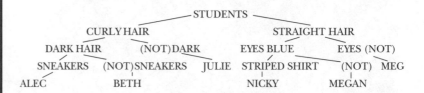

8. Explain to the students that this resulting dichotomous People Key can now be used by anyone to name or identify any student in the class. Invite another teacher, the principal, or a parent to use the key. Select a student specimen to stand in the front of the class. Ask the adult to run through the choices given in the key to see whether they can name their chosen specimen.

Dress Up a Twig

Objective:
Students will learn the structure and function of the parts of a winter twig and how twigs can be used to identify trees.

Grade Level: 3-6

Groupings: Entire class

Materials: A twig with buds; three party hats; paper or felt cutout of a leaf; tape; paper leaf scars cut from construction paper; adhesive dots or labels; paper, pencils, crayons.

Time Allotment: 20 minutes

Directions:

1. Show the class your *Twigger of America* card (page 118) and tell them that you are an official member of this national organization. Explain that most people identify trees by the shapes of their leaves, but twiggers can identify trees without their leaves. Have the students guess what clues, other than leaves, can be used to identify and distinguish trees.

2. Explain to the class that a *Twigger of America* looks very carefully at the twigs of trees. Choose a volunteer to help you teach the class about the parts of a twig. Explain that you will dress up this volunteer as a twig.

3. Hold up a real twig. Ask the class what is at the end of the twig (a bud). Place a party hat (inside of which is a cutout leaf) on the volunteer twig's head to represent this bud. Explain that the bud at the tip of the twig is called the **terminal bud.** Ask the students what might be inside the bud (leaves or flowers). Have the volunteer look inside his or her bud to see if the students' guesses are correct. Stress that in all the winter buds on trees are next year's leaves or flowers. Be sure to point out that different types of trees have distinctively different buds. They may be different sizes, shapes, colors, or have different smells.

4. Ask the students whether they see any other buds along the sides or side branches of the real twig. The side buds are called **lateral buds.** Explain that the volunteer's arms represent side branches and the lateral buds are often at the tips of these branches. Place matching party hats on the hands of the volunteer twig to represent lateral buds.

5. Tell the class that the arrangement of these lateral buds and branches is important in identifying trees. They can be arranged in one of two ways. Some trees have **opposite branching.** Have the volunteer stretch his or her branches (arms) out to the sides. Point out that one bud (hand) and branch (arm) is directly across from or opposite the other. Ask the class to imitate this type of branching pattern. Tell them that only a few types of trees have opposite branching. They are often called MAD HORSE trees; the letters in the word "mad" are the first letters of the names of three trees, and the horse represents a fourth. All these trees have opposite branching. Can the students guess what the trees are?

a. *Pass out freshly cut twigs to the class and have them identify the different parts. Have the students draw and label the parts of their twigs.*

b. *Place a few freshly cut twigs in water inside the classroom in late winter or early spring. This will force them to open or bloom indoors.*

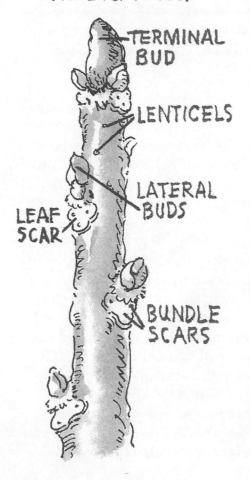

THE BIG TWIG

TERMINAL BUD

LENTICELS

LATERAL BUDS

LEAF SCAR

BUNDLE SCARS

Directions: (continued)

(The *m* stands for *maple*, the *a* for *ash*, and the *d* for a tree that barks, or *dogwood*; *horse* stand for *horse chestnut*.) As a joke, you might have the students keep their hands up in the air while you are explaining this and ask them if they would be mad, too, if they had to stand around this way all day.

6. Next use the volunteer twig to demonstrate the second branching type, called lazy or **alternate branching**. Have the volunteer hold one arm up in the air and the other down to the side. Point out that in this type of branching, you do not find buds or branches across from one another, but rather alternating along either side of the stem. Most trees have alternate branching.

7. Explain that twigs have other parts that aid in identification. Along the twigs there are **leaf scars** where last year's leaves were attached. Use tape to attach paper cutout leaf scars beneath each of the three buds on your volunteer twig. Point out that there may be marks, or **bundle scars**, on the leaf scar that form a pattern of tiny dots or lines. The bundle scars mark the place where veins ran from the leaf stem to the twig. Ask the students if they can see a design in the volunteer's leaf scar.

8. Another feature the students may see scattered over the surface of a twig are tiny holes or breaks in the bark. These are called **lenticels** and allow for air exchange. Place sticky dots all over the volunteer twig to represent lenticels.

9. Now your twig is complete. Review all the parts and the two types of branching patterns. Give your volunteer twig a round of applause.

Twig Match

Objective:
Students will develop their observation and twig identification skills.

Grade Level: 3-6

Groupings: Individuals and small groups

Materials: *Twigger of America* cards (page 118); at least one twig for every student (be sure to have at least two twigs from each species of tree available); paper and pencils.

Time Allotment: 30-45 minutes

Directions:
*This activity works best if it follows **Dress Up a Twig** (page 115) and is done after the leaves have fallen from the trees. If possible, choose trees that grow in or around the school yard. Cut the twigs no more than a week ahead of time.*

1. Tell the students that as part of their tree studies, they are going to be initiated into the "Twigger of America Club", an honorary club for people who are knowledgeable about trees. Show them a *Twigger of America* card and explain that they must pass a few tests before they can become official members.

2. Explain that a *Twigger of America* can identify trees even without their leaves. This is quite a challenge, as leaves are usually used in tree identification. Pass out twigs to the students and review the important parts (see **Dress Up a Twig**, page 115). You might want to give students a copy of the **The Big Twig** (page 116).

3. Give the students a few minutes to carefully observe their twigs noting any distinguishing characteristics. Then, inform them that one or more students in the class has the same type of twig that they do. When you say "Go," have the students find the matching twigs among their classmates.

4. Once the students have found their matches, have them work together to write accurate descriptions of their twigs. Be sure to explain that they are not describing one of their twigs specifically, but their type of twig in general. Have them note the following characteristics: overall color of the twig, color and shape of the buds, the type of branching pattern (alternate or opposite), presence or absence of lenticels (including their color and shape), shape of leaf scar, and any other characteristics such as smell, texture, or thorns. You might make a list of these characteristics on the blackboard or create a worksheet for students to complete.

Extensions:

a. *Have the groups match their twig to a tree growing in the school yard.*

b. *Hand out a twig to each student and have him or her draw and label it. Use hand lenses to make detailed drawings of the leaf and bundle scars. Then put several twigs in a pile. Have students swap drawings, then see if they can match twigs and drawings.*

c. *Hold a twig relay race. Divide the students into two even lines. Stand several feet away from the students. Have two piles of twigs, one to give to the students and another pile that contains at least one match for each twig in the first pile. Be sure to keep these piles separate. Have the first student from each line run up to you. Give each of them a different twig from pile number one. They now need to find its match in pile number two. Once they have chosen a match, they need to verify it with you. If correct, they return the two twigs to their respective piles and run back to their line. They tag the next team member, who repeats the process. The race continues until everyone has had a chance to play. Congratulate the teams. You might wait until now to award them their* Twigger of America *cards.*

Directions: (continued)

5. When the students finish their descriptions, have one member of each group bring up two twigs and their group's description. Have all the groups place their twigs in a central location.

6. Collect the twig descriptions. Explain that you will be shuffling them and passing a new description to each of the groups. Each group should read the new description and note important clues. When you say "Go," one person from each group may come up and select one twig that matches the written description they have. Have the group look over the chosen twig and decide whether it is the one described.

7. When all the groups have decided upon a match, each group can report the key characteristics they used to match the written description to their chosen twig. The group that wrote the description can verify the guess and/or give additional clues to help with the correct selection.

8. When all the twig matches have been verified, have each group use a winter twig field guide to determine what type of twig they have.

9. Congratulate the students and award them their *Twigger of America* cards.

Life Cycle Sort

Objective:
Students will learn about the different developmental stages in the life of an organism.

Grade Level: 3-6

Groupings: Small groups

Materials: A selection of photographs of one individual from infancy through adulthood; *Tree Life Cycle* cards (page 121 - 22) hung on long strings.

Time Allotment: 30 minutes

Directions:

1. Explain that you have just received a loose collection of photographs of an individual over the years and you'd like the students' help putting them in chronological order. Ask them to brainstorm a list of the important events or stages in a person's life that might be recorded in the photographs. Record their ideas on the blackboard. Once the list is complete, work together to sequence their suggestions in chronological order.

2. Randomly label your photographs and lay them in a central location for the students to observe. Allow time for the students to study the photographs. Have them guess the proper sequence and record their guesses using the labels. When everyone has finished, ask the class what they think the right order is. Have them match the photos to the stages and events they brainstormed.

3. Explain that all living things go through different stages of development in their lives just as we do. The sequence of these stages from beginning to end is called a **life cycle.** Can they think of any examples in nature? (Egg, tadpole, frog; egg, chick, chicken; calf, heifer, cow; puppy, dog)

4. Tell the class you have pictures of a tree throughout its life. Once again, they are out of order. Ask them to put these in the correct sequence but explain there is an extra challenge. They will need to do the sorting without talking. Lead a quick discussion on ways other than talking to communicate sequence order.

5. Divide the class into two or three groups depending on class size. You can adjust the number of *Tree Life Cycle* cards used, but try to use the same stages of the life cycle in every group if possible. For example: for a class of 21 students, divide the class into three groups and use the same seven *Tree Life Cycle* cards in each group.

6. Have the students in each group stand in a circle. Hang one of the cards around each student's neck with the picture on his or her back. Explain that they may look at everyone's card except their own. (If this is too difficult for your students, hang the *Tree Life Cycle* cards around the student's neck facing forward.)

Extensions:

a. *Go on a life cycle scavenger hunt. See whether the students can find all the stages of a tree life cycle in and around the school yard or nearby woods.*

b. *Plant seeds and observe the various stages of growth in an indoor classroom garden. Make life cycle cards for common garden plants and have the students do a similar sequencing activity.*

Directions: (continued)

7. When you say "Go," have the students carefully observe everyone's pictures and arrange themselves in order from the beginning to the end of a tree's life. When a group finishes, have them signal by sitting down in order. Remind them to be sure to check the order before signalling they have finished.

8. When all the groups are finished, ask each student to look carefully at the life cycle stages represented in the pictures on the backs of the students on either side. By seeing what comes before and after, can they guess what stage of a tree's life is represented on their card?

9. As a class, review the tree life cycle using the order determined by the group that finished first. Begin by asking the first student in line what stage is represented on his or her card. Get input from the first student in the other group(s). Have these students turn their cards so that they are facing forward, revealing their picture and confirming their guesses. Continue in the same manner, having each student guess and confirm the stage represented in his or her *Tree Life Cycle* card.

10. Review the life cycle order. Finish by making comparisons between the stages in a tree's life and ours.

Tree Life Cycle Cards

Tree Life Cycle Cards

A Tree's Birthday

Objective:
Students will learn to identify the rings on a tree trunk cross section and will learn what these rings can indicate about a tree's life cycle.

Grade Level: 1-3

Groupings: Entire class, in pairs

Materials: Tree birthday party invitations; cross-sectional slices of tree trunks or branches (these should be pre-cut from small to medium-sized logs); magnifying glasses; sandpaper; vegetable oil; push pins with string and small cards attached; six large cards; party hats; cake.

Time Allotment: 45 minutes

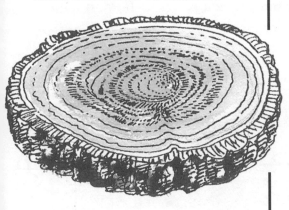

Directions:

1. Before this activity begins, put an invitation to a tree's birthday party in each student's desk or cubby. It should list the time, date, and purpose of the party.

2. Discuss with the class how we keep track of how old we are. Use a birth certificate, photo albums, calendars and/or a birthday book to show how we record birthdays and other important dates and events. Explain that trees also have a record of their ages.

3. Have students work in pairs. Give each pair a magnifying glass and a tree cross-section. Explain that foresters call these cross sections "tree cookies." Can the students tell how their tree kept track of its age? Let them observe their tree cookie and identify any special features they see. Ask them to record their observations by writing and/or drawing what they see.

4. After the students have examined their tree cookies, discuss their findings. Ask them to explain how they think trees keep track of their ages.

5. Explain that each year a tree grows wider by making new wood. When the tree starts growing in the spring, the new wood cells are very big and appear light in color. These light color bands of wood, visible in the tree cookies, are called **spring wood**. The wider the band, the more the tree grew. Later in the year, when tree growth starts to slow down, the new wood cells are smaller and closer together. These appear as dark rings in the tree cookies and are called **summer wood**. Every dark ring of summer wood marks the end of one year's growth.

6. Explain that the number of rings in their tree cookies corresponds to the number of years the tree has been growing. How can they determine the age of their tree? (Count the dark rings. The total will equal the tree's age.)

7. How old are the trees? Have each pair work together to count the rings in their tree cookie. To make the rings darker and easier to count, have the students sand their tree cookie with sandpaper and rub a few drops of vegetable oil over the sanded surface. Have the students record the age of their tree on a small card.

Extension:

a. *Look over old weather reports and statistics. Record the years in which there were major droughts, record rainfalls, severe ice storms, etc. in your area. Look at tree rings from these years to see whether there is a correlation between tree growth and climatic events.*

Directions: (continued)

8. On each of the larger cards, write one of the following categories: 1-25 years old, 26-50, 51-75, 76-100, 101-125, and 126+. Spread these cards on the floor in a line. Have the students create a graph by laying their tree cookies in a vertical or horizontal line next to the card labeled with their tree's age.

9. Correlate the tree rings to calendar years. Explain to the students that the outermost ring represents the present year. If they subtract the total number of rings from the present year, they can learn when the tree was born. For example, if the outer ring = 1994, and the tree has 30 rings, then the tree was born in 1964.

10. Use the tree rings as a time line for important events in the lives of the students and their families. Give each student a set of five push pins which have small cards attached by pieces of string. On one side of each card, have the students write an important event in their life or the life of someone in their family; on the other side have them write the year in which the event happened. For example: 1985, I was born; 1990, I started school; 1991, my baby sister was born. Have students place the push pins in the tree ring that matches the year when each event happened.

11. To close the activity, hand out party hats, and have the students sing happy birthday to their tree cookie and celebrate with a piece of cake!

Teacher Credit: Jodi Lane, Robinson School, Starksboro, VT.

Stories in the Rings

• EXHIBIT •

Materials:
Poster board; markers; index cards; scissors; string; push pins; Velcro circles.

Design:

1. Make a large cross-section of a tree (12 to 15 inches in diameter) out of poster board. Trace around various large circular household items such as garbage can lids or mixing bowls to make the outer rings. The smaller, inner rings can be drawn by tracing smaller circular objects or using a pencil and compass.

2. Make several smaller tree cross-sections (4 to 8 inches in diameter), each with different ring widths, patterns and markings (see **Reading the Rings**, page 126 for specific ideas). Glue a small circle of hooked Velcro to the center of each of these cross-sections.

3. Make a label describing what made the specific markings on each of the smaller tree cross-sections. Put the labels on the exhibit near the smaller tree cross-sections (but not next to its match). Attach a piece of string to the description. To the free end of the string, attach a fuzzy circle of Velcro.

4. Create an answer card that explains, in pictures and words, each description/cross-section match. Put the answer cards in a labelled envelope on the exhibit.

READING *the* RINGS

Various factors influence a tree's growth. The effects of these are recorded in the tree's annual growth rings.

Broken branches.

Tree leaning over or tree knocked down.

Years of drought or insect damage.

Sugaring scars.

Heart rot.

Selective cutting.

Forest fire, lightening strike, bark chews (by porcupine, mouse, beaver), or logging damage.

Design: (continued)

5. Write the following background information and directions on or near the exhibit.

Background Information:

Each year as a tree grows, it makes a new ring of wood. The outermost ring was the last one made before the tree was cut, and it represents the present year. We can count the rings to determine a tree's age and use simple math (subtraction) to calculate the year when past events occurred. The size and shape of tree rings can reveal what happened throughout a tree's life. A wide ring tells us that the tree grew a lot that year. A narrow ring means the tree was not able to grow very much. Injuries to the tree leave marks and scars in the wood.

Directions for the larger tree cross-section:

Write an important event on one side of a card and the date on the other. Using a push pin, attach the card to the proper ring in this large tree cross-section. Remember, the outermost ring is the present year.

Directions for the smaller cross-sections:

Look closely at the rings in these small cross-sections. Can you guess what happened to the tree by reading the story in its rings? Use the strings to match each description to a tree cross-section. Check your guesses on the answer cards.

Activity:

1. Each student should write at least one important event and its date and year on a slip of paper and attach it to the corresponding tree ring using a push pin. Review these event cards as a class.

2. Students may work alone or in pairs to match each small tree cross-section to the description of its markings. Have students check their choices using the answer card.

Paper Making

Objective:
Students will learn how to make recycled paper.

Grade Level: 2-6

Groupings: Small groups

Materials: Examples of recycled paper products; scrap paper; water; natural materials (see below); 1-2 kitchen blenders; iron, cloth and large kitchen strainer (all optional). Per group: large container; wide mouth jar; dish basins; sponges; pieces of window screen (cut to the size of the paper you want and duct taped around the edges); newsprint.

Time Allotment: 1 hour

**NATURAL MATERIALS
for PAPER MAKING**

*Leaves (green, brown or colored)
Grass clippings
Flower petals (roses, marigold,
dandelions, violets)
Milkweed silk
Scented herbs
Onion skins*

Extensions:
a. *Experiment with different shapes and sizes of window screen to create interesting paper shapes. Plastic window screen stretched over circular embroidery hoops makes wonderful circles of paper.*

Directions:
This activity works best if it is done on two consecutive days. Collect the natural materials and prepare the paper pulp on the first day and make the paper on the second day.

1. Tell the students that in 1992 each person in the United States threw away about 262 pounds of paper (of a total of 1,480 pounds of trash). That is a lot of paper! Brainstorm a list of all the paper products people use and record the list on the blackboard. What happens to all of this paper? (Some of it is recycled, but most of it is used just once and thrown away.)

2. Show the students examples of recycled paper products; greeting cards, wrapping paper, computer and copy machine paper, toilet paper, handmade stationery. Explain that they will be making recycled paper from scrap paper in the classroom and natural materials.

3. Divide the class into small working groups. Have them rip their scrap paper into one to two inch pieces. Each student should make about two cups of shredded paper. Have each group put all their pieces together in a large container. Cover these with water and soak them overnight. The soaking makes it easier for the blender to process the paper scraps. Have the students collect some natural materials and soak them separately.

4. Have each group put one handful of their wet paper pieces and three to four cups of water in a wide mouth jar. Have them pour this mixture into the blender. Process the wet paper pieces and water in the blender for several seconds, until fairly smooth. This blending creates a mixture called a **slurry**, composed of water and paper **pulp**. Pour the slurry into a dish basin. Have the groups continue making slurry until their basins are half full. Blend the natural materials separately and combine with the slurry in the basin. Add water until the basin is 3/4 full.

5. Hand out the screens to the students and explain that the screen will be used to catch the paper pulp. When the paper pulp dries, it will be a new sheet of paper.

6. One student in each group should stir the slurry in the

Extensions: (continued)

b. *Research the discovery and history of paper making.*

c. *Have each student keep a tally of the number of times and the types of paper he or she uses in one day.*

d. *Save the paper that is used in the classroom for a week. Weigh it and multiply by the number of weeks of the school year to find out how much paper the class uses. Brainstorm ways to recycle this paper.*

PAPERMAKING THEN *and* NOW

Paper has been around for a long time. In 105 B.C. a man in China named Tsai-Lun watched some wasps as they chewed up wood and molded it into thin sheets to build their nest. Impressed with the nest's texture and inspired by their methods, Tsai-Lun mashed rags, bamboo and mulberry wood into a liquid pulp. He filtered the pulp on a flat screen, lifted out a thin sheet formed from the fibers, let it dry and the first sheet paper was made!

Paper making has come a long way since then, but the basic process is similar. Every piece of paper still begins with a tree. Logs are sent to

Directions: (continued)

dish basin with his or her hand. This insures that the paper pulp is suspended in the water. Have another lower the piece of screen at an angle under the slurry. When the screen is completely under the slurry, have the student slowly lift it out, keeping it as flat as possible and catching the paper pulp on the surface of the screen. If the paper pulp layer is too thin, strain off some water from the basin and try again. If it is too thick, dilute the slurry with water.

7. Have the student hold the screen and paper pulp over the basin for a few seconds to let the excess water drip off. Then, quickly and carefully, have the student flip the screen and paper pulp over onto several thicknesses of newsprint.

8. Keeping everything in place, have them sponge the screen to soak up excess water in the pulp. Squeeze out the excess water from the sponge into the slurry bucket. Continue sponging until the paper seems fairly dry.

9. When their new sheet of paper is dry enough, it will separate readily from the screen and remain attached to the newsprint. Have the students slowly lift one corner of the screen. If the screen and paper pulp separate, they can gently lift the screen from the paper. If the screen and paper pulp stick together, they need to sponge off more water.

*paper pulp factories where the bark is removed and the logs are then shredded. The wood chips are then added to a digester, which works like a large pressure cooker to separate the **cellulose** and **lignin fibers** which make up wood into fiber bundles. Inside a blow tank, these bundles are burst apart into individual fibers. These fibers are then run over screen drums, washed, filtered and refined.*

These fibers then go into a head box where they are pumped as a watery pulp onto rolling wire screen mats. Water drains off and the mats vibrate slightly to help the fibers interlock into sheets. Different types of paper are made by variations in the amount of pulp pumped onto the rolling mats, the speed of the mat and the speed of the vibrations.

The sheets then pass through a long series of rollers which press out any remaining moisture. Next, steam heated drying drums dry the paper, and finally, a process called calendaring polishes and smooths out wrinkles. Large sheets of paper are wound onto rolls which can be cut to produce a wide array of paper products.

Directions: (continued)

10. Have each student set the new sheet of paper aside, still attached to the newsprint, in a safe place to dry. Have each student label the newsprint with his or her name.

11. While the paper is still damp, it may be covered with a piece of smooth cloth and ironed (with the assistance of the teacher or other supervisor).

12. When the paper is fully dry, peel the newsprint off. Use the new paper as stationery, greeting cards, or for any other creative project. The quality of the paper varies depending on the type of scrap paper used to create the slurry and the natural materials added. Some kinds of paper will be more difficult to write on than others.

***Important clean up note:** do not put extra paper pulp down the drain. The drain will clog. Strain as much of the pulp out as you can with the screen or a large kitchen strainer and discard it in the waste basket. Pour the rest of the water outdoors.*

Recycled Paper Beads

Materials: Paper, scissors, ruler, a bag of 8 or 10 penny nails, white glue, colored pencils, paints, markers, old knitting needles, white candles or paraffin wax, empty soup or coffee can, pot, cup, string or yarn, blunt plastic darning needles.

1. Have the students collect a variety of paper for their creations. Suggest magazines, catalogs, gift wrap, construction paper, and brown paper bags. Different papers create different effects. Brown bags make wood colored beads, and manila school paper makes ivory colored beads.

2. Begin by having the students cut their paper into long strips. The strips can be 6 to 18 inches long and 1/2 to 2 inches wide. The size and shape of the strip will determine the shape of the bead. Long rectangles make cylindrical beads, long triangles make cone-shaped beads. Have the students experiment with different shapes and sizes. They may want to measure and mark their paper with a ruler and pencil before cutting.

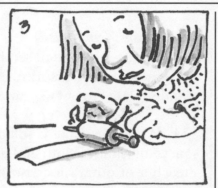

3. Next have the students place one end of their paper against the shank of an 8 or 10 penny nail. Direct them to roll the paper tightly and evenly away from them, keeping the edges neat.

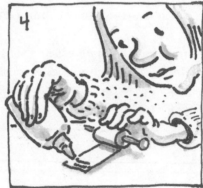

4. When they have rolled all but the very end, have them add a line of glue to the inside edge and press it down on the bead. Remind them to hold it tightly until the glue sets.

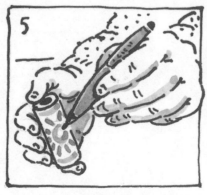

5. If they are using white or plain paper, they may decorate it using colored pencils, paint and/or markers.

6. If you are working with older students, have them add a professional finish to the beads. While the students are rolling their beads, place white candle stubs inside an empty coffee or soup can. Make a double boiler by placing this can into a pot of water and heating it to melt the wax.

7. Remove the can from the water bath and place it in a central location. Have the students place a bead on an old knitting needle and dip it into the wax for the count of three. (The temperature of the wax is tricky; if it is too hot, it doesn't coat the beads well. If it is too cool, it gets cloudy and clumps.) You may need to reheat the wax periodically or heat several cans of wax to switch on and off as they cool. Redip the beads one or two times, letting them cool and set in be tween.

8. Have the students balance the knitting needle with the bead on it across a cup and let it cool completely. They can then use their fingernails to scrape off any excess wax and then rub them with their finger to add a shine.

9. Then, using blunt darning needles, have the students string the beads to make colorful necklaces, bracelets or other jewelry!

Air Cycle Boogie

Objective:

Students will understand and demonstrate the fundamental oxygen/carbon dioxide exchange between plants and animals.

Grade Level: 3-5

Groupings: Entire class

Materials: None.

Time Allotment: 20 minutes

Extension:

a. *Have the students go on an air fact-finding hunt. Suggest they interview weathermen to find out the role of air in weather predictions, doctors to discover how important air is to people, or a greenhouse operator to learn how plants use air. Have them look into the effects of air pollution on plants and animals and research the greenhouse effect and ozone depletion.*

Directions:

1. Ask the class to think about how plants and animals depend on one another. Brainstorm and record on the blackboard what plants give animals (food, shelter, oxygen) and what animals give plants (fertilizer, aid in pollination, seed dispersal, carbon dioxide). Explain that the class will act out a cycle that is essential for life on earth. This cycle, called the air cycle, has been going on between plants and animals for millions of years.

2. Divide the students into two lines facing each other. Explain that one line will represent the plants, the other the animals. Ask each student to pick a specific type of plant or animal he or she would like to be and tell the class what it is. Explain that the air cycle is like a well choreographed dance; in fact, students will actually be doing a dance, the *Air Cycle Boogie*. Tell them that each group will have a starting cue and a certain sequence of movements to perform as their part of the dance.

3. Explain that the plants will start the *Air Cycle Boogie*. Ask them what four things plants need to grow (air, water, soil, sun). Explain that the plants' starting cue is *carbon dioxide*, the kind of gas in the air they need to live. Direct the plants to boogie like this:

a) When the plants hear the words carbon dioxide, they pretend to breathe it in. Have them reach out their arms and pull in carbon dioxide while saying, "Carbon dioxide, aaaah."

b) Then they drink up water and nutrients from the soil through their roots. Have them bend down to the ground and rise up slowly while making slurping noises, chanting, "Water and soil nutrients."

c) Next they will do something only plants can do — make food from sunlight. Have them jump into the air with their arms outstretched and shout, "Hooray, sun!" Older students might chant, "Pho-to-syn-the-sis!" while moving their arms to the beat.

d) Lastly, the plants breathe out oxygen. Have them wave their hands in front of their faces while saying, "Oxygen."

Practice this half of the dance one or two times to be sure the students in the plant group know the sequence.

BREATH *of* FRESH AIR

Life on earth as we know it would never have been possible without the air cycle, in which green plants, in the process called photosynthesis, take in carbon dioxide and release oxygen. Many hundreds of millions of years ago, before living things appeared on earth, the earth's atmosphere contained little or no oxygen. Primitive algae-like plants began conducting photosynthesis and creating oxygen, allowing more complex life forms to develop. Scientists say that the oxygen in earth's atmosphere comes mainly from plants. You can see plants giving off oxygen by carefully watching green plants in an aquarium in good light. Watch for oxygen bubbles rising occasionally to the surface. Although you can't see it, grass growing on a 100 by 100 foot plot releases enough oxygen every day to meet the needs of a family of four.

Directions: (continued)

4. Ask the students what the animals need to live (air, food, water). Explain that they just received their starting cue from the plants: *oxygen*, the gas in the air that animals need to live. Direct them to boogie as follows:

a) The animals pretend to breathe in oxygen. Have them reach out their arms and pull in the air while saying, "Oxygen."

b) They then eat food and drink water. Have them imitate eating and drinking.

c) When they are full of energy, the animals will do something plants can't do —move around. Have them dance in place.

d) Lastly, the animals breathe out carbon dioxide. Have them wave their hands in front of their faces while saying, "Carbon dioxide."

Again, have the animals practice the sequence, reminding them to say the key words or phrases. Point out that the air cycle is now complete, as the animals' last line, "Carbon dioxide," is the starting cue for the plants.

5. Guide the plants and animals through the dance together in slow motion. Make sure you stress all the important steps in the process. Then pick up the speed. You might have them try to do the dance as fast as they can, as dramatically, or as quietly. Try freezing the action at key points in the boogie. End the dance with everyone taking a bow.

Catch a Snowflake

Objective:
To observe and classify different types of snowflakes.

Grade Level: 2-5

Groupings: Individuals or pairs

Materials: Shoeboxes; Krylon plastic spray (can be purchased at a hardware store); acetate sheets cut to fit inside the shoebox; cardboard cut to the same size as acetate sheets; spring-type wooden clothespins (two per pair); plastic storage bags; ruler.

Time Allotment: 30 minutes

Directions:
This activity is done during a snowfall. All the materials should be kept in plastic bags in the freezer or outdoors at least two hours prior to the actual collecting.

1. Introduce your students to Wilson "Snowflake" Bentley (see **Snowflake Snapshots**, page 134). He believed that no two snowflakes are alike and took over 5,000 photographs to prove it. Recently, scientists have been challenging this assumption. Ask your students' opinions and tally the results. Explain that they will be collecting data to help resolve the controversy.

2. Take your class and the materials outdoors to a spot that is sheltered. Record weather conditions: temperature, wind direction, wind speed, and moisture.

3. Pass out acetate sheet, cardboard and two clothespins to each student. Have the students place the acetate sheet on top of the cardboard and clip these together with at least two spring-type clothespins.

4. While gripping the clothespin, hold each acetate sheet away from yourself and the students. One at a time, spray each sheet with Krylon. Allow the excess to drip off one corner.

5. Immediately after spraying, hand the sheet to a student. Caution them to hold the clothespins gently and not to touch the Krylon. Have them hold the acetate sheet out horizontally in front of them so a few snowflakes fall onto the Krylon covered surface.

Extensions:

a. *Chill a piece of black felt and use it to collect snowflakes. From the **Snowflake Key** (page 136), determine the crystal type of each flake and keep a running tally for each snowfall. Record weather conditions each time you catch snowflakes to see how weather factors affect the type of snow crystals formed.*

b. *Look at pictures of snowflakes, including photographs taken by Wilson "Snowflake" Bentley.*

c. *Make snow shake jars. Have the students bring in small jars with tight fitting lids. Have the students affix floral clay (available at a florist shop or craft store) to the inside of the lid. Stick small branches of evergreens and twigs into the clay to create a miniature forest. Encourage your students to use their imagination to create little creatures from a variety of materials (twist-ties, pebbles, toothpicks, etc.) to place in the forest. Fill the jar with water, add silver sparkles for snow, and close the lid securely. Then shake for snow!*

d. *Have the students draw their replica snowflake. Use a ruler and protractor to make a perfect snowflake. Compare the students' drawings. Do any two snowflakes match?*

Directions: (continued)

6. Once they have collected a sample of snowflakes, have them place the acetate sheet, Krylon-side-up, inside their shoebox. Have them close the box to prevent additional snowflakes from landing on the acetate sheet.

7. Leave the closed shoeboxes in a cold place for one hour. The Krylon will dry and harden, and the snowflake will disappear, leaving its imprint or replica.

8. The replica snowflake can be observed with a hand lens, microscope, or overhead projector. Have students compare their snowflake replicas to the replicas pictured in the *Snowflake Key* (page 136) to discover what type of snow crystals the class has collected.

9. Tally the snow crystal types found. Did the snowfall consist of more than one type of snow crystal?

10. Using a millimeter ruler, try measuring the replica snowflakes. What is the diameter of the largest snowflake? The smallest? Graph the class results. Finally, carefully compare snowflake replicas. Are any two identical?

SNOWFLAKE SNAPSHOTS

Beginning in the 1880's, Wilson A. "Snowflake" Bentley, of Jericho, Vermont, made some 5,300 microphotographs of snowflakes. He caught snowflakes on a cold board covered with black velvet and photographed them with an old-fashioned bellows camera focused through a microscope in his refrigerated studio. Snowflake Bentley had to work fast, before his subjects melted. It wasn't until 1940 that a way of preserving snowflake impressions was discovered, a process similar to the method used in this activity.

Make a Snowflake

Objective:
Students will make a paper six-sided snowflake.

Grade Level: 1-5

Groupings: Individuals

Materials: Square pieces of paper and scissors.

Time Allotment: 15 minutes

Extension:
a. *Have students make their favorite snowflake shapes out of felt. Fold the felt as you would to make paper cutout snowflakes. Cut the felt and glue it to a block of wood. When it is dry, use paint or ink to make snowflake stamps.*

Directions:

1. Start with a square piece of paper.

2. Fold the paper in half to form a right triangle.

3. Fold in the acute angle corners to form a cone.

4. Fold the cone in half length-wise.

5. Cut the top off the cone as shown by the dotted line.

6. Cut designs and shapes into your wedge.

7. Open your six-sided snowflake!

Snowflake Key

NAME	SHAPES
HEXAGONAL PLATES	
STELLAR CRYSTALS	
HEXAGONAL COLUMNS	
NEEDLES	
SPATIAL DENDRITES	
CAPPED COLUMNS	
IRREGULAR CRYSTALS	

Snow Melt

Objective:
Students will observe and measure the conversion of snow to water.

Grade Level: 2-5

Groupings: Pairs

Materials: Clear quart containers with lids; homemade paper rulers (strips of paper marked in inches or centimeters) or rubber bands; several scales or balances.

Time Allotment: 20 minutes

Directions:

1. Ask the students what they think makes up snow. How might they prove it? Explain that they will do a simple experiment to find out this and other important things about snow.

2. Divide the class into pairs. Have the students weigh their empty quart containers and record the weights.

3. Have the students collect the cleanest snow they can find. Weigh the snow-filled containers. Record the weight. Have them subtract the weight of the empty container from the weight of the snow-filled container to find the weight of the snow itself.

4. Tape the paper ruler vertically to the side of the jar. Ask the students how high they think the water will be when the snow melts. Have them mark their predictions on the ruler. (For younger students, place rubber bands around the jar instead of paper rulers to mark each student's prediction.)

5. Have the students cover the containers, set them aside, and record the time. Ask them to predict how long it will take for all of the snow to melt. Will the melted snow weigh more or less or the same as the unmelted snow? Record predictions.

6. Have the students check the containers periodically until all of the snow has melted and record the time.

7. Have the students record the weight and water levels of the melted snow in the containers. Did the weight of the snow change after it melted? (It should be the same.)

a. *Test the melted snow water for purity. Examine two coffee filters closely with a hand lens. Record any markings. Place the coffee filters in two different funnels. Pour the melted snow water through one coffee filter. As a control, pour distilled or filtered water through the second filter. Examine both coffee filters with a hand lens. What do you see? Discuss differences and possible explanations.*

b. *Many people have heard of acid rain. Snow can be acidic also. Test the pH of the melted snow with litmus paper or pH solution. Follow package directions and use the chart provided to determine results. As a control, also test the pH of distilled water. Compare and analyze the results. Are acid rain and acid snow essentially the same thing?*

c. *Try **Snow Melt** during another snowfall. Is there a difference in the water content?*

Directions: (continued)

8. Have the students compare the results to their predictions. Discuss differences and possible explanations. (The water level of the melted snow will be less than that of the snow because of the volume of the air spaces between the snow crystals.)

9. Have the class share their results.

SNOW SEEDS

Snow seeds don't come in packets, but you probably have a few in your pocket. Reach down deep and see whether you can pull out any bits of lint or dust. Snowflakes start in clouds as ice crystals that form around tiny particles of dust or, very often, sea salt. The crystals may grow and join together with others to form the flakes that fall in snowstorms. The snowflakes that we see are usually not single snow crystals, but rather aggregates of crystals.

A Blanket of Snow

Objective:
Students will discover the insulating effect of snow and understand that temperature varies according to snow depth.

Grade Level: 3-5

Groupings: Small groups

Materials: (per group) Outdoor thermometer; meter or yardstick; paper; pencil and clipboard for outdoor recording.

Time Allotment: 30 minutes

Directions:
For best results, this activity should be done on a winter day when the temperature is in the 20 degree range or less and when there has been at least seven inches of snow on the ground for several days.

1. Ask the students whether they have heard of the phrase, "a blanket of snow." What does a blanket do? Does snow really act as a blanket, keeping what's underneath warm? Does the thickness of the snow have an effect? Is a heavy blanket warmer than a thin blanket?

2. Divide the class into small groups. Furnish each group with a set of materials and assign an area of the school yard to investigate. Brainstorm with the students ways to discover, using the materials provided, whether the snow acts as a blanket.

3. The groups should collect the following data at each location: a) air temperature; b) temperature under the snow, at ground level; c) depth of the snow; d) temperature under the snow at a depth of two inches from the snow's surface. Include any other parameters that the students find interesting.

4. Have the groups take the above measurements at different locations in your test area: under trees, near buildings, in snow drifts, in the open. Have each group collect data from three to five different locations. Stress the importance of gathering multiple data.

Extensions:

a. *Have the students construct snow gauges to record snowfall amounts over the winter. A glass jar that fits inside a large metal coffee can makes a good gauge. Mark the glass jar in inches or centimeters with a permanent marker. Place the gauges outside where they will not be disturbed. (Try sprinkling a little water on the ground around the base of the coffee can to freeze it in place. This will prevent it from being blown around in a storm.) After each snowfall, compare and record results. Compare class measurements with local weather predictions.*

b. *Use cotton balls on a bar graph to keep track of the amount of snow that falls over the winter.*

Directions: (continued)

5. Back in the classroom, have each group analyze their data. Compare air temperature to the temperature recorded at two inches under the snow. Compare these temperatures to the temperature recorded at ground level. What conclusions can be drawn from results? (In every case, the ground level readings will be near 32° Fahrenheit.)

6. Using the students' findings, discuss the influence of snow depth on temperature. Do plants and animals benefit from a blanket of snow? What happens in a winter with little snowfall and subfreezing temperatures? Is there any truth to the phrase, "a blanket of snow"?

SNUG *in the* SNOW

Near ground level under the snow cover, in the subnivean layer of snow, is an entire network of pathways, tunnels, and nests where small animals pursue their winter lives. Shrews, mice, voles, and others winter in the subnivean layer, where the insulating snow keeps the temperature constant at around 32° Fahrenheit.

The Language of Snow

Objective:
Students will learn to distinguish different kinds and qualities of snow.

Grade Level: 3-5

Groupings: 2-4 students

Materials: Map or globe; library books on the Eskimos or Inuits.

Time Allotment: 30 minutes

Directions:

1. Some snow is good for making snowballs and snowmen, and some is not; some snow is good for sledding, and some is not; some snow feels dry, some feels wet; some snow squeaks when you step on it, and some doesn't. Ask students to describe different kinds of snow and ice. Record their descriptions. Can they think of special names to describe the different types of snow? How many such names can the students think of (e.g. snow, hail, sleet)?

2. Explain that in certain places, snow is a part of life for most of the year. People who live in these places develop a large vocabulary to describe snow. The Eskimos or Inuits are one such people. They live in the Kobuk valley of Alaska and have over ten words to describe different types of snow.

3. Locate the Kobuk valley in Alaska on a map. Have the students research the weather throughout the year, including daily temperature, day length, and snowfall.

4. Divide the students into small groups. Give each group one of the Inuit words for snow and its definition. Have each group use the word in a short poem, haiku, cinquain, or song in order to explain its meaning.

5. When all the groups have finished, have each group read their work out loud. The rest of the class then tries to guess the meaning of the Inuit word used.

6. Ask the groups to make up their own secret language of snow. Have each group write a story about winter that

Extensions:

a. *Make a pair of Eskimo snow goggles. Use poster board for the goggles and cut out as shown. Have each student hold the goggles up to his or her face and have a partner gently mark a dot on the goggles over the student's eyes with a marker or other blunt writing instrument. Remove the goggles and carefully push a pencil point through the dot. Cut out slits for the eye holes. Staple a piece of elastic to the sides. The students can decorate their goggles. Then head outside on a bright snowy day and test them out.*

b. *Have the students keep journals of snow conditions over a month or two, characterizing snow using the Inuit vocabulary or their invented vocabularies.*

Directions: (continued)

includes five new snow words. Stress that the meaning of the new word needs to be clear from the way it is used in the sentence/story. Have each group create their own dictionary for their new words.

7. Have the groups exchange stories. Each group should try to discover the meanings of the new words. After recording their guesses, use the created dictionaries to find the answers.

SNOW VOCABULARY
of the Inuits of the Kobuk Valley, Alaska

ANNUI - *Falling snow.*
API - *Snow on the ground.*
PUKAK - *Sugar snow, hard round crystals that act like ball bearings rolling over one another. This is the snow that can cause avalanches.*
QALI - *Snow that collects on the branches of trees.*
SIQOQ - *Swirling or drifting snow.*
UPSIK - *Wind-beaten snow.*
KIMOAGRUK - *A snow drift.*
QAMANIQ - *A bowl-shaped hollow of snow around the base of a tree.*
SIQOQTOAQ - *Snow with a hard crust on top.*

* from THE SECRET LANGUAGE OF SNOW, T. Williams and T. Major (Sierra Club Press, 1984).

Mello Jello

Objective:
Students will observe the effects of insulation on temperature.

Grade Level: 2-5

Groupings: Pairs

Materials: Jello mix; hot plate; film canisters with lids (2 per pair); thermometer; masking tape; measuring tape; assortment of possible insulating materials: Styrofoam peanuts, sawdust, newspapers, aluminum foil, paper cups, bubble wrap, etc.

Time Allotment: 45 minutes (plus time for the Jello to firm).

AIR POCKET POWER
Insulation is any material that is used to keep temperature from changing. Usually insulation works by capturing small pockets of air and holding them around whatever is being insulated. In Mello Jello, for example, it's not the Styrofoam peanuts themselves that keep the Jello warm; it's the air spaces between the peanuts.

Directions:

1. Ask the students to define insulation. Why is it used? What types of things are insulated? Why is insulation important in winter? Brainstorm a list of materials that might be good insulation. Ask the students to bring in insulation materials from home to share with the class. (Stress that students not bring in standard fiberglass insulation.)

2. Have the students work together to sort the insulation materials. Group similar materials together. As they are working, boil water and make the Jello.

3. Divide the class into pairs. Explain that each pair will get two film canisters filled with warm liquid Jello. Using the materials brought from home and those provided in the classroom, they will insulate one of their canisters in order to keep the Jello as warm as possible when placed outdoors. The other canister won't be insulated at all. Both canisters will be set outdoors and later compared.

4. Each pair should prepare a list of the insulating materials they would like to use. Remind them to think about the order in which they would like to use these materials. For example, they might wrap a Jello canister in newspaper, then in bubble wrap, then in rags.

5. Give each pair two canisters of warm Jello. On a piece of masking tape fixed to the canisters, have them write their names and label the canisters #1 and #2. Each pair should work quickly to record the temperature of the warm Jello in both canisters. Allow them several minutes to make and record additional observations about their Jello such as its color and consistency.

6. When you say, "Go," all the students should put lids on both of their Jello canisters. Have them set canister #1 aside. They then have 15 minutes to work on insulating canister #2. Each pair should label their insulated package with their names, and measure and record its height and width.

7. The students should then place both their insulated and uninsulated canisters outdoors for 30 - 60 minutes.

8. Back in the classroom, each pair should record exactly

Extensions:

a. *Discuss how people improve the insulation in their homes (plastic on windows, hay bales around the foundation, weather stripping, etc.). Ask the students what might be done to improve your school's insulation?*

b. *Repeat the experiment using snow as insulation. Have the students place canisters filled with warm Jello in three different locations: on top of the snow, two inches under the snow, and eight inches under the snow. Compare results.*

c. *Discuss ways animals insulate themselves and their homes in winter.*

Directions: (continued)

how they insulated their canister, noting the materials used, the order in which they were used, and where the insulated package was placed outside. Have them predict and record what might happen to their insulated Jello. Will it gel or freeze? Will it remain a warm liquid? What will the final temperature be? Ask them to make similar predictions for the uninsulated Jello.

9. When the allotted time has passed, the class should collect all the canisters. Have each pair take the temperature of the uninsulated Jello immediately upon returning to the classroom. Then, working as quickly as possible, they should unwrap their insulated packages and take the temperature of the insulated Jello. Have the students note any changes in the consistency of the Jello in each container.

10. Have the pairs compare their results. Did any pair still have liquid Jello? Was any Jello warmer than 40 degrees? What types and amounts of insulation worked best? Who had the largest package? Did the amount of insulation have an effect on the final temperature? What are the qualities of good insulation?

Coping with Cold

Objective:
Students will learn about the winter survival strategies of New England animals.

Grade Level: K-3

Groupings: Entire class

Materials: Set of cards listing the four winter adaptations (hibernation, migration, dormancy, remaining active) with string for hanging cards around students' necks; props to represent these adaptations such as an alarm clock (set for spring), a suitcase, a bathrobe, and a warm winter coat; MOUSEKIN'S WOODLAND SLEEPERS by Edna Miller (Simon & Schuster, 1970 – *out of print*); and pictures of animals or animal puppets.

Time Allotment: 30 minutes

Directions:

1. Discuss with the class the season of winter and how it affects people. What changes do the students and their families make in their dress, food, homes, vehicles?

2. What about animals? How do they adapt to winter? Do they make similar changes in their coats, food, homes, and ways of travel? Using the students' ideas, highlight the following four winter survival strategies: **hibernation, migration, dormancy and remaining active.** (See *New England Mammals in Winter*, page 147 - 48.)

3. Choose four students to be the experts on the four strategies. Call them up one at a time and hang a winter adaptation sign around their neck. Assign props to each student to symbolize or define the winter adaptation. For example, an alarm clock "set for spring" can represent hibernation, a suitcase for migration, a bathrobe for dormancy, and a warm winter coat for remaining active.

4. Explain that you will be reading MOUSEKIN'S WOODLAND SLEEPERS, a story about how different animals adapt to winter. Challenge the students to discover what winter survival strategies the various animals in the story are using. Stop throughout the story to ask the students how the animals described are adapting to winter.

5. Have the four winter survival strategy experts stand in the front of the class. Pass out pictures of animals or animal puppets to the rest of the students. Have each student decide which strategy their animal uses to adapt to winter. When you

Extension:

a. Adapt MOUSEKIN'S WOODLAND SLEEPERS by Edna Miller (Simon & Schuster, 1970 – OUT OF PRINT) into a big book. Shorten the story so it contains only the animals' winter activities.

b. Look into where some common birds go in the winter. Trace their migration routes on world maps and calculate the distance travelled.

c. Certain active animals such as the snowshoe hare, short-tailed weasel, and ermine, change color in winter. Discuss with your class the benefits of camouflage.

d. Involve your class in researching more about hibernating mammals. How long do they hibernate? What are some unique physical changes the animals experience? To dispell a common myth, have the students compare their findings to the winter activities of a bear.

e. During the winter thaws, look for signs that some common dormant animals are out and about (tracks, droppings, food, homes, etc.).

Directions: (continued)

say "Go," each student hands his or her picture to the expert wearing the sign that matches the animal's winter survival strategy.

6. Review their choices. Add more information as needed and use the Miller story for reference.

HIBERNATION HAPPENINGS

Bears are animals that everyone thinks of as hibernators, but in fact bears don't really hibernate. In their dens in winter, bears become dormant, entering a deep but intermittent sleep. Occasionally on warm winter days they may wake, leave their dens, and range about. True hibernation, by contrast, is an almost death-like state characterized by profound physical changes. Unlike the body functions of a dormant animal, a hibernator's metabolism slows greatly. A woodchuck's body temperature drops to about 37° Fahrenheit, and its heart rate drops to as slow as three or four beats per minute. True hibernation, a radical energy-saving adaptation, is practiced in New England by only three types of animals: the woodchuck, several species of bat, and two kinds of jumping mice.

New England Mammals in Winter

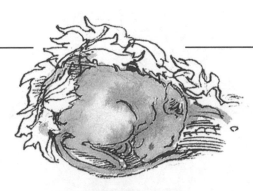

HIBERNATE

(deep sleep for a prolonged amount of time)

SPECIES	WINTER HABITAT	WINTER FOOD SOURCE
Little Brown Bat and other bat species	Caves	Doesn't eat during winter
Woodland Jumping Mouse & Meadow Jumping Mouse	Underground, below frost line	Doesn't eat during winter
Woodchuck	Burrows, below frostline	Doesn't eat during winter

DORMANT

(wakes up and moves about occasionally)

SPECIES	WINTER HABITAT	WINTER FOOD SOURCE
Black Bear	Caves, under fallen trees	Doesn't eat during winter
Eastern Chipmunk	Burrows, below frostline	Seeds & nuts stored in caches
Raccoon	Hollow trees, under rocks; city & suburbs	Whatever is available; prefers nuts & berries, eats frogs, clams, snails, crayfish, occasionally birds or small rodents
Striped Skunk	Open fields or woods, city & suburbs	Berries, roots, insects, eggs, small animals

ACTIVE

(well adapted to winter & food source available)

SPECIES	WINTER HABITAT	WINTER FOOD SOURCE
Coyote	Open fields & woods	Small or medium sized animals
White Tailed Deer	Sheltered woods, usually evergreen	Buds, twigs, apples, evergreen foliage
Red Fox	Open fields, woods farmland, suburbs	Fruit, mice, rabbits, insects, carrion (some stored in caches)
Snowshoe Hare & Cottontail Rabbit	Above ground nests in woods & brush	Buds, twigs, own droppings
Eastern Mole (semi-active)	Tunnels below frostline	Insects, spiders, slugs, seeds
Meadow Vole	Tunnels under snow & leaf litter in meadows	Seeds, roots, stems, bark
White-footed Mouse & Deer Mouse	Nests in walls, logs, stumps, under tree roots	Berries, buds, seeds, nuts, bark, greens, insects, human scraps
Porcupine	Dens in rocks, holes in trees, under trees	Evergreen foliage, bark & twigs
Eastern Gray Squirrel	Tree dens or leaf nests	Acorns, nuts, seeds
Short-tailed Weasel	Open fields & woods	Small rodents, insects, amphibians

Sole Search

Objective:
Students will use observation skills to distinguish different footprints.

Grade Level: K-3

Groupings: Entire class

Materials: Paper and crayons.

Time Allotment: 30 minutes

Directions:
1. Tell the class that you went to the *Sherlock Holmes Track Detective School* and learned how to recognize animals and people by their tracks. Tell the students they can become track detectives, too.

2. Pass out paper and crayons to each student. Have them remove their right shoes and make rubbings of the soles. Demonstrate to the class how a rubbing is made by holding the paper against the sole of the shoe and rubbing the side of a crayon over the paper to make an impression of the sole.

3. When the rubbings are finished, have the students put their right shoes back on. Then have them place their rubbing on the ground, line up their left shoes on top of the rubbings, and trace the outline of their left shoes.

4. Collect the footprint rubbings and have the students place their left shoe in a central spot.

5. Explain to the students that you will pass out one of the footprint rubbings to each student. Remind them not to accept their own rubbings. Have the students look at this footprint carefully, noting any distinguishing characteristics or clues. Their detective mission is to find the shoe that matches the footprint. When you say, "Go," the students begin to sort through the pile of shoes for the correct match to their print.

Extensions:

a. *Sort the footprint rubbings into groups based on various characteristics: size, design of tread, crayon color, etc. Have students guess what characteristic you used to sort the prints. Then let the students do the sorting.*

b. *Have the students make their thumb prints on two different colored pieces of paper. Collect one print and have the students place the other face-up in a central location. Mix up the prints, pass them out, and challenge the students find the matching finger print. It is best to do this activity with small groups.*

Directions: (continued)

6. Once the students have found matches, have them sit in a circle to review and check the shoes and prints. Have each detective point out the distinguishing characteristics of his or her footprint and the matching character in the chosen shoe. Finally, have them locate the owner and return the shoe and rubbing.

WHO GOES THERE?

Ev - ery - where that you go,——— In white flu - ffy snow——— you see an - i - mal tracks,——— an - i - mal tracks,——— Tracks run - ning this way and that Now tell me who walked here? A white tailed deer. Now who jumped there? A snow - shoe hare. And who wad - dled here? I know it's a skunk. And they all made tracks 'round the old tree trunk.

Sharp Eyes

Objective:
Students will sharpen observation skills by determining small changes in a partner's appearance.

Grade Level: 1-5

Groupings: Entire class, in pairs

Materials: None

Time Allotment: 10 minutes

Directions:

1. Come into class dressed as a typical detective (borrow a Sherlock Holmes hat, trench coat and magnifying glass). Ask the class if they know who you are pretending to be. Generate ideas about what detectives are, what they do and what special skills or attributes they have, stressing good observation and listening skills. Tell the students that in this activity they will each be a detective.

2. Divide the class into two equal groups. Have them stand in two lines so every student is directly opposite another student.

3. Explain that they will all get a chance to make a small change in their appearance. Make suggestions and demonstrate a few examples. Have all the students observe you, then ask them to close their eyes while you make a change. You might untie a shoe, push up your sleeve, or take off a watch. Can they guess what you've changed?

4. Choose one side to be the detectives first. Tell the detectives that it is their mission to observe everything about their partner or specimen's appearance. Explain that they are to study their specimen very carefully for one minute (or less), and then the detectives will hide their eyes and the specimens will change one small thing about the way they look.

Extensions:

a. *Change something in the classroom. Challenge the students to observe what is different.*

b. *Have the students work in pairs. Have one student secretly set up a collection of small items (no more than ten) under a bandana. Have the partner lift the bandana to observe this collection. After a minute or less, have the observer close his or her eyes while the other student removes one of the objects. Uncover the collection again to see whether the observer can determine what is missing. Trade places and try again.*

Directions: (continued)

5. Give the detectives time to examine their specimen. Then have the detectives turn around (no peeking) to let the specimens change.

6. When all the specimens are ready, have the detectives turn back and try to determine how their specimen has changed. If a detective is having trouble, have both students turn around again. Let the specimen change back to the way he or she was originally. The detective will usually recognize the change on the second try.

7. Have the groups switch roles, and let the specimens have a chance playing detective.

Predator-Prey

Objective:
Students will understand and dramatize predator-prey relationships.

Grade Level: 1-5

Groupings: Entire class

Materials: Pictures of local animals (enough for every two students); two blindfolds (paper bags or the students' hats work well); two maracas or other noise makers.

Time Allotment: 20 minutes

Directions:

1. Pass out pictures of the animals to the class, having students share pictures as needed. Ask the students to think about the type of food their animal eats.

2. Ask the class to divide themselves into two different groups. One group will include animals who eat only plants. They are called **herbivores**. The second group will include all the animals who eat other animals. Some of the animals in the second group eat other animals and nothing else; these are called **carnivores**. Other animals in the second group, called **omnivores**, eat plants as well as other animals. Review the animals in each of the groups and make the necessary corrections.

3. Review the types of food herbivores might eat. Explain that herbivores are themselves often eaten by carnivores and omnivores. Herbivores that are hunted by carnivores and omnivores are called **prey**, and the carnivores and omnivores that do the hunting are called **predators**.

4. Ask the carnivores and omnivores if they see someone in the herbivore group they might like to have for lunch. Review their choices.

5. After some predator-prey relationships are established, collect the animal pictures. Have the students form a circle. Ask them to imagine that the circle is the boundary of a forest where predators and their prey live. Each student in the circle is a tree. Have them take root and stand quietly.

6. Ask the students to name a predator that lives in your area. Choose a student to be that predator and to come into the center of the circle. Ask the class what that predator's prey would be. Select another student to come into the center of the circle to represent the prey.

7. Explain to the students that the predator will be hunting its prey inside the forest circle. What senses might the predator use to catch its prey? How might the prey keep from being caught?

Extensions:

a. *Use animal pictures in a variety of sorting games in which students match predator and prey species. Students can separate the animals into groups based on food source—herbivore, carnivore, or omnivore.*

b. *Create a "Concentration" game based on predator-prey relationships. Select pictures of predators and prey species. Add an equal number of matching cards with the word "predator" and "prey" written on them. Mix the cards and turn them face down in rows. Two students play by taking turns turning over two cards at a time to find a match of a predator's picture with the word "predator" or a prey's picture with the word "prey." The game continues until all the matches are found.*

c. *Borrow a collection of skulls from your state Fish and Wildlife Department or a local college zoology department. Have the class look carefully at the teeth of carnivores and herbivores. Have the students (who are omnivores themselves) feel their own teeth. Compare and contrast their teeth with those of other animals.*

d. *For delightful stories featuring a variety of herbivores, carnivores, predators and prey, read* DR. DESOTO *by William Steig (Farrar, Strauss & Giroux, 1982) and* MICE TWICE *by Josephine Low (Macmillian, 1980).*

Directions: (continued)

8. Explain that this predator will be hunting its prey on a very dark night. They will wear blindfolds to simulate this situation. Stress that their sense of hearing will now become very important. Give the predator and the prey a maraca, and explain that as they move, they *must* both shake their maraca. Make sure everyone else is quiet (after all, trees cannot talk).

9. Blindfold the two students and move them to different places in the circle. When you say, "Go," the predator should try to find the prey by listening for the noise of the prey's maraca. When the prey is touched, the game is over. To make the activity more or less difficult, change the size of the circle.

10. Repeat the activity to give other students a chance to be a different predator and its prey.

Who Am I?

Objective:

Students will learn effective questioning techniques through a review activity on the habits of New England animals in the winter.

Grade Level: 2-6

Groupings: Small groups or entire class

Materials: Pictures of animals hung on long strings.

Time Allotment: 15 minutes

Directions:

This is a good review activity to a unit on animals in winter and winter tracking. It works best if the students are familiar with the material presented in **Coping with Cold** *(pages 145 - 46),* **Pitter Patter** *(pages 157 - 60), and* **Predator-Prey** *(pages 153 - 54), and have done some outdoor tracking.*

1. Explain to the students that they will be playing a winter animal guessing game. The object of the game is to guess the identity of a mystery animal by asking simple yes or no questions. Explain that this game is often played at the *Sherlock Holmes Track Detective School* to help the students learn how to gather clues quickly.

2. Break the students into small groups. Have them brainstorm a list of questions, based on the winter habits of animals, that can help them to discover the identity of an animal. Bring all the groups together and compile a class list of questions. Highlight the winter survival strategy used by the animal (hibernation, migration, dormancy, remaining active); the track pattern the animal leaves as it moves through the snow (walker, hopper, waddler, bounder); and the kind of food the animal eats (carnivore, omnivore, herbivore, predator, prey).

3. Explain that you will hang a picture of an animal around one student's neck but the picture will be on the student's back so he or she cannot see it. Instruct that student to turn so that everyone else has a chance to see the picture. Using

Extension:

a. *Put a mystery animal card on every students' back. When you say "Go," have the students ask each other yes and no questions to discover the identity of their animal. When an animal's identity is discovered, the student may turn the card so it is facing forward. Have all the students continue to answer questions until everyone has identified his or her animal. Time the class to see how long it takes.*

Directions: (continued)

the list of questions generated by the class, have the student try to guess the identity of the mystery animal. Remind the other students that they may only answer yes or no. (If you feel that your students need more help developing their questioning skills, have a student hang a card around your neck and demonstrate the activity.)

4. Keep track of the number of questions the student asks to identify the mystery animal. When the student guesses correctly, let that student chose the next mystery animal. Play the game again, giving all the students a chance to do the guessing.

Pitter Patter

Objective:

Students will learn to observe animals by studying their tracks and will understand how animals can be grouped according to the way they move.

Grade Level: 1-5

Groupings: Entire class

Materials: Track pattern cards (see step # 5); index cards showing various animal footprints; *Track Pattern Cards* (page 161); string, rolls of paper or window shades (see step #6).

Time Allotment: 20 minutes

Directions:

1. *Pitter Patter* is the key activity to a unit on tracking. Show the class your **Sherlock Holmes Track Detective Card** (see page 170) and explain that you went to a special animal tracking school and learned to be a track detective. Ask the students whether they would like to become track detectives. Tell them you can initiate new detectives if they can discover and learn the secret tracking formula.

2. Gather the class around you. Explain that the secret tracking formula will help them focus on important outdoor tracking clues in the woods and fields. Explain that the formula is top secret, and so it is necessary to whisper.

3. Caution the students to listen carefully as you will be giving important clues to the formula. Give the following clues slowly and see whether the students can guess the three words in the secret formula. Pause to let them fill in the italicized word. The tracking formula consists of three words that all begin with the letter *P*. The first clue students should look for when tracking is the animals' foot*print*. Once they discover a foot*print*, they need to determine the design that the footprints make in the snow. This design keeps repeating itself and is called a track *pattern*. The last thing they need to discover in tracking is where the animal lives or if it has a secret hiding *place*.

4. Have the students repeat the secret formula: *pattern, print, place.* Explain that it is important to use this formula to identify and study animals when they're outdoors tracking. When they find a trail, they should first identify the track pattern. This can help to narrow down the possible animals that might have made the track. Next look for a good, clear, detailed footprint. This is one of the best tracking clues but often is difficult to find. Last, students should be sure to notice the place where the tracks are found. They should try to discover where the tracks are going to or coming from. These places give the last important clue to the animal's identity.

5. Explain to the students that animals walk in four basic track patterns. You will teach the class to recognize these patterns. They will need to learn these before they go outside tracking. Make the track pattern cards from twelve 3" x 5"

Extensions:

a. *While outdoors, use a ruler to measure the tracks. When you find an animal's trail, measure the **stride**, or the distance between two tracks; some trackers also measure the distance between the first and third track because it tells you its approximate overall length. Also measure the **straddle**, the distance across the tracks, from the outside of the first to the outside of the second. This measurement can tell you how wide the animal is. Use a field guide to compare these measurements with the animal's true dimensions.*

b. *Make your own tracks in the snow. Compare walking and running tracks. Measure the stride. What happens to the distance between footprints when you start to run? Have the students create their own track patterns while others try to guess how they were made.*

c. *Play track charades. Have the students act out stories about different animals. Remind them to try to move in the track patterns appropriate for their animals. Use the following stories, or have the students make up their own.*
• *You are an owl. Swoop down to catch a mouse, leaving your wing prints in the snow.*

• *You are a rabbit nibbling on some low branches. You hear a gunshot. Quickly hop into the woods, stopping often to listen for danger. Hide under a low bush.*

• *You are a mouse hopping through the forest. You leave a long track behind you as your tail drags on the snow.*

Directions: (continued)

index cards. Draw a single large oval on eight of the cards, and then cut four cards in half and draw single small circles on them, giving you a total of sixteen track-pattern cards. You will use these cards to demonstrate the four track patterns.

6. Begin with the perfect or straight-walking pattern. Place six cards on the floor in the correct pattern. With older students you might lay down the first two or three cards correctly and then see if they can complete the pattern.

Ask for a volunteer to try to walk in this pattern with feet on the first two prints, and hands on the next two. To walk in this pattern, the students will have to move their right hand and left foot at the same time (and likewise their left hand and right foot). As their hand moves forward, their foot goes onto the card where their hand was. Show the students the footprints of all the animals who walk in this pattern and have them guess who they are. Use a roll of paper or a white window shade stamped with various animal footprints in rows (see ***Moving Along***, page 160).

7. Give all the students a chance to imitate this pattern. Have them imagine they are one of the straight-walkers and let them practice walking around the room in the straight-walker pattern.

8. Using the track pattern cards, lay out the hopper pat-

tern on the floor. Ask the students what animal might move in this pattern. Explain that hoppers have one pair of feet that is larger than the other pair. Can they guess which tracks are made by the front feet and which by the rear? Which way is this animal headed? Point out that the

• You are a raccoon waddling along a stream. Stop and go down to the stream to look for food.

• You are a weasel bounding through the snow with long strides. Suddenly you tunnel under the snow in search of mice.

hopper's pattern is interesting because the larger hind feet land in front of the smaller front feet. Ask the student how an animal might do this. Have a volunteer demonstrate. On all fours, the volunteer hopper places the hands between the widespread legs. Moving, the arms swing ahead first to take the body's weight. The back feet follow, swinging around to the outside of the hands and landing slightly forward of them. Again, show the class footprints of other hoppers and let the students hop around like one of these animals.

• You are one of a small herd of deer walking single-file through the deep snow. Stop to graze. Suddenly, one of the herd hears a sound – danger!! Flick up your tail and run for cover.

• You are a dog out alone on a sunny afternoon. Run around and explore the neighborhood, sniffing as you go.

• You are a lone coyote on a hilltop at night. Give a howl and head out across a field in search of your dinner.

9. Next, lay out the waddler pattern. This is one of the more difficult patterns to imitate. See whether the class can figure

out the waddler's method of walking from its track pattern. Ask for a volunteer waddler. The waddler's weight shifts to the right as both the left hand and foot move forward at the same time, then shifts to the left as the right hand and foot move in their turn. When done slowly and with some exaggeration, waddling can give a clear impression of an animal slowly lumbering along. Show the class footprints of waddlers. Explain that they are usually slow-moving animals that don't need speed because they have other means of

MOVING ALONG

PERFECT or STRAIGHT WALKING *is the most common gait for felines (house cat, bobcat), canines (dog, fox, coyote), and ungulates (cow, sheep, deer, moose).*

HOPPING *is the gait used by cottontail rabbits, snowshoe hares, squirrels, chipmunks, mice, voles and shrews.*

WADDLERS *are mostly heavy-set mammals such as beaver, porcupine, muskrat, raccoon, skunk, opossum and bear.*

BOUNDING *is the common gait for most of the weasel family — short and long-tailed weasel, mink, otter, marten and fisher.*

Directions: (continued)

defense (e.g., the skunk has its smell, the porcupine its quills, the bear its size, and the raccoon its sharp teeth). Have the class slowly waddle about, pretending they are one of the waddlers.

10. Lay out the last track pattern, that of the bounders. (These tracks are seldom seen in urban or suburban areas, so you might decide to omit this pattern.)

Explain that all members of the weasel family except the skunk are bounders. These animals have long, narrow bodies and very short legs. Moving, they look like a spring or a Slinky. Have a volunteer bounder place his or her hands and feet together in one spot, then leap or bound forward so that all fours land together. Show the class a typical weasel footprint. Explain that in order to identify tracks of the several different members of the weasel family, one would need to look closely at the size of the print and at the place it was found. Let the students bound around like weasels.

11. Review the four track patterns briefly. Pass out copies of the *Track Pattern Card* to your students. Have them fold it in half along the dotted line and protect it for outdoor use by covering it with contact paper, laminating it or simply placing it in a plastic baggie. Punch two holes in the top and add string so it can be worn around the neck. Then take the class outside in search of real animal tracks. Have them use their *Track Pattern Card* to help them identify the tracks they find.

Track Pattern Card

Okay, Track Detectives, you are on your own! Use the secret code, and in dirt, mud, or snow, identify tracks wherever you go!

First, what **PATTERN** are the tracks in?

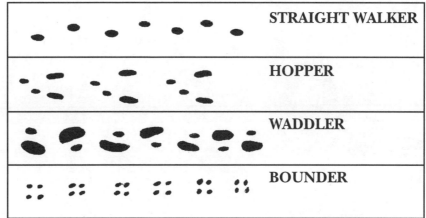

	STRAIGHT WALKER
	HOPPER
	WADDLER
	BOUNDER

What **PLACE** are they found? Remember to look for homes, leftover food scraps, and other clues such as feathers, fur, blood, scat, etc. left at the scene.

- -

Now check the **PRINT** of the animal's foot. Notice the overall shape, measure its size, note the presence or absence of claws, and count the number of toes.

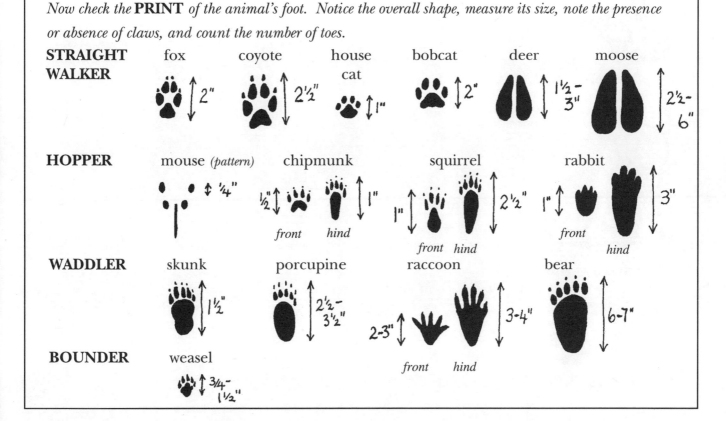

STRAIGHT WALKER fox 2"   coyote 2½"   house cat 1"   bobcat 2"   deer 1½ – 3"   moose 2½ – 6"

HOPPER mouse *(pattern)* ¼"   chipmunk ½" 1" *front hind*   squirrel 1" 2½" *front hind*   rabbit 1" 3" *front hind*

WADDLER skunk 1½"   porcupine 2½ – 3½"   raccoon 2-3" 3-4" *front hind*   bear 6-7"

BOUNDER weasel ¾ – 1½"

Animal Tracks Worksheet

Draw the **PATTERN** *for each animal.*

White Tailed Deer

Fox

Raccoon

Gray Squirrel

Cottontail Rabbit

White-footed Mouse

Striped Skunk

Track Stamps

Objective:
Students will learn about various animals' tracks by making stamps and prints of their tracks.

Grade Level: 4-5

Groupings: Entire Class

Materials: Photocopies of *Forest Animal Track Templates* (page 165 - 66); scissors; Dr. Scholl's foot and shoe padding (available at drugstores); ink pads; paper; small (2 1/2" x 4") blocks of wood.

Time Allotment: 45 minutes

Directions:

1. Ask the students to think about the different kinds of animals that might live in the nearby woods and fields. List suggested animals on the board. Ask students how they might tell for certain whether a particular kind of animal lives in their area. Point out that in winter it's easy to find signs of the animals in an area by the footprints or tracks they leave.

2. Explain that different animals have distinct footprints. One at a time, show the students the footprints cut from the track template sheet, making sure the animals' names are not visible. Challenge the students to match footprints with one of the animals from the list on the board.

3. Explain to the students that they will make a track stamp of their favorite animal. Have multiple copies of track templates available for the students to choose from. Have each student pick a footprint and carefully cut out the various parts of the print from the template sheet. It is not necessary to cut out claws.

4. Pass out a piece of foot and shoe padding to every two students. Have each student place his or her cutout footprint templates on the padding (as close together as possible) and trace around them. Then they can cut out their footprints. Scraps of padding can be used for claws.

5. Pass out one or two wood blocks to each student. (If the front and hind feet of their animal are different, they will need two blocks of wood.) Have students attach their cutout footprints to the smoothest side of their wood blocks by peeling the protective backing off the padding and sticking the padding's adhesive surface to the wood. Ask the students

Extensions:

a. Use the track stamps to make **Track Stories** (see page 169) on mural paper with stamp pads.

b. Create greeting cards using the track stamps. Paste a cut-out animal or draw a picture of an animal and its habitat, then make a track.

c. Make track stamps using the **Farm Animal Track Templates** (see page 167) Make a farm scene and add tracks. Compare tracks of farm animals with those of wild animals.

d. Make an assortment of track print cards. Discuss similarities and differences in prints. Have the students work in small groups to sort the track print cards in as many ways as possible.

e. Play Track Twister (see extension a. on page 10).

Directions: (continued)

to refer to the footprint templates to help them place the various footprint parts in the proper configuration.

6. Pass out ink pads and paper, and let the students test their track stamps!

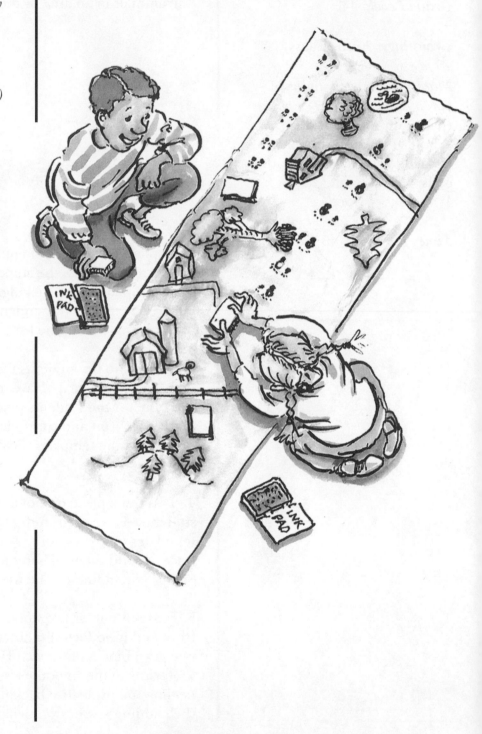

Forest Animal Track Templates

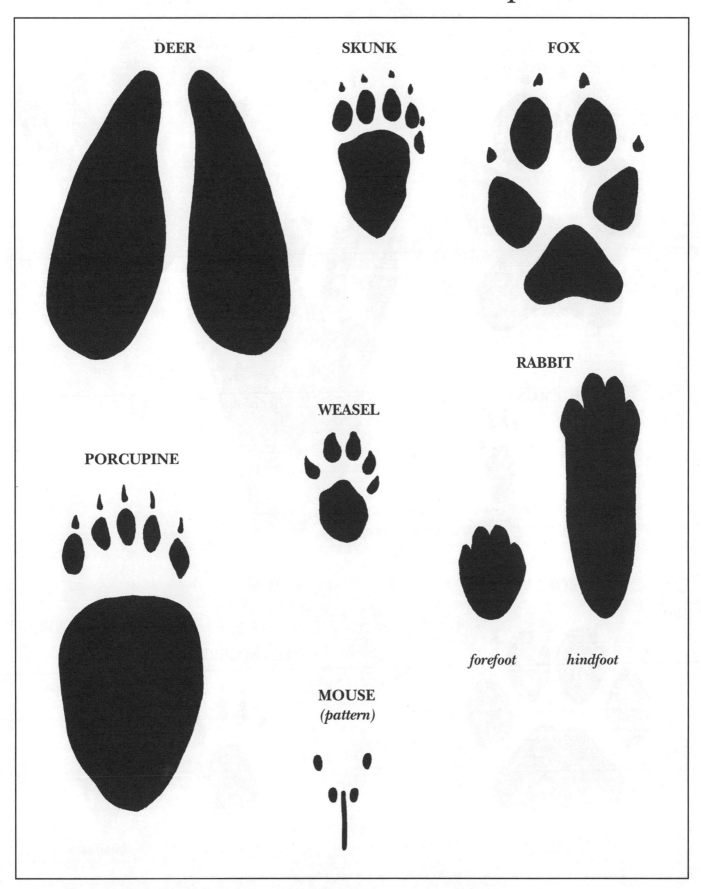

DEER

SKUNK

FOX

RABBIT

WEASEL

PORCUPINE

forefoot *hindfoot*

MOUSE
(pattern)

Forest Animal Track Templates

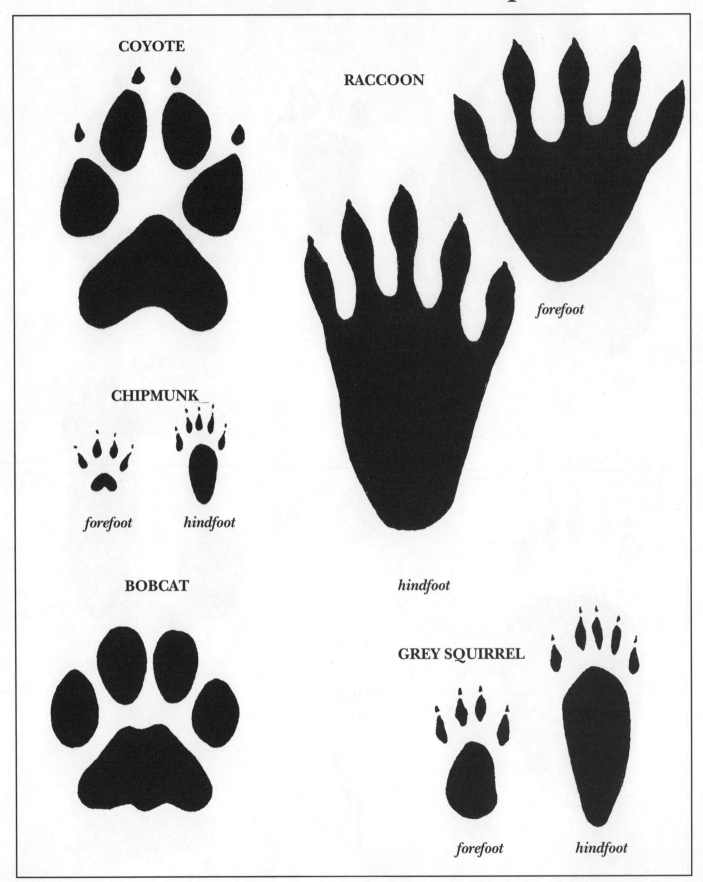

COYOTE

RACCOON

forefoot

CHIPMUNK

forefoot   *hindfoot*

hindfoot

BOBCAT

GREY SQUIRREL

forefoot   *hindfoot*

Farm Animal Track Templates

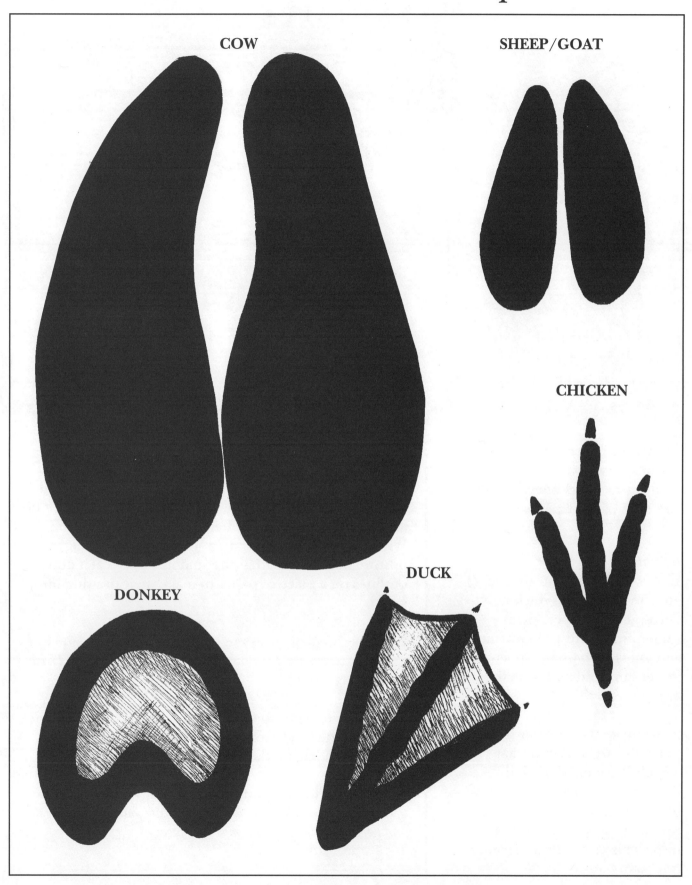

COW

SHEEP/GOAT

CHICKEN

DUCK

DONKEY

Tricky Tracks
• EXHIBIT •

Materials: Paper lunch bag; crayons; newsprint; track stamps (see *Track Stamps*, page 163); ink pads; paper; scissors.

Activity:

1. Allow the students time to observe a mounted track story. On a piece of paper, each student writes his or her name and guess as to what happened in the story and adds it to the bag.

2. At the end of the day or week, the artists reveal what actually happened in their track stories. Read the guesses to the class. The student whose guess is the closest can display his or her drawing and track story next.

Design:

1. Involve your students in the creation of this exhibit. Have the children work in pairs. Explain that they will be drawing a life-size detective. They should think about how a detective might look. What clothes might he wear? What sort of accessories might he carry? What might his posture be? Suggest that the students trace each other's outlines on a piece of paper to make their drawing life-size.

2. When the detectives are complete, have the pairs work together to create a track story on newsprint. (See *Track Stories*, page 169.)

3. Choose one group to begin the exhibit. Mount their detective and track story on the bulletin board. Attach a paper lunch bag marked "Your Guesses."

4. Write the following directions on or near the exhibit: *What happened here? Can you guess? Write your answer on a slip of paper and place it in the paper lunch bag.*

Track Stories

Objective:
Students will use their knowledge of animal behavior and relationships to make predator-prey stories using Track Stamps.

Grade Level: 2-5

Groupings: 2-4 students

Directions:
*This is a culminating activity to a unit on tracking. It works best if you have done the following activities with your class: **Pitter Patter** (page 157), **Predator-Prey** (page 153), and **Track Stamps** (page 163). With younger students, create a set of track stamps on your own.*

1. Take the class outdoors to nearby woods and fields to find animal tracks. Have the students use the secret Sherlock Holmes tracking formula (see **Pitter Patter**, page 157) to identify tracks, noting the *place* where the tracks are found, their *pattern*, and their *print* size and shape. Use this information to make guesses about whose tracks they have found and what the animals might have been doing. Return to the classroom and list observations on the board.

Materials: Mural paper; stamp pads; animal track stamps (see *Track Stamps,* page 163); crayons; sample track story, *Sherlock Holmes Track Detective Cards* (page 170).

Time Allotment: 45 minutes

2. Divide the students into small groups and assign each group two different animals (one animal will be a predator, the other its prey). Caution them to keep their animals secret. Explain to the students that they will be using footprints to tell a story about these two animals.

3. Show the students an empty piece of mural paper. Have them imagine that it is snow. Explain that the groups will use crayons to draw the place or habitat where their two animals live in the winter. The setting might be a field, a forest, a cave, a den under a tree, or inside a hollow log.

4. Hold up an example of a finished track stamp. Ask the students to guess what kind of animal it is from the footprint. Explain that each group will receive track stamps of their two animals. The prints made from these stamps will be important clues in the stories the students will tell.

Extensions:

a. *Display your class' Track Stories in the hallway. Ask other students in the school to guess what happened in each of the stories. Provide a bag for guesses and announce the winner(s) over the public address system.*

b. *Have the students write about their Track Stories.*

c. *Have the students research an animal and then write a Who Am I? riddle using the information. The riddle can be attached to an illustration of the animal's habitat. Include its tracks, having them lead to a lift-up flap, under which is the animal's name and picture.*

Directions: (continued)

5. Remind the students of the four different track patterns learned in *Pitter Patter* (page 158 - 59). You might want to hang up a chart illustrating the four patterns with examples of the various animals that make them. Tell the students that their job will be to complete their stories by stamping tracks on the paper in the correct patterns for their animals.

6. Hold up a finished track story, preferably one that uses the track stamp you have shown. Ask the students to guess what the tracks show. What were the animals doing? Explain that the students will be making similar stories. Then they will take turns guessing each others' stories.

7. Begin by passing out only mural paper and crayons. Have them first draw their animals' habitats. Caution them not to draw a picture of their animal. Once the setting is drawn, have the students agree on a story about the two animals.

8. Give the students their two track stamps and ink pads. Check to see that they know their animals' track patterns. Give them time to complete their Track Stories.

9. Collect the finished stories. Hold them up one at a time and let the class play detective, guessing who the animals were and what happened in each story . Let the artists verify their guesses.

10. Congratulate the class and award them their *Sherlock Holmes Track Detective* cards. Remind them to keep on tracking!

Animal Homes in Winter
• E X H I B I T •

Materials: Poster board; two large envelopes; crayons or markers; animal pictures; string; plastic sandwich bag; push-pins.

Activity:
1. Each student chooses an animal from the envelope and hangs its picture on the winter scene where he or she thinks the animal would be found. Students then check their answers using the answer cards.

ANIMALS THAT:
- overwinter in the barn:
  cow, sheep, chicken
- overwinter in the pond, either in the mud or in the water beneath the ice:
  turtle, frog, fish
- overwinter inside trees: *raccoon*
- overwinter in burrows underground:
  skunk, woodchuck, chipmunk, garter snake
- remain active in tunnels under snow:
  mouse, vole
- remain active in trees:
  gray squirrel, owl, porcupine
- remain active in open snowy fields:
  rabbit, red fox

Design:
1. Draw an outdoor winter scene on several pieces of poster board. Be sure to include a tree, a small pond, a large underground area, a barn and a snowy field.

2. Draw or cut out pictures of animals and mount them on small pieces of poster board. Attach string loops to the backs of each animal picture (to hang from push pins on the exhibit). Include at least one animal from each of the groups listed to the left.

3. Using this information, write an answer card for each animal whose picture you include explaining what that animal does in winter.

4. Label one of the large envelopes "ANIMALS," and the other "ANSWERS." Attach them to the exhibit and fill the proper envelope with the animals and answers. Fill a plastic bag with push-pins and place it on one side of the exhibit.

5. Write the following directions on or near the exhibit:
   Where do you think animals live during the winter? Pick an animal and give it a home by attaching it to the bulletin board with a push-pin. Then, find the answer card to see if you guessed correctly.

Do Not Disturb

• E X H I B I T •

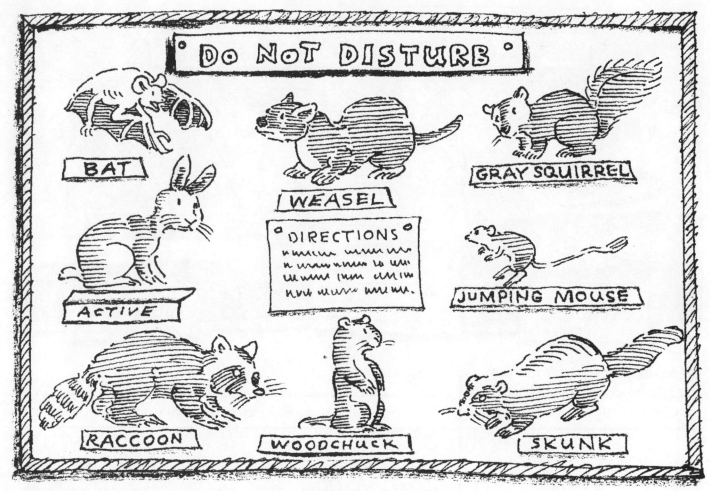

Materials: Pictures of mammals; sturdy construction paper.

Activity:

1. Students may work alone or in pairs to guess what each of the mammals pictured does in winter. They lift the flaps to check their guesses.

SUGGESTED MAMMALS
for the EXHIBIT
Groundhog or Woodchuck
Cottontail Rabbit, Gray Squirrel
Jumping Mouse, Striped Skunk, Little
Brown Bat, Raccoon
Short-tailed weasel or Ermine

Design:

1. Draw or cut out pictures of common New England mammals. Be sure to include the three types of true hibernators: a groundhog or woodchuck, a jumping mouse, and a little brown bat. Mount the pictures on a bulletin board.

2. Beneath each mammal mount a lift-up flap made from the sturdy construction paper. Label the outside with the mammal's name. Under each flap describe what that animal does in winter. Use *New England Mammals in Winter* (pages 147 - 48) for answers.

3. Write the following directions on or near the exhibit:
Only three types of mammals in New England truly hibernate during the winter. Can you guess who they are? What do the other animals do in winter? Make your guess and lift up the flap for the answer.

Sneaky Pete

Objective:
To observe birds and their winter feeding habits.

Grade Level: K-6

Groupings: Entire class

Materials: Clothing to make a scarecrow; pillowcase; yarn; newspaper for stuffing; large-brimmed hat; lawn chair or other chair suitable for outdoor use; lunch tray and birdseed.

Time Allotment: 30 minutes

Directions:

1. Discuss the fact that not all birds migrate as winter approaches. Explain to the students that food is the determining factor; if a bird is able to find enough food, it does not need to expend the enormous amount of energy needed to migrate. What kinds of birds spend the winter in your state? What kinds of things might they eat?

2. In this activity the students will set up a special feeding station for the birds. Stress the responsibility of feeding birds. Once you start, they come to depend on you for food. If you forget to feed them and they can not find another food source quickly enough, they could die.

3. Explain to the students that they will be making a scarecrow named Sneaky Pete. Instead of scaring the birds, this scarecrow will be their friend and hold a tray of birdseed.

4. Help the students create Sneaky Pete by stuffing newspaper in old clothes. Make a head out of an old pillowcase. Draw a face and use yarn for hair. Devise ways to attach the parts together to make your Sneaky Pete scarecrow.

5. When Sneaky Pete is finished, have the class set him up on a chair in a protected area outdoors. Place a large-brimmed hat on his head that shades his face. Put a lunch tray on his lap and fill it with birdseed. Sprinkle some seed on his shoulders and head.

6. Give the birds plenty of time to find Sneaky Pete and to get adjusted to their new friend. Have students replenish the lunch tray daily. Have the class observe and record the happenings at the feeder for a week.

7. Now it's time to get sneaky! Replace Sneaky Pete with a student from the class. Have the student sit as still and as quietly as possible in Sneaky Pete's chair. Put Sneaky Pete's hat on the student's head and place the tray full of birdseed on the student's lap. Sprinkle more birdseed on the student's head and shoulders.

Extensions:

a. *Make pine cone bird feeders. Have the students bring pine cones to class. Have them spread peanut butter on their pine cones and roll them in birdseed. Tie a piece of string around each cone and hang them outside on a branch for the birds. See **For the Birds** (page 178) for other feeder ideas.*

b. *Create a bird sighting record for the class. Post a large sheet of paper near your feeders. Have the students record the kinds of birds that visit the feeder. Have several bird field guides on hand to help with identification.*

Directions: (continued)

8. Have the rest of the class watch from a nearby window or hide quietly. Within minutes, some birds should arrive and land in the lap of the new Sneaky Pete. It is a great way for the students to get good look at birds up close! Throughout the winter, let all the students in the class take a turn replacing Sneaky Pete.

Fill the Bill

Objective:
Students will learn why different birds have different beaks.

Grade Level: 3-6

Groupings: Pairs and small groups

Materials: Peanuts in the shell (25 per pair); masking tape; representational bird foods (see Bird Beak Stations page 177); 7 paper cups; one set per group of beak-tools (see page 177); bird field guides; pictures or mounted specimens (to borrow, contact the state Fish and Wildlife Department or a local university).

Time Allotment: 30 - 45 minutes

Directions:
1. Begin with a discussion of animal adaptation. What does it mean? What are some examples of animal adaptations? Do people have any special adaptations?

2. Explain to the students you will be testing their hand skills with a simple activity. They will be working in pairs. One student will scatter peanuts in the shell on the floor. When you say "Go," the other student will have one minute to gather and shell as many peanuts as possible. Have each student count the number he or she was able to shell and record it on the blackboard. Then let their partner have a turn. As a class, review the numbers collected and calculate an average.

3. Repeat the same activity after each student has his or her thumbs taped securely to the side of their hands. Again record the number of peanuts shelled and calculate an average. Compare to the first average. What accounts for the differences? (Opposable thumbs are a special adaptation which aid in grasping actions, picking things up, and manipulating tools and food.)

4. Show the class pictures of birds with different types of beaks. Explain that each bird's beak is specially adapted to its food source. Ask the students what type of habitat these birds live in and what foods they might eat.

5. Tell the students you have set up seven stations representing different types of food for common New England birds. At each of the stations, explain to the students the type of food represented. At each station, place an index card that labels each food type as a reminder.

6. Divide the class into small groups and give each group a bag containing ten different beak-tools. Explain that each tool represents a different type of bird beak. They will experiment with these beak-tools by using them to collect food at each of the stations in order determine which beak is best adapted for gathering a particular food.

Extension:

a. *Explain to the students that not only are birds' beaks adapted to their food source, but their feet are also adapted to help forage for food in a particular environment. Have the students look up the following birds in field guides and observe their feet. Ask them to draw a picture of their feet and describe how they are adapted to their food source.*

1. DUCKS AND GEESE
(Webbed feet to swim and eat aquatic life.)

2. HAWKS AND OWLS
(Feet with talons for holding and tearing meat.)

3. PHEASANT AND GROUSE
(Scratching feet to search for insects and seeds in the dirt.)

4. HERONS AND EGRETS
(Wading feet to walk in shallow water looking for aquatic life.)

5. WOODPECKERS AND SAPSUCKERS
(Climbing feet, to look for insects in dead trees.)

Directions: (continued)

7. Have each group begin at a different station. The groups will have 2-3 minutes at each station to test their beak-tools. When the allotted time is up, signal for the groups to move to a new station. Have the students record their beak-tool choice for each station. When students are uncertain of which tool is best adapted for a particular food, ask them to perform the following test. For 30 seconds, use one of the tools to gather food and place it in the paper cup provided at each station. Record the amount. Repeat using the alternate beak-tool choices. The tool that allows them to put the most food into the cup in 30 seconds is the one they should consider best adapted.

8. When everyone has finished, review the beak-tool choices for each station. Discuss how and why particular tools work best to gather the different foods. Were some tools able to gather more than one type of food? Did any two beak-tools work equally well for one type of food? Using the tools as models, what do they envision each beak type to look like. Have them illustrate their ideas.

9. Using field guides, pictures of birds, or stuffed bird specimens, have the students match up their beak illustrations to actual birds beaks.

BIRD BEAK STATIONS

STATION	REPRESENTATIVE FOOD	ACTUAL FOOD	BEAK TOOL	BIRDS
1.	Water in a narrow vase	Nectar in a flower	Drinking straw	Hummingbird
2.	Mixed nuts in the shell	Seeds	Nutcracker	Finches Grosbeaks
3.	Rice on a log	Crawling insects	Tweezers	Nuthatches Warblers
4.	Gummy worms in a large coffee can filled with wet oatmeal	Worms in mud	Chopsticks	Woodcock Robins
5.	Puffed rice floating in a a large bowl of water	Floating aquatic vegetation	Teaspoon strainer	Ducks
6.	Popcorn thrown through the air	Flying insects	Kitchen strainer	Nighthawk Whippoorwill
7.	Mini-marshmallows inside an upside-down egg carton with holes cut in each of the 12 sections	Insects in wood	Nutmeat pick	Woodpeckers

For the Birds

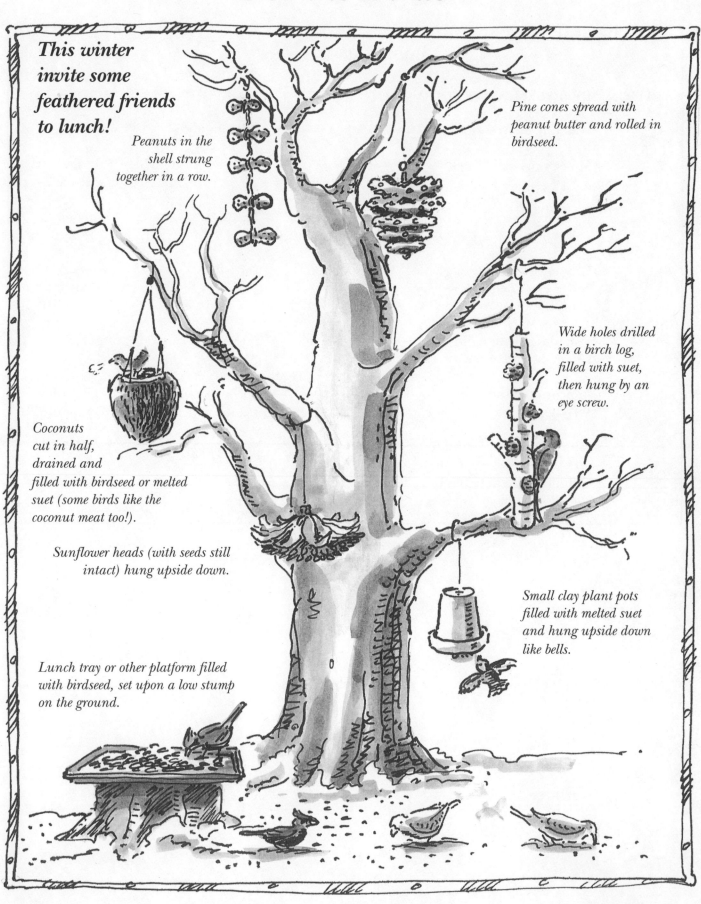

This winter invite some feathered friends to lunch!

Peanuts in the shell strung together in a row.

Pine cones spread with peanut butter and rolled in birdseed.

Coconuts cut in half, drained and filled with birdseed or melted suet (some birds like the coconut meat too!).

Wide holes drilled in a birch log, filled with suet, then hung by an eye screw.

Sunflower heads (with seeds still intact) hung upside down.

Small clay plant pots filled with melted suet and hung upside down like bells.

Lunch tray or other platform filled with birdseed, set upon a low stump on the ground.

SPRING ACTIVITIES

How Sugaring Began

Objective:
Students will use their imaginations to create original legends on the origins of maple sugaring.

Grade Level: 2 - 5

Groupings: Small groups

Materials: Assortment of art supplies such as paper; crayons; markers; string; tape; or glue; any readily available props such as clothing, containers, or sticks.

Time Allotment: 30 minutes

Directions:

1. Ask the students to define legends. A legend is a story based on fact that centers on an actual person, place or event. It is elaborated on and enhanced with additional information interweaving fact with folklore. Can they think of any examples of common legends? (Johnny Appleseed, John Henry, Paul Bunyon, Bigfoot, Sleepy Hollow, the Christmas Rose.) Explain that they will have the chance to create and dramatize their own legend about how maple sugaring began.

2. Divide the students into small cooperative groups. Explain that they may choose any setting or time period for their legend, from the time of the dinosaurs to the recent past. Encourage them to use their imaginations to develop an original legend. The only requirement is that sap must be turned into syrup in the conventional way (by boiling sap from maple trees) by the end of the story. Ask that anyone familiar with a sugaring legend not mention it so their group can create a completely new story.

3. Provide time for each group to develop a story line and record it. They will then need to adapt this story for "the stage." Suggest possibilities for the presentation: the use of a narrator, character lines, audience participation.

4. Encourage the use of creative props and costumes. Provide general supplies and allow time for thoughtful creations.

5. Provide time for each group to practice and refine their presentation, then let each group enact their legend. Compare and contrast the different class legends.

Extensions:

a. *Share a different legend about maple sugaring with the class. Consider acting out the legend as your students did, with costumes and props.*

b. *Create a class book of sugaring legends.*

Directions: (continued)

6. Tell the class the Woksis Legend (see below).

THE WOKSIS LEGEND

Once there was a brave Iroquois chief named Woksis. He lived in the woods of New England with his family. Woksis went hunting everyday. One day in early March, the hunting was especially good. He easily tracked a small deer through the snow. There would be fresh venison for supper the next day. After cleaning and gutting the deer, he hung it in a nearby tree. He threw his tomahawk into the tree and left it there for the night. The next morning he went out hunting, taking his tomahawk with him. The night before had been very cold and the snow had a thick solid crust which held him up as he stalked away. Woksis' squaw, Moqua, and their two children worked hard all morning preparing the deer, cutting it into pieces for dinner and storage. By afternoon, the air had warmed and they took a short break to enjoy the sunshine. When Moqua started the fire for supper, she realized that they had forgotten to gather water. The snow was now very soft and slushy and would make the walk to the stream long and hard. The two children got their collecting bucket which was sitting beneath the tree where Woksis had left his tomahawk the night before. In the bucket they noticed a clear liquid collecting. It was running from the gash the tomahawk left in the tree. It tasted like water. The bucket was more than half full, so they decided to fill the cooking pots with it. As their venison boiled, the liquid became thick and dark and a wonderful smell arose from the pot. When Woksis returned, he remarked on the delicious smell. He dipped his finger into the now thick sticky brown liquid and pronounced it sweet. His children told him where they gathered the sweet water and from that day forward, every spring, they boiled the sweet water from the maple trees to make maple syrup.

* Other sources for sugaring legends include KEEPERS OF THE EARTH *by M. Caduto and J. Bruchac (Fulcrum, 1988) and* THE MAPLE SUGARING STORY *by Betty Lockhart (Perceptions, Inc., 1990).*

Eye Spy

Objective:
Students will learn about the maple sugaring process through an observation and recall memory game.

Grade Level: 2-5

Groupings: Entire class

Materials: A blanket and a collection of at least 15 objects related to maple sugaring (see below).

Time Allotment:
15-20 minutes

SUGARING OBJECTS

drill and 7/16 inch bit
thermometer
hammer
hydrometer and cup
collection of different types of
  spouts/taps
wool felt or cheesecloth filter
plastic pipeline in different sizes
funnel
metal and/or wooden buckets
several empty syrup containers
bucket lids
color grading set
snowshoes
pancake mix
yoke
candy molds
matches
maple sugar candy
firewood
mokuk

Directions:
This is a good introductory or review activity to any science unit. It works well when done before and after a unit to measure how familiar the students have become with the subject.

1. Tell the class the story of two children who were inspired by HARRIET THE SPY by Louise Fitzhugh (Dell, 1978). They devised a game, "Eye Spy," to sharpen their memory and observation skills. Explain that one child would place a collection of related articles under a blanket. He or she would lift the blanket and the other child would carefully observe the objects underneath. After a period of time, the objects would be covered. The child would try to name or describe from memory all the objects under the blanket and guess how they were related. They each took turns assembling and hiding objects and guessing their identities until their detective skills were greatly improved.

2. Have the class gather around a blanket under which you have hidden a collection of at least 15 maple sugaring tools or related objects. Be sure that everyone can observe the objects. Explain that they will now have the chance to test their memory and observation skills with a game of "Eye Spy."

3. Explain to the class that they will have 30 seconds to observe the collection of objects. Their goal is to remember as many objects as possible and to guess the relationships of the objects to one another. When the allotted observation time is up, have the students return to their desks to write, draw or describe all the objects they remember. Do they see a relationship between the objects?

Extensions:

a. *Allow the class to observe the same collection of objects. Have them close their eyes. Remove one of the objects. Have them open their eyes. Can they guess what is missing?*

b. *Assign the children to small groups. Ask them to work together to sort the sugaring objects into groups. Let the rest of the class observe their groupings and make a guess at their sorting criteria (see* **People Key***, page 113).*

Directions: (continued)

4. Ask each students to count up the number of objects he or she recorded. At this time, reveal how many objects were actually under the blanket. Who remembered the greatest number of objects? Ask this student to share one of the objects on their list. Does he, she or anyone else know what it is or how it it used?

5. Ask each student to share an object and its identity and use.

6. Explain any unidentified objects and their use. As a review, take the students through the maple sugaring process from start to finish, object by object.

MAPLE SUGARING GLOSSARY

ARCH - the portion of the evaporator beneath the pans in which the fire is built.

EVAPORATOR - a device used for boiling maple sap to produce maple syrup.

FILTER - a piece of material, usually wool felt, through which syrup is passed to remove impurities.

GRADING SET - a set of color standards, approved by the government, used to classify different color grades of maple syrup.

HYDROMETER - an instrument used to measure the density (specific gravity) of syrup. Specific gravity gives an exact reading of the sugar content. Sap becomes syrup when it is boiled down to 66% sugar.

MOKUK - a traditional birch bark container used by Native Americans for holding maple sugar.

PAN - the upper portion of the evaporator, often divided into sections, in which the sap is boiled.

PIPELINE - a system of flexible plastic pipes that carry sap from trees to large storage tanks at the sugar house. Sap either flows by gravity downhill or with the assistance of vacuum pumps.

REVERSE OSMOSIS - a high-pressure process involving the use of special membrane filters that partially removes the water from sap, greatly shortening the boiling time.

SAP - a clear colorless liquid found in trees. The sap in sugar maples contains a small percentage of sugar, usually about 2 %.

SHEETING OR APRONING - a simple visual test done to see if hot sap is approaching the thickness of syrup. If a scoop of hot sap slides off the edge of the scoop in one sticky sheet or curtain, then it is the approximate consistency of syrup.

SINZIBUCKWUD - the Algonquin word for maple syrup, meaning "drawn from wood."

SPILE - a wooden spout that channels the flow of sap from the tree.

SUGAR BUSH - a grove of sugar maple trees that are tapped for syrup.

SUGARHOUSE - a building where sap is boiled down to syrup.

SUGAR SAND OR NITER - naturally occurring mineral impurities that precipitate out during boiling and are removed by filtration.

TAP - a metal or plastic spout that channels the flow of maple sap from the tree to a container or pipeline.

TAP HOLE - a hole drilled 2-3" deep into the sapwood of a maple tree, out of which sap flows.

VACUUM PUMPS - machines connected to the pipeline that create a vacuum within the lines to help the sap flow from the tree to the storage tanks at the sugarhouse.

Back in Time

Objective:
Students will learn about the history of maple sugaring.

Grade Level: K-3

Groupings: Small groups

Materials: This activity involves setting up three stations in the woods using props to represent different historical time periods. Try working with other teachers to set up the stations on the school grounds and solicit parents' help in obtaining the props.

NATIVE AMERICANS:
maple tree with a V-shaped gash; hewn wooden trough or large birch bark basket; birch bark mokuk filled with maple sugar; fire pit with stones in the center; sticks; hollow stump for boiling; bag of popcorn; tomahawk; snowshoes.

COLONISTS:
several stems of Staghorn Sumac; wooden spile; wooden bucket; 1-3 kettles on wood frames over representative fire; horseshoe or yoke with collecting buckets.

20TH CENTURY SUGAR MAKERS: *metal buckets; metal spouts; hand drill and bit (or battery or gasoline powered drill).*

Cardboard arrows to mark trails between stations.

Time Allotment: 30 minutes

Directions:
This activity works best if groups of 8-10 students visit each station with the teacher or an adult volunteer.

1. Ask the students if they would like to go back in time to see if the legends they've heard about maple sugaring are indeed true. Use the following chant or have the class create their own. Have them make up a series of accompanying motions. Bring the students fairly close to the first station (Native American) before beginning the chant then let them discover the station and props for themselves.

> *It's back in time we want to go*
> *To see if the legends they tell are so*
> *How maple sugaring came to be*
> *Repeat these words and follow me*
> *To learn about the times before*
> *Back we go to days of yore*

2. Ask the students how far back in time they think they have gone. Any guesses as to the date? (Any date before 1600.) Who was sugaring here? Using clues from the objects found, ask them to reconstruct how Native Americans tapped the trees. How did they gather the sap? How did they heat the sap? How do they think they ate the finished product? How did the Native Americans pick up the hot stones and transfer them to the hollow stumps without burning their hands? Have a mokuk of maple sugar or popcorn sprinkled with maple syrup or sugar to sample before leaving this station.

> *Native Americans gashed the trees with a tomahawk and inserted bark chips or later, long Sumac spiles or Elderberry. They collected the sap in large birch bark baskets or hand hewn wooden troughs. Hot stones from the fire were placed with sticks (used like chopsticks) in a hollow stump with the sap to heat it. They turned the sap into sugar, which they carried in birch bark mokuks and ate sprinkled over foods, like popcorn.*

3. Ask the students if this is how we sugar today. Who learned to sugar from the Native Americans? (The first colonists.) Explain that they need to continue on in time to see the changes in sugaring throughout history. Use the following chant, reversing any accompanying motions used in the first chant. (Since they took you backwards, reversing

Extensions:

a. *Obtain some plastic tubing and other modern equipment and create another station (the final station in step #6 becomes early 20th century, this new station is mid to late 20th century). String the tubing between trees to collect sap. Have the students count the number of trees attached by tubing. Or coil the tubing on the ground and tag trees that would be tapped. (Or have the students identify the maples that could be tapped with the tubing.)*

b. *Obtain a plastic syrup bag (available from Leader Evaporator Co., 25 Stowell St., St. Albans, VT, (802) 524-4966 or G.H. Grimm Co., P.O. Box 130, Rutland, VT, (802) 775-5411). Ask the students to study it to see whether they can figure out when it was used. Is it a future invention or improvement? (The sap bag was patented in 1954, around same time tubing became popular, so it never caught on.) Have the students list the pros and cons of using sap bags.*

Directions: (continued)

them brings you forward, of course.) Have small clues or markers on nearby trees to lead the way to the next station.

> *Forward we go in history*
> *To see who next tapped the maple tree*
> *New tools and changes we're sure to find*
> *Hurry now, don't get left behind*
> *Repeat these words and don't delay*
> *Look for clues to point the way*

4. Who is sugaring here? What year do they think it is? (1600 to 1800.) How did the colonists tap the trees? How did they gather and boil the sap? How does the class think the colonists ate the end product? Let the students try carrying sap with the yoke and two buckets. Let the class discover an old journal made from yellowed paper (use Chapter 10 of FARMER BOY, by Laura Ingalls Wilder, [Harper Collins, 1961] to create the text) or a sweet treat made with maple syrup.

The colonists tapped the trees with an augur or drill and used wooden spiles. They collected the sap in wooden buckets and hauled it to the boiling area using shoulder yokes or horses. The sap was heated in three kettles, transferring the sap to one bucket as it got thicker and closer to syrup. The colonists usually ate it as sugar, either granulated or in blocks.

5. Ask the students again if that is how sugaring is done today. Chant the following poem to continue on in the history of sugaring and return to the present day.

> *We've travelled back in history*
> *To learn who tapped the maple tree*
> *Now forward in time we want to go*
> *Back to the time that we all know*
> *Lead us back to the present day*
> *And sugaring, the modern way*

6. Lead a similar discussion to help the students understand how sugaring is done today. Have the children use the drill and bit to tap a tree, and insert the metal tap. Later, collect the sap and boil it down in the classroom. Follow up with a visit to a working sugaring operation with the latest equipment.

Make a Mokuk

Objective:
Students will make a maple sugar container similar to those used hundreds of years ago by Native Americans.

Grade Level: 1 - 4

Groupings: Entire class

Materials:
Copy of mokuk pattern (page 188), one for each student; heavy construction paper; stapler; pencils; scissors; string; hole punch; and crayons, markers, or paint.

Time Allotment: 20 minutes

NATIVE AMERICAN DESIGNS

Directions:

1. Brainstorm a list of what Native Americans might have used as maple sugar containers since they did not have glass, plastic or metal. Explain how they made small containers of birch bark called **mokuks**. Compare mokuks to the students' container ideas.

2. Explain to the students they will be making their own mokuks out of paper. Give each student a copy of the mokuk pattern. Ask them to cut the pattern out along the solid lines.

3. Have them place the pattern on a piece of heavy construction paper and trace around it. Remind them to add any dotted lines and markings to their tracing and cut out the mokuk.

4. Have the students turn their mokuks over and decorate the outside. They can paint them to look like birch bark, and/or decorate them with original designs or Native American designs.

5. When they have finished, have them fold the mokuk along the dotted lines and tape it together. Provide staplers so they can add a staple or two as reinforcement.

6. Have the students punch holes in their mokuk using the circle markings as guides. They can then attach a piece of string as a handle.

Mokuk Pattern

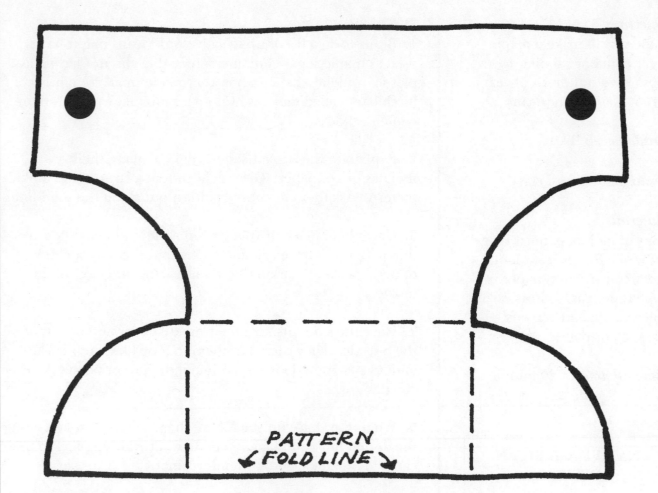

PATTERN
FOLD LINE

INSTRUCTIONS

1. Make copies of this page for each of the students in your class. Photocopy the template onto the top of a sheet of 8 1/2" x 11" paper and post the instructions elsewhere.

2. Pass out the templates to the students. Have them fold the paper in half along the pattern fold line. Direct them to cut out the pattern along the solid lines and add the dotted lines on the opposite side.

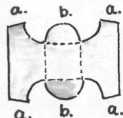

3. Open and place the pattern on a piece of poster board or heavyweight paper. Trace around the pattern, mark in the dotted lines, and cut it out.

4. It is easier to decorate the mokuk while it is flat. Use Native American designs or make up your own.

5. Fold the paper mokuk along the dotted lines to create the base.

6. On one side, fold in flap **b**. On the same side, bring **a** flaps together and overlap them on top

of flap **b**. Staple or tape these flaps together from the inside to create one side of the mokuk.

7. Repeat this process on the opposite side. The top opening of the mokuk will be narrower than the base.

8. Punch holes in the sides of your mokuk and attach string to form a handle.

Sumac Spiles

Objective:

To make maple sugaring taps similar to those used hundreds of years ago by Native Americans.

Grade Level: 4-6

Groupings: Pairs

Materials: *(per pair)* Staghorn sumac branches (3/4" in diameter, cut in 5-6" lengths); 4" pieces of straightened coat hanger, duct taped at one end to form a handle; pruning shears; pocket knives; collecting bucket. (Teacher will need a hand or portable drill with a 7/16" bit.)

Time Allotment: 30-45 minutes

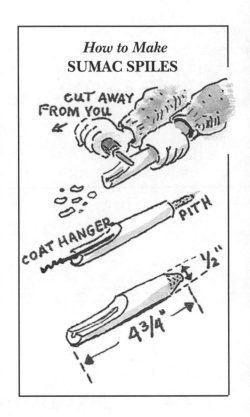

How to Make
SUMAC SPILES

CUT AWAY FROM YOU

PITH

COAT HANGER

1/2"

4 3/4"

Directions:

1. Ask the students to pretend they are the first sugar makers. How would they tap their trees to get the sap out? Brainstorm and record a list of the tools they might have used to drill the tree, to channel the sap out of the tree into a container, and to collect the sap before boiling.

2. Explain that they will be making a tap similar to those used hundreds of years ago. The Native Americans used twigs that had a soft central core, or pith, to make their taps or **spiles.** This pith could be pushed out easily, leaving an open hole through which the sap could flow. Compare this spile to their original ideas.

3. Staghorn sumac (Rhusty Phina) is a common eastern shrub with a soft pith. It has thick velvety twigs and the branches are topped with fuzzy red berries. If it is available in or near the school yard, have your students refer to field guides to identify it. Select and cut straight stems that are long enough for one or more 5" lengths. Have the students measure and mark the stems at 5-6" intervals. Teachers use pruning shears to cut the stems into sections.

4. If you have not cut the sumac as a class, distribute the precut sections. Review pocket knife safety. Set strict rules for proper and appropriate use. Direct them to shave off 2 -3 inches from the top of the sumac stem as shown. They may leave the bark on or peel it off the stem as they choose.

5. After cautioning the students again about safety, have them use a straightened length of coat hanger to poke out the central pith from their spile. This creates the hollow center.

6. Direct them to use their knives to whittle the round unshaven end to a tapered point. The whittled end should be smaller than 1/2" to fit into a standard 7/16" tap hole. Have them use a ruler to measure and record the diameter. If this end is greater then 1/2", they will need a larger drill bit to drill their tap hole.

7. Use these homemade spiles to tap nearby maple trees (See *Measuring Monsters and Midgets*, page 191). Drill a hole in the

Extensions:

a. *Make a collection of various types and styles of taps or spiles. Ask the students to compare and contrast them, sort them into groups, place them in chronological order, etc.*

b. *Use a field guide to northeastern plants to identify Red and Black Elderberry (Sambucus pubens, s. canadensis). These plants also have hollow piths and were traditionally used as sugaring spiles. Try making spiles from these plants.*

Directions: (continued)

tree and insert the spile. Place collecting buckets on the ground under these spiles as they were placed hundreds of years ago.

Measuring Monsters and Midgets

Objective:
Students will learn how to measure circumference and apply the rule which determines the number of taps allowed per tree.

Grade Level: 2-4

Groupings: Pairs

Materials:
Measuring tapes, one for each pair; copies of the *Circumference Chart* (page 192), one for each pair; drill and 7/16" bit.

Time Allotment: 20 minutes

Directions:
1. Ask the class how sugar makers get sap from maple trees. Show them a drill and bit, and explain that a hole is drilled into the sapwood of the tree to a depth of 2-3 inches. When the weather conditions are right, the sap flows out of this hole.

2. Explain that a tree must be a certain size before it can be tapped. Sugar makers measure maple trees not by how tall they are, but by how big around they are, or their **circumference.** Use a measuring tape to demonstrate how to measure circumference. Have the students pretend that you are maple tree. Hold one end of the measuring tape and have a student wrap the rest of the tape around your waist. Tell the class your circumference measurement.

3. Show students the *Circumference Chart* and review how big a tree has to be before it can get one, two, or three taps. Ask the students how many taps you would get if you were a maple tree.

Extensions:

a. *For younger students, have the class measure trees with three different colored pieces of string. One string should measure 30 inches, another 54 inches, and the last 72 inches. Students wrap the strings around the trees. If the tree is smaller in circumference than the 30-inch string, it should not be tapped. If it is bigger than the 30-inch string, it can get at least one tap. If the tree is bigger than the 54-inch string, it can have at least two taps. For a very large tree, see if the circumference is bigger than the 72-inch string. If so, then it gets three taps!*

b. *Use the measuring tape or the pieces of different colored string to measure various objects in the classroom.*

CIRCUMFERENCE CHART

Circumference* of tree must be equal to or greater than . . .

30 inches = 1 Tap
54 inches = 2 Taps
72 inches = 3 Taps

* Circumference = inches around the tree

Directions: (continued)

4. Group the students in pairs. Give each pair a measuring tape. Explain that they will be taking turns pretending to be a maple tree while their partner measures their circumference. How many taps would they get? Remind the students to switch roles so that each knows his or her circumference. Record and graph the class results.

5. Take the class outdoors to measure trees in the school yard. If you find a maple tree that is over 30 inches in circumference, try using a drill and bit to tap the tree.

SWEET TAPPING

*When winter weather changes to that magical combination of cold nights followed by warm days, it is time to tap into some sweetness. Trees are first checked to see if they "measure up" (see **Circumference Chart**, left). The sugar maker then decides where to tap the tree. First, old tap holes are found. The wood around old holes is scarred and dead and does not contain any sap. Next, the height of the tap hole is determined. It is necessary to vary the height from year to year to prevent the tap hole scars from encircling the tree, weakening or even killing it. Then, using a drill and 7/16 inch bit, a hole is drilled 2 1/2 to 3 inches deep in the trunk of a tree. The hole is often drilled with a slight upward angle so when the tap is in place gravity helps the sap run into the bucket. Some sugar makers advise tapping on the south side of the tree because it warms first in the day. Others suggest tapping over a big root or large branch for the most sap. But wherever tapped, the sound of sap dripping in a bucket is a sweet spring sound to any ears.*

Sap to Syrup Race

Objective:
Students will learn how much sap is needed to make a gallon of syrup.

Grade Level: K-6

Groupings: Entire class

Materials:
A quart of sap (tap a tree, get it from a local sugar maker, or simulate sap by diluting sugar or syrup in water at a 1:40 ratio); 40 or more gallon jugs filled with water; two 1/3 cup measures; large funnel; one empty gallon syrup container.

Time Allotment: 20 minutes

Directions:
A week before you do this activity, ask the students to bring in plastic gallon milk jugs from home. It won't take long to collect 40 or more gallons needed for this activity. You can also obtain jugs at your local recycling center.

1. Ask the students to describe sap. What do they think it looks like? How does it smell? How does it taste? Put some sap in a clear container and water in another. Number the containers #1 and #2. Ask the students which one they think is water and which one they think is sap. Have them indicate their guess by raising their hands for one or the other container. Then have them test their guess by tasting a small sample from each container. How would they define sap now?

2. Explain that sap is mostly water. By boiling the sap, most of the water is evaporated (that is, it turns into water vapor or steam), and sugar is concentrated in the remaining liquid forming maple syrup. Explain to the students that it takes a lot of sap and a lot of hard work to make a gallon of syrup. Have the students guess how much sap it takes to make a gallon of syrup. Record their guesses.

3. Divide the class into two teams. Set up the milk jugs outdoors or in large indoor space such as the gymnasium or cafeteria. Cluster small groups of jugs throughout the area. Explain to the students that each cluster of jugs represents the sap buckets on a maple tree. They will race to collect the sap, carry it to the "sugarhouse" and "boil it" down into syrup.

4. Designate a small area as the sugarhouse. Explain that they will bring each jug of sap they collect here to the sugarhouse. To simulate the evaporation process, the students will measure and pour off 1/3 cup of water from their gallon jug. Then, using a funnel, they will pour this "syrup" into an empty syrup container. They then will place their gallon jug of "steam" outside the sugarhouse in a designated area.

Extensions:

a. *Tap a tree with the class and keep a sap collection chart. Have the students record the amount of sap collected each day for a week. Ask them to predict how much syrup could be made with the amount of sap they collected. Boil the sap down in class and compare actual results to the students' predictions. How do they account for differences?*

b. *Discuss the fact that some trees are sweeter than others. It takes less sap from these trees to make syrup. Show the class* **Maple Math** *(right) and have them calculate the number of gallons of sap needed for trees with different sugar concentrations.*

THE MAPLE RULE

"How many gallons of sap are needed to make a gallon of syrup?"

*You ask me how the problem's solved
It is easy, all you do
Divide the number eighty six
By sugar content true*

*Thus three percent takes twenty nine
And five but seventeen
The average say is two percent
Takes forty three is seen*

*The richer the sap without a doubt
Will save you many a dime
In quality and fuel cost
Not to mention boiling time*

*- An excerpt from
" The Maple Rule of Eighty- Six"
by C. H. Jones.*

Directions: (continued)

5. When they are finished, they will run back and tag the next person in their line who will repeat this process. The two groups will continue to collect sap and "boil it down" until the gallon syrup container is full.

6. When the container is full, stop the race. Determine which group collected the most sap by checking their number of jugs of "steam" and congratulate them. Then, more importantly, ask the students how many gallons of sap were gathered by both groups to make one gallon of syrup. Compare and discuss the answer with the guesses they made in step #2.

MAPLE MATH

The number of gallons of sap needed to make a gallon of syrup varies with the sugar content of the tree. Using a special instrument called a **sap refractometer**, *a sugar maker can determine the sugar content of maple trees in the sugar bush. By using the Jones Rule of 86, he or she then can calculate the amount of sap needed to produce a gallon of syrup. Simply divide 86 by the % sugar concentration to determine the number of gallons of sap needed. The average sugar concentration of maple trees is 2%. Using the formula: 86 divided by 2 = 43. Rounded off, this is the standard figure of 40 gallons used as the sap to syrup ratio. As the sugar concentration of trees increases, the amount of time and fuel needed to make the syrup decreases. As you can guess, trees with high sugar concentrations are highly desirable. Researchers have been working at the Proctor Maple Research Lab in Underhill, Vermont to clone sweet sap trees so that someday a whole sweet sugar bush can be planted. The sweetest tree on record is in St. Johnsbury Vermont — with a sugar concentration of 10%! How many gallons of sap are needed to make a gallon of syrup from this tree?*

Fit to be Thinned

Objective:
Students will learn how a forest can be turned into a productive sugar bush by considering and altering various factors important to tree growth.

Grade Level: 3-6

Groupings: Entire class

Materials: *Tree Identification Cards* (page 196).

Time Allotment: 20 minutes

Directions:

1. Although the maple sugaring season occurs only in early spring (late February through early April), a maple sugar maker works throughout the year to prepare for the season. Explain to the students that they will be doing an activity to discover what these sugar makers need to consider to help the maple trees in their forest produce the most sap.

2. Choose one or two students to be the sugar makers. Explain that they just bought land and need to survey their new forest. Set the forest boundaries in the classroom with an area of approximately 12-15 square feet. Describe the forest as having several different sizes of trees growing close together. The remaining students will play the role of the trees. Have the students arrange themselves as trees within the forest boundaries.

3. Introduce yourself as a forester who can help the sugar makers learn how to manage their forest as a sugar bush. Ask the trees to name five things that they need in order to grow well (sun, soil, water, air and space). Visit each tree and randomly hang a *Tree Identification Card* around his or her neck. Each card identifies the tree and describes its age, health and growth. One by one, the trees can introduce themselves using this information.

Extensions:

a. *Explain that there are many different management goals for any particular forest. One person might manage the forest for increased wildlife, another might want a good supply of firewood, and yet another might want to produce lumber. Choose a forester to act out the management strategies that might be appropriate for these different uses.*

b. *Make a school yard management plan, taking into consideration any factors important in the placement of new trees: where shade is needed; where open space is needed for play areas; school yard traffic patterns; tree species suitable for your region; appropriate permission. Then, plant a tree in your school yard.*

TREE IDENTIFICATION CARDS
For each card, draw the tree on one side and write the description on the other.

A big maple tree with some dead branches (2)

A maple tree with a small crown (2)

A maple sapling (2)

A maple seedling (2)

A young healthy maple tree (2)

A large crowned maple tree (2)

A standing dead tree

An big healthy oak tree

A small shagbark hickory tree

A young beech tree

An old beech tree

An old pine tree

A healthy white birch tree

A small basswood tree

Directions: (continued)

4. Explain that maple trees with wide spreading branches produce the most sap. Trees with wide spreading branches are said to have big crowns. Have the trees raise their branches (arms) in the air to check the size of their crown. Do any of the trees touch one another? What resources are they competing for? (Sunlight, space.)

5. How can the sugar makers improve sap production and help the trees develop large crowns? (If they remove some of the trees, they will reduce competition for sunlight and space.) Explain that this process of removing trees is called selective cutting, or thinning, and is an important forest management technique. Compare cutting trees to thinning and weeding the garden. Remind the sugar makers that the decision to cut should take into consideration several factors, including the tree's present health, type, and age. What would happen if too many trees were thinned out? Too few? Point out the importance of nurturing young trees and planting new ones so that the forest can regenerate over the years.

6. Have the sugar makers visit each tree. Through careful observation of the tree and its neighbors, they need to decide whether or not it should be cut. Have them pretend to cut down chosen trees. As trees are cut down, ask them to move to the area designated as the woodpile.

7. Once the sugar bush is thinned, ask the students how it might change over the years and how they will manage it.

Be a Sugar Maker

Objective:
Students will learn about the various tools used to boil down sap to syrup.

Grade Level: K-3

Groupings: Entire class

Materials: Two large rectangular cardboard boxes (one painted black); aluminum foil; toilet paper tubes; circular piece of cardboard about 3 inches in diameter; brass brads; shoe box; assortment of common household items to represent sugaring tools (see page 198).

Time Allotment: 40 minutes (20 minutes if evaporator is made in advance)

Directions:
1. Involve the class in creating a mini-evaporator for the classroom. Cut the flaps off the top of a large rectangular cardboard box and cover it with aluminum foil. Use the two long top flaps as dividers in the evaporator pan. Cut a square notch towards one end along the bottom edge of each. Cover each divider with foil. Tape them securely to the box with the notches at the bottom; the left divider has the notch at the bottom of the pan, the right at the top. Cut a hole in the lower right side of the pan and insert a toilet paper tube as the draw-off spout. Attach a circular piece of cardboard to the top of the toilet paper tube with a brass brad to turn as the faucet.

2. Cover a shoe box with foil to use as the preheater pan. Cut a hole on the left side of the preheater and create a drain spout and faucet as you did above. Place the preheater pan on top of and at the back of the evaporator pan.

3. To make the firebox, use the black cardboard box. Open the flaps at one end to create doors. Set the evaporator and preheater pan atop this firebox and you and your students are ready to be sugar makers.

4. Gather the assortment of household items to represent tools used in a maple sugaring operation. Pass the tools out to pairs of students and have them try to guess how they might be used. Have them compare tools and share ideas with each other.

5. Explain that you will be going through a day in the life of Arnie and Louise, two sugar makers. As you tell their story, have the student holding the prop you are mentioning come to the evaporator and pantomime how the sugar maker would use the tool in the sugarhouse. Use the following story and questions or create your own.

> *Arnie gets ready to fire up the evaporator. Who can help him with this task?*
> *(Let the student wear the fire gloves or pot holders, put some kindling in the arch beneath the evaporator, and imitate striking a match.)*

PREHEATER PAN

MINI-EVAPORATOR

FIREBOX

SUGARING TOOLS :

- ☐ Potholders or fire gloves
- ☐ Empty box of matches
- ☐ Ruler
- ☐ Thermometer
- ☐ Kitchen strainer to use as sap and syrup strainer
- ☐ Kitchen ladle or scoop to use as a sugaring scoop
- ☐ Empty cream container to use as de-foamer
- ☐ Funnel with coffee filter or piece of wool felt to use as a filtering tank
- ☐ Syrup container
- ☐ Drinking straw with a ball of clay attached to the bottom and a tall plastic cup to represent a hydrometer and hydrometer cup (fill the cup with water and add or remove clay to make the straw float upright)
- ☐ Three small clear containers filled with water and different amounts of vanilla to represent a grading set.

Directions: (continued)

Louise checks the level of sap in the pan. She wants to keep 1 - 1 1/2 inches of sap in the pan. Who can help her measure this?
(Student with ruler.)

Once the sap starts cooking, Louise wants to check the temperature. What can she use and who can help her?
(Student with the thermometer.)

The temperature gets too hot, and the sap starts boiling over the pan. Louise quickly needs to add a drop of a rich, thick liquid to make the bubbles disappear. Quickly, who can help?
(Student with the cream container.)

The level of sap in the pan has fallen below 1 1/2 inches. Arnie needs to add some sap to the preheater pan. The sap has some small twigs, bits of leaves and dust in it. How can he clean the sap? Who can help him?
(Student with the kitchen strainer.)

Louise thinks the sap is close to becoming maple syrup. She wants to check by seeing if it pours off quickly like water or more slowly like a sticky gooey sheet. Who can help her scoop up sap to check?
(Student with the ladle or shovel.)

Extensions:

a. *Cut out and enlarge pictures of real matching sugaring tools and have the students compare and match them with the household items they used. Contact the Leader Evaporator Co., 25 Stowell St., St. Albans, VT 05478 (802) 524-4966 or G.H. Grimm Co., P.O. Box 130, Rutland, VT, (802) 524-4966 for a catalog of sugaring equipment.*

b. *Play sugar maker charades. Have students draw a card with a picture or the name of a sugaring tool on it. Ask them to act out using that tool in the sugarhouse. Have the rest of the class guess which tool they are using and what exactly they are doing.*

c. *Have the students work in pairs to write riddles about the various tools used in maple sugaring, from tapping the tree to making syrup in the sugarhouse. Read the riddles and guess the tool.*

d. *Have the students put the tools in the order that they are usually used in the sugarhouse.*

Directions: (continued)

It's almost syrup. Now Arnie needs to fill up a tall cup and use a special tool that measures exactly how thick the syrup is. It has to be just the right concentration, thickness, and sweetness to be sold as real maple syrup. What is the name of this tool and what does it look like?
(Student with the Hydrometer and cup.)

Hooray! It's maple syrup. But it looks a bit cloudy. That's because it contains small particles of sugar sand which form as the syrup boils. The particles are so small you can hardly see them, but they have to be removed to make the syrup clear. What can he use to remove them?
(Student with the funnel and coffee filter.)

The syrup is nice and clear. Now Louise and Arnie need to decide on its grade. Is it light, medium or dark amber? Who can help them?
(Student with the grading set.)

Mix and Match Maple Vocabulary

• EXHIBIT •

Materials:

Paper; crayons; paint; markers; poster board; stapler; Velcro and/or felt.

MAPLE SUGARING VOCABULARY WORDS

boil	*pan*
bucket	*pancakes*
collect	*sap*
drill	*spring*
evaporator	*sugar bush*
filter	*sugarhouse*
fire	*sugar maker*
hammer	*syrup*
maple tree	*tap*
metal bucket	*temperature*

Activity:

1. Have the students work alone or in pairs to match the words with the sentences.

Design:

1. Let the students help you in the design of this exhibit. Give each child a maple sugaring vocabulary word (see left and the **Maple Sugaring Glossary,** page 184) and have them illustrate it using the medium of their choice.

2. Give each student a strip of poster board and ask them to write a sentence using their vocabulary word but leaving a blank spot in the sentence where the word would go. On a smaller piece of poster board, have them write their word. Help them staple a piece of hooked Velcro to the blank spot in their sentence and a piece of felt or fuzzy Velcro to the back of their word.

3. Make a Maple Sugaring Dictionary from poster board. On the inside, staple pieces of hooked Velcro for the vocabulary words. Ask the students to put their vocabulary word in the Dictionary.

4. Collect all the artwork and sentences. Create the exhibit by placing the artwork with the accompanying sentence below it on a bulletin board.

5. Write the following directions on or near the exhibit:
   Read the sentences and see whether you can fill in the blank with a word from the Maple Sugaring Dictionary.

Maple Password

Objective:
Students will learn and review maple sugaring vocabulary.

Grade Level: 2-6

Groupings: Entire class

Materials:
Paper; two envelopes; index cards.

Time Allotment:
20 minutes for Password, plus the creation of the "Maple Sugaring Dictionary."

Directions:

1. Explain to the students that they will create a class "Maple Sugaring Dictionary." Break them into groups and assign each group several letters of the alphabet. Ask each group to brainstorm a list of words related to sugaring for each of their letters. Bring the groups together to share their lists with the rest of the class. Add important words from the *Maple Sugaring Glossary* (page 184), if necessary. The dictionary can be an ongoing project if started at the beginning of a unit. Challenge the students to create the most complete sugaring dictionary possible. Suggest that whenever they hear or read a new word specific to sugaring, they add it to an ongoing master list for inclusion in the final dictionary. Have the students talk to local sugar makers or read publications on sugaring and sugaring equipment to help make the list as complete as possible.

2. When the lists are complete, ask each group to define their words. Let them be responsible for alphabetizing and writing up their pages in the dictionary. (For older students, have them refer to standard dictionaries as a guide for format.) Give the students time to look through the completed class dictionary.

3. Now the class is ready to play a game of *Maple Password.* Divide the students into two teams and have them quickly review their sugaring vocabulary.

4. As they are reviewing, select several words from their dictionary and write each word on three separate index cards. Place two of the index cards into two separate envelopes. Ask each team to further divide themselves into pairs. Have the first pair from each team come forward and sit in four chairs at the front of the room.

5. Explain that during each round, both teams will receive the same vocabulary word. One person from each pair will see the vocabulary word. They will take turns giving one word clues to their partners to help them guess the word. Let the students decide which of the pair will see the word and give clues. Have the students who are guessing the words turn their backs to the class and have the other two come forward.

Extensions:

a. *Make a set of flat paper buckets that are strung with string to be worn around the students' necks. On half of the bucket cards, write a sentence which uses one of the vocabulary words from the "Maple Sugaring Dictionary." Leave a blank in the sentence where the word belongs. On the remaining cards, write the missing words. Distribute all the buckets and explain that each student must find the student with the word that completes the sentence properly. For older students, place the buckets on the students' backs and have them works as a group to pair each other up. Then let the "word" student guess their word and fill in the blank as they read the sentence on their partner's back.*

b. *Create a class book of sugaring riddles using words from the dictionary. Ask pairs of students to write a riddle about a sugaring word using information from its definition. Have them fold and staple a piece of construction paper to create a pocket. Ask them to write their riddle on the outside of the pocket. On an index card, have them illustrate their word on one side and on the back write the word and its definition. Have them slip this card into the pocket. Have the pairs share their riddles with the class. Then bind these pages together to form a "Sugaring Riddles Dictionary."*

Directions: (continued)

6. Pass these students an envelope with the word written inside. Show the "audience" the same word written on the third index card. Remind them they must remain silent. When everyone has seen the word, collect the envelopes and place all three cards in a paper bag. Now have the team members sit side-by-side facing the audience to begin the game.

7. Choose a team to begin giving the clues. (The teams alternate giving clues until the word is guessed.) Remind them that they have the same word and should listen closely to the other team's clues and guesses because it can help them.

8. The first team to guess the word receives a point. The game continues with the next pair from each team repeating the process with a new word. The team that won the last round gets to choose who will give the first clue.

Sugaring Tools Through Time
•EXHIBIT•

Materials:

Black or brown poster board; construction paper; markers; drawings or pictures of sugaring tools (sugaring catalog from Leader Evaporator Co., 25 Stowell St., St. Albans, VT, (802) 524-4966 or G.H. Grimm Co., P.O. Box 130, Rutland, VT, 05702, (802) 775-5411 are good references); a large plastic freezer bag and a small sandwich bag; push pins.

Design:

1. Cut out four tree silhouettes from black or brown poster board. Make sure that the trunks are wide enough to fit an 8 1/2 by 11 inch piece of construction paper in the center. Line up the four silhouettes and secure them to the wall.

2. Write the following stories (or similar ones) on construction paper. Use a different color marker for the bold words. Mount each story on one of the tree trunks.

*Sinzibuckwud is the Algonquin Indian word for maple sugaring. It means "drawn from wood." To get the maple sap, Native Americans would make a V-shaped gash in maple trees with a **tomahawk or hatchet**. Sometimes bark chips were placed into the gash to help the sap flow into a **hewn wooden trough or birch bark basket** placed on the ground beneath the tree. **Stones** were heated in a **fire pit** then placed into a **hollowed-out stump** filled with sap to make it boil. The sap was boiled down to maple sugar which they stored in small birch bark containers called **mokuks**.*

*The first colonists learned about maple sugaring from the Native Americans. They used a 1/2 inch **auger** to drill holes in the trees. The Native Americans showed the colonists how to carve **wooden spiles** from the twigs of staghorn sumac and elderberry. The sap dripped into **wooden buckets** placed on the ground beneath the spile. They gathered the sap from these buckets using a **shoulder yoke and two firkins** or buckets. They boiled the sap down in **big iron kettle** over an open fire. Often three different kettles were used. A large kettle was used to boil fresh sap; a medium kettle held thicker sap that had been boiling for a while; and a small kettle was for sap that was almost syrup. This method lightened the color and improved the flavor and quality of the finished syrup and sugar. They poured the sugar into **blocks or molds** for storage.*

Activity:

1. Have the children work in pairs. Ask them to read each of the stories then match the pictures in the plastic bag with one of the time periods. Use a push pin to hang the tool on or near the correct tree.

Design: (continued)

*As time went on, the fine art of maple sugaring kept improving. **Hand drills** were used to tap the trees. Wooden buckets and spiles were replaced with **galvanized metal buckets** and **metal taps** which were stronger and lasted longer. The buckets had lids to keep out rain and dirt. Sap buckets were collected with a **sled pulled by work horses**. They hauled the sap to a sugarhouse. Inside, the sap was boiled in a **flat open pan** over an enclosed **firebox**. This enclosed firebox or arch burned more efficiently and used less wood. Syrup was put in **cans and bottles** and used for barter or to sell.*

*Today maple sugaring is done with modern equipment. **Power drills** with gasoline engines or batteries are used to tap thousands of trees in a sugar bush. **Plastic taps** and **pipeline or tubing** is run through the sugar bush, carrying the sap downhill by gravity through larger **plastic mainlines** to **large storage containers** or directly to the sugarhouse. The sap is boiled down in a **large evaporator with a preheater pan**. The pan is partitioned into sections and often has dropped flues that increase the surface area and speed up the boiling process. The syrup is tested to meet specifications, graded by color and packed hot in **metal or plastic containers**. You can buy Grade A light amber (fancy), medium amber or dark amber to put on your pancakes, waffles or ice cream. Which one is your favorite?*

3. Draw or collect the following pictures of sugaring tools:

NATIVE AMERICAN: *tomahawk or hatchet, hewn wooden trough or birch bark basket, stones in a open fire pit, hollowed-out stump, mokuk.*
COLONIAL: *auger, wooden spile, wooden bucket, shoulder yoke with firkins/buckets, black iron kettles, blocks or molds.*
RECENT PAST: *hand drill and bit, metal buckets with lids, metal taps, sled pulled by horses, flat open pan with firebox, cans or bottles.*
PRESENT DAY/MODERN: *power drill, plastic taps, pipeline or tubing, mainline, modern arch and partitioned evaporator, metal or plastic containers.*

4. Place all of the pictures into a large plastic bag. Hang this to one side of the exhibit with another plastic bag full of push pins.

5. Write the following directions on or near the exhibit:

Below you will find some of the tools used throughout history for maple sugaring. Read the stories on the trees and try to match the tools to the proper period in history. Use a push pin to attach the tool to matching tree.

From Sap to Syrup
· E X H I B I T ·

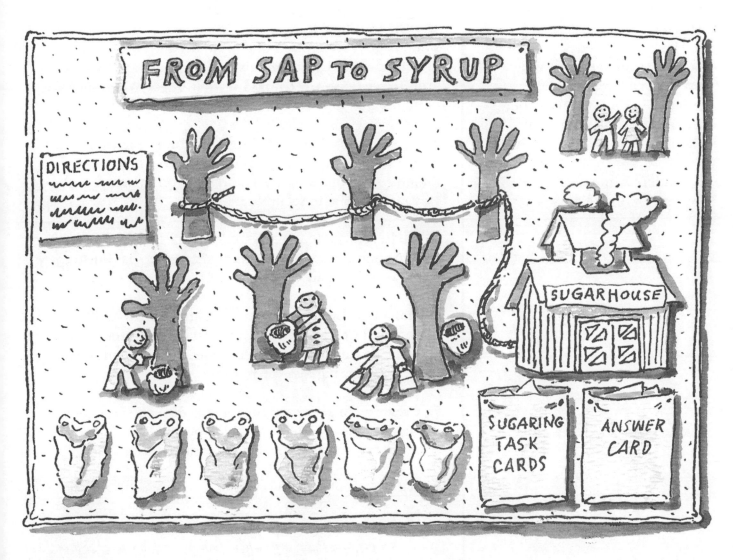

Materials:
Mural paper; drawing paper; crayons; brown construction paper; aluminum foil; scissors; glue or tape; plastic sandwich bags; an envelope.

Design:
1. Involve your class in the creation of this exhibit. Brainstorm a list of all the tasks performed to change sap to syrup. Write these steps on the blackboard.

2. Pass out drawing paper and crayons to the students. Ask them to draw pictures of themselves working at one of these tasks. As they are drawing, transfer the important sugaring tasks to separate index cards. These cards will be used for a sequencing activity as part of the exhibit.

3. Show the class a sheet of mural paper, approximately 5-6 feet long, on which you have drawn a sugar house. Pass out brown construction paper to the students and explain that they will be making maple trees for a class sugar bush. Ask the

Activity:

1. Have the students work in pairs to arrange the sugaring task cards in chronological order. Ask them to place their ordered cards in the row of plastic bags beneath the exhibit.

2. Students can check their sequence with the answer card.

Design: *(continued)*

students to trace around one of their hands with their fingers spread. Have them extend this tracing down their arms to create sturdy trunks for their trees. When they are done tracing, have them carefully cut out their trees.

4. Pass a 6-inch square of aluminum foil to each student. Explain that they will fashion the foil into a tiny, three-dimensional collecting bucket to hang on their trees. Provide tape or glue to secure the buckets.

5. As they finish, have each student attach his or her tree, drawing and bucket to the mural. Students that finish early can add other details to the mural.

6. Hang the completed mural and attach a row of clear plastic sandwich bags beneath it. Attach an envelope labelled "Sugaring Task Cards" to one side of the mural and place the sugaring task cards inside.

7. Create an answer card that details the correct sequence of sugaring tasks. Attach an envelope labelled "Answer Card" to the mural and place the answer card in it.

8. Write the following directions on or near the exhibit:

Read over the sugaring task cards. In what order does a sugar maker perform these steps when making maple syrup? Place the cards in order in the row of plastic bags beneath the mural.

Teacher Credit: Bonnie O'Day, Central School, So. Burlington, VT.

Take a Peek Inside a Maple Tree
• E X H I B I T •

Materials:
Poster board; heavy weight construction paper; a sheet of acetate; scissors; markers; stapler; and tape.

Design:
1. From brown poster board, cut out a large tree silhouette. (To make this exhibit sturdy enough to withstand years of use, use canvas or another heavy fabric to construct the tree.)

2. Use five different colors of construction paper to make lift-up flaps; each flap represents one of the five layers of the tree. Use brown paper for the outer bark, green paper for the inner bark, clear acetate for the cambium (glue a small sheet of white paper to the center), yellow or ivory paper for the sapwood, and red paper for the heartwood.

3. Write riddles on one side of each piece of construction paper and the answer on the other side. Be sure to turn the paper accordingly so the answer appears right side up. Use the following riddles or create your own.

I cover the tree	*I carry sugar from the leaves*
Just like your skin	*Throughout the tree*
Providing protection	*When you scratch the tree*
To the layers within	*you're hurting me*
Who am I?	*Can you guess my name?*
I am the outer bark	**I am the inner bark.**
I'm not very big	*Full of water and minerals*
You can't see me	*Going up and down*
But I make the rings	*At sugaring time*
Inside the tree	*I'm where the sap is found*
What am I called?	*Do you know my name?*
I am the cambium.	**I am the sapwood.**

I'm right in the very middle
At the very heart
Strong wood but not alive
So rot can sometimes start
What am I called?
I am the heartwood.

4. With a stapler, attach the layers in the correct order to the center of the tree.

Activity:
1. Students can work individually or in pairs. Have them take turns reading the riddle on the outside of each flap and then guessing the answer.

2. Have them lift the flap to check their answers.

The Inside Story

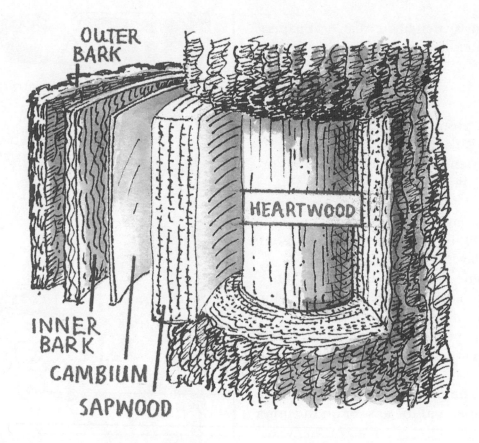

The first layer of the tree is the **OUTER BARK.** The outer bark is the tree's skin. It protects the tree from injury and disease. It is made of dead **phloem** cells that split and shift in various patterns. Each type of tree has its own special bark pattern.

The second layer is the **INNER BARK.** Just like your digestive system, it is for food transport. The inner bark is green and made of live phloem cells. These cells are full of sugars which they carry throughout the tree. The sugars are made in the leaves by the process **photosynthesis.**

The third layer is the **CAMBIUM,** and it is invisible. Well, not really, but you need a microscope to see it, because the cambium is only two cell layers thick. Each growing season, the cambium makes new sapwood or **xylem** cells which form the rings you see in the wood. It also makes new inner bark or phloem cells.

The fourth layer is the **SAPWOOD.** Minerals and water go up and down and all around in the sapwood. The sapwood has thick-walled cells that are like the plumbing system or veins of the tree. The sapwood is the new wood or xylem of the tree.

At the center of the tree is the dead **HEARTWOOD.** The heartwood is usually strong, and it provides the tree's support. The heartwood is dead sapwood. The cells no longer carry water and minerals throughout the tree because they are plugged up with a thick resin-like substance. Heartwood is often darker in color than the young sapwood.

Heartwood-Sapwood

Objective:
Students will learn how the external and internal parts of a tree trunk work.

Grade Level: 2-5

Groupings: Entire class

Materials: Cross-sectional slices of a 6-8" diameter log; index cards with strings attached, labelled as follows: "Heartwood" (1-2 cards); "Sapwood" (6-8 cards); "Bark" (12-15 cards); and "Cambium" (1-5 cards). (See *The Inside Story,* page 208, for reference.) Use a number of cards based on the number of students in the class.

Time Allotment: 15 minutes

Directions:

1. Pass out cross-sectional slices of a tree to every two or three students. Explain that foresters call these cross sections "tree cookies." Look at the tree cookies and discuss what the students see inside. Explain to the class that they will be referring to these tree cookies as they build their own class tree.

2. Ask the students to look at the darker wood in the center of their tree cookies. Can they guess what the wood at the heart of a tree is called? (**Heartwood.**) Hang the heartwood sign around a student's neck and have him or her stand in the center of the room. Explain that the heartwood is very strong and helps hold up the tree. Do the students know what is inside their bodies that holds them up? (Compare the heartwood to bones and muscles.) Have the heartwood student make some muscles to make sure that the student is strong enough for the job. Have the student dramatize the function of heartwood by flexing his or her muscles, announcing, "I'm big, I'm strong, I hold up the tree, I'm heartwood!"

3. On the tree cookie, point out the lighter wood that is closest to the bark and surrounds the heartwood. Explain that this wood is alive and full of sap. Can they guess its name? (**Sapwood.**) Pick out six students to be the sapwood. Hang sapwood cards around their necks and let them join hands in a circle around the heartwood. What is the function of the sapwood? (To carry water and minerals throughout the tree.) Have the sapwood students imitate this function by raising and lowering their hands and chanting together, "Sap going up, sap going down, sap going up, sap going down."

4. Ask the students what is on the outer edge of the tree cookie? (**Bark.**) What does the bark do for the tree? (It protects the tree from weather, animals, insects, and disease.) As you select students for this role, ask them to bark and growl to show that they will be good protection for the tree. Hang bark cards around their necks, and have them form a circle around the sapwood. Explain that the bark has two parts and two functions: 1) the outer bark is protection, like the students' skin; and 2) the inner bark serves as the tree's food conductor, carrying food from the leaves to the rest of the tree to help it grow. These students dramatize the role of

Extensions:

a. *Celebrate the students' new knowledge by enjoying homemade sugar cookies that have been decorated with rings of icing. Review the parts of the trees as you eat them. Explain that each ring represents one year in the tree's life. How old are their edible tree cookies?*

b. *At sugaring time, build a class tree like the one in this activity. Tap it using a make-believe drill and bit. Pretend to drill into the sapwood. Do not drill into the heartwood—since it is dead wood, there isn't any sap inside. Pull out the drill and let some sap drip out in the form of sapwood students.*

c. *Explain the importance of temperature in maple sap flow. A tree needs cold nights followed by warm days in order for its sap to run. On cold nights, when the temperature is below 32° Fahrenheit, the sap is frozen and does not move. When the temperature rises above 32° the following day, the sap starts moving. Build a tree and play a game of "Maple Freeze Flow." Ask the students representing each tree layer to perform their motions, but have only the sapwood students say their accompanying lines. When you call out a temperature below 32°, the sapwood must freeze. When you call a temperature above 32°, the sapwood starts moving and repeating their lines again.*

Directions: (continued)

the bark by raising their hands over their heads. As they lower them, they chant, "Food going down, food going down." Then, as they raise their hands over their heads again, they growl and bark.

5. Finally, explain that one part of the tree is missing. It is a microscopic layer between the bark and the sapwood. Does anyone know what it is called? (**Cambium**.) The cambium helps the tree grow bigger every year by adding a new ring of sapwood and new layer of inner bark. Explain to the remaining students that they will perform the role of this active, growing part of the tree. Hang cambium cards around their necks. Place them between the sapwood and the bark. Have them run around this circle chanting, "I make new wood, I make new bark, I make new wood, I make new bark."

6. Review and practice each group's role by having the heartwood, sapwood, cambium and bark repeat their lines with the accompanying motions.

7. As the grand finale, have the whole tree perform together. Have the heartwood begin and let each successive layer join in until everyone is performing in unison!

Little Sprout

Objective:
Students will learn about the parts of a seed and their function.

Grade Level: K-3

Groupings: Entire class, in pairs

Materials: Adult backpack filled with crumbled paper so it looks full but is light enough to wear comfortably; large jacket or rain poncho; tape; paper labels for the seed parts (see illustration, page 212); high energy snack like GORP stashed in the main compartment of the backpack; water bottle with attached straw; hat (preferably green); dry lima beans, soaked overnight (three to four per pair); hand lenses.

Time Allotment: 20 minutes

Extensions:

a. *With the students, germinate some of the left over lima bean seeds. Have them stuff a clear plastic cup full of paper towel and thoroughly wet the towel. Have them put some lima bean seeds along the inside of the cup so they are visible from the outside (between the paper towel and the inner surface). Will the seeds be able to germinate without soil? How long will it take? Ask them to record their predictions. Remind them to keep the toweling moist and observe and record if and when the seeds germinate.*

b. *Have a snack of peanuts in the shell. Have the students carefully*

Directions:

1. Dress up a student as a well-prepared hiker. Have him or her put the backpack on, then the rain jacket. Introduce the individual to the class as "Sprout," a seedy character, and explain that she or he has come to help teach the students about seeds. Explain that Sprout and seeds have a lot in common. Do the students see any similarities? Tell the students that you do, and will help them recognize them.

2. Ask the students what a well-prepared hiker wears to protect his or herself from the wind, rain, and cold. (A coat.) Explain that seeds also have coats for protection. Attach the seed coat label to the coat the volunteer is wearing. Explain that when the conditions  change, Sprout can take his or her coat off and enjoy the warm sunny weather. Similarly, when conditions are right for growth, the seed absorbs water, the seed coat cracks open and the seed begins to sprout roots and leaves, or **germinate**. Have the volunteer remove his or her coat and hang it so that the seed coat label is clearly visible.

3. Ask the students what else a well-prepared hiker brings. (A backpack with supplies.) Let Sprout discover the snack in the main compartment of the backpack. (This can be shared at the end of the activity — it can even have some peanuts or other edible seeds inside to dissect!) Explain that seeds also have a supply of stored food. Our hiker's food is stored in a backpack. A seed stores its food in **cotyledons**. Attach the cotyledon label to the backpack. Cotyledons provide the plant with the initial energy to germinate and grow. Once the plant has established itself, the cotyledons fall off.

4. Sprout expends a lot of energy hiking and eventually gets thirsty. What else is important to bring along on a hiking

Extensions: (continued)

remove the outer shell and dissect the two peanut seeds inside. Can they locate the seed coat? (The brown papery covering.) The cotyledons? (The nut meat they eat.) The embryo? (The tiny plant tucked inside.)

c. *Create templates for the seed parts and have the students make a larger-than-life seeds. Use waxed paper for the seed coating and colored construction paper for the cotyledon, roots, and shoot. Attach them all together with a brass fastener. Ask the students to make their seed germinate by swiveling out the root and shoot.*

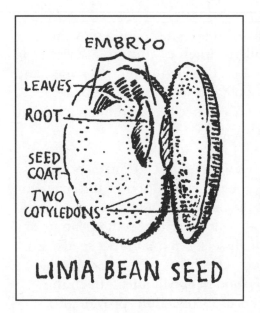

LIMA BEAN SEED

Directions: (continued)

trip? (A water bottle.) Have Sprout remove the water bottle from the backpack. Plants also need water and minerals to help them grow. How do the plants get this water and minerals? (Roots.) Attach the root label to the straw of the water bottle.

5. Ask the students what other item is useful to have on a hiking trip, especially on bright and sunny days. (A hat.) Have Sprout remove a hat from the backpack and place it on his or her head. Compare the hat to the first green leaves a seedling puts out to absorb sunlight. Attach the leaves label to the hat. The leaves use sunlight to make food for the plant. This process of making food from sunlight is unique to plants and is called **photosynthesis.** Soon the cotyledons will fall off and the plant is now able to get energy from the sun. Have the volunteer remove the backpack and place it next to the seed coat.

6. Explain that the leaves and roots grew from a tiny plant inside the seed called the **embryo**. Place an embryo label around the volunteer's neck showing the connection between these two parts. Review the various parts of the seed and their functions using the props.

7. Explain to the students that they will now dissect a real seed to find and observe these different parts. Have the students work in pairs and give each pair 3-4 pre-soaked lima beans. Have them carefully rub the seed between their fingers. What do they notice about the outside of the seed? (It has a thin moveable covering.) Have them carefully peel off the outer covering. What part of the seed is this and what is its function? (It is the seed coat and it protects the seed.)

8. Inside the seed coat are large fleshy structures that form the bulk of the seed. What are these? (The cotyledons.) What is their function? (They are stored food that the plant uses to get started growing.) Have the students carefully split these in half lengthwise. What do they see tucked inside along the inner curve of the cotyledon? (A tiny plant or embryo, made up of the first leaves and root.) Have them use their hand lenses to get a closer look and then make a drawing of their seed and label the parts.

A-maze-ing Plants

Objective:
Students will demonstrate and observe the effect of light on plant growth.

Grade Level: 2-6

Groupings: Small groups or entire class

Materials: *(per group)* Several house plants grown on a windowsill in such a way that they are leaning in one direction; small potted plant (runner beans or sprouted potato plants work well); cardboard box with inner divider; utility knife (to be used by the teacher only); scissors; duct tape; flashlight.

Time Allotment: 45 minutes for set-up, two weeks for results

Extensions:

a. *Have the class set up two separate control experiments. Using the same type of plant, place one inside a cardboard box without any openings. Ask the students to record their predictions on how this plant will grow, noting differences in size, color, appearance. Grow a second plant completely unenclosed. Again have them record growth predictions, noting size, length, color and appearance.*

b. *Hang a maze box from the ceiling with the opening on the bottom of the box. Will the plant defy gravity and grow upside down to get to the light?*

Directions:

1. Show the students the house plants you have been growing on the windowsill. What do they observe about the way they are growing? (The plants lean in one direction, towards the window.) How can they explain this growth? (The plants grow toward the sunlight). Go on a scavenger hunt in and around the school to look for other plants' growth responses to light. Discuss and compare students observations and examples.

2. Explain that they will set up an experiment to see just how far some plants will grow to get light. Divide the students into small groups and give each group a small potted bean or potato plant (or have them sprout their own) and a cardboard box with an inner divider. Explain to the students that they will shut the plant inside the box with only one opening for sunlight. Have them place the box on its side and cut a hole in the upper side to let in light. (They will need adult assistance to cut through the cardboard.)

3. With the box in this position, ask them to place their plant in one of the sections in the bottom of the box. Explain that they will create a maze of light from the top of the box to the plant at the bottom by cutting holes in the various levels of the divider. Ask the group to decide upon a sunlight path and mark the openings. Have them remove the inner divider to cut the holes.

ON *the* BRIGHT SIDE

Plants can't move, or can they? Even though plants are firmly rooted in the ground, they can still respond to changes in their environment by changing patterns in their growth. Sunlight is one essential ingredient for plant growth, and plants have been known to 'bend over backwards' to get their share. Auxin, a growth hormone in plant stems, helps regulate shoot growth. When the auxin concentration is uniform around the stem, the shoot grows upright. But when sunlight varies, auxin is broken down on the sunnier side of the stem. The higher concentration of auxin on the shady side causes it to grow more and bend toward the light, until the sunlight and hence the auxin concentration around the stem, is once again in balance. This bending toward light is called **phototropism,** *and it is a commonly observed response of plants in and around your home. It is why house plants lean towards the window, why trees branch over the road creating a shady tunnel, and why fallen trees turn at their tips and grow upright again.*

Directions: (continued)

4. Have them water their plant thoroughly and place it inside the box. Provide duct tape to secure the plant to the base of the box and seal the box closed. Ask them to check for other openings by shining a flashlight into the hole and looking forplaces where light escapes. Ask them to seal with tape any openings as another light source could interfere with the experiment.

5. Ask the students what will happen to the plant inside their boxes? Have each group record their predictions. Suggest they make a drawing of their maze and predict where the plant will grow. Will the plant be able to work its way through the maze to the light? If so, how long will it take? How long will it take to reach certain points along the way?

6. Have the groups place their boxes in sunny locations, either in windows or under grow lights. Explain that they will open their box once or twice a week to water the plant. Have them observe and record the plant's growth by marking it inside the maze box. Have them measure the length of their plant and note its appearance and health. After two weeks, have the groups compare their a-maze-ing results.

Zigzag Seeds

Objective:
Students will observe the effect of gravity on seeds.

Grade Level: 2-4

Groupings: Small groups

Materials: *(per group)* At least 4-6 flat seeds (pumpkin, cucumber, squash); paper towels; spray water bottle; two panes of Plexiglas measuring about 5"x 6"; two large rubber bands; rectangular pan filled with water; grease pencil.

Time Allotment: 15 minutes set-up, several weeks for results

Extension:
a. *Ask the groups to draw a simple zigzag pattern and try to get a seedling to follow it. Ask them to predict the number and orientation of the turns it will take to copy the pattern. Then have them perform the experiment. Did the results match their predictions?*

Directions:
1. Seeds fall from the fruits of plants and can land in just about any orientation. Ask the students what they think happens to a seed that lands upside down. Does it germinate? If so, do the roots come out above the ground and the shoots grown down? Or does the plant know to turn itself around? How? Make a list of the students' ideas and theories on this subject.

2. Have the students work in small groups to set up an experiment to see whether seeds 'know' up from down. Give each group several seeds, two pieces of Plexiglas, and some paper towels. Have them fold the paper towels to fit on top of one piece of Plexiglas and use a spray bottle to thoroughly wet the paper towel.

3. Have them observe their seeds and make a detailed drawing of one. Ask them to guess what is the top of the seed and what is the bottom, and record their guesses. Ask them to arrange their seeds on the top of the paper towel in any orientation, with growing space between the seeds. They may choose to place all of their seeds in the same orientation or vary them. Have them make a diagram of their seed arrangement noting the orientation of each.

4. Have them place the second piece of Plexiglas on top of the seed layer, as if they were making a sandwich and the Plexiglas was the bread. Have at least two students work together to place two rubber bands around the whole assembly, holding the seeds tightly in place. Have them label the top, bottom, left and right side of the Plexiglas with a grease pencil.

WHAT'S UP?

How does a little seed buried underground know which way it should grow? Believe it or not, seedlings are not completely 'in the dark.' They can sense up from down! This principle is called **geotropism.** *Plants, like the rest of us, are under the influence of gravity. Gravity is a strong, constant force that exerts an influence on all life on Earth. That's why it takes energy to lift things off the ground, from something as small as a pin to something as large as an airplane. Gravity is also the reason why all things, including us, fall down. Certain growth controlling substances within plants are sensitive to gravity. Plants respond to this pull of gravity by orienting shoot growth up and root growth down. When a plant's vertical orientation changes, it causes an imbalance in these substances on the upper and lower sides of the shoot and root. The plant grows more on one side of the shoot or root (the lower side of the shoot and the upper side of the root) until the plant curves back to its normal vertical orientation and the growth controlling substances are in equilibrium once again.*

Directions: (continued)

5. Have them fill a basin with one inch of water and place the bottom of the Plexiglas seed sandwich into the basin. Remind them to be sure that the paper towel is at or below water level so it can act as a wick and keep the seeds moist.

6. Ask the students to predict and record when their seeds will germinate and the orientation of the emerging roots and shoots on each.

7. Have the students observe their seeds daily and record the germination date, noting root and shoot orientations. (In all cases the shoot will grow up and the root will grow down.) Have the groups compare results.

8. Ask them to let the shoot and root grow until they are about 1/2 inch long. Have them turn the Plexiglas sandwich so a different side is facing up. What will happen to the newly established seedling? Have them record their predictions? (The plant will turn until the shoot is facing up and the root down.)

9. Ask them to observe and record the seedlings' growth in response to this change in orientation. What would happen if they turned the Plexiglas seed sandwich again? And again? Have them make predictions and test their guesses. How do they explain their results?

Root with a View

Objective:
Students will observe root growth in response to water source.

Grade Level: 2-4

Groupings: Small groups

Materials: *(per group)* Waxed half gallon cardboard milk carton; pre-cut Plexiglas or acetate, cut to fit tightly into the milk carton; waterproof glue or other available sealant; strong tape such as strapping, duct, electrical, or packaging; piece of cardboard cut to the same dimensions as the side of the milk carton; potting soil; small clay flowerpot; clay; bean seeds; grease pencil; utility knife (to be used by the teacher only).

Time Allotment: 30 minutes for set-up, several weeks for observation and results

Extensions:
a. *Ask the group to gently remove one of the plants and its roots, using a spoon. Using a hand lens or magnifying glass, have them observe the roots up close to see the root hairs. Or germinate seeds in paper towels and after the roots are several inches long, observe them. See the activity* **Zig Zag Seeds** *(page 215) for another source of roots.*

b. *Use the root view boxes to see if and how roots respond to obstacles in the soil. Have the group bury a large*

Directions:
This works best if done over two days, the first day to make the root view box and the second to begin the experiment.

1. Ask the students what they do when they are thirsty. Can plants find their way to water when they are 'thirsty'? Explain they will set up an experiment to see how sensitive roots are to water and whether they will grow towards a water source.

2. Have each group construct their own root view box. Give them a milk carton. Have them cut off one side, creating a top opening when the box is laid horizontally. With this opening on top, explain that one side will be cut to form a large window for root viewing. Ask them to measure and draw a half inch border all around one side of the carton. It works best if the teacher or another adult cuts this opening with a utility knife. Have them lay the box with the window side down and apply some waterproof glue to the inside border. Have them place their piece of Plexiglas or acetate into the box, press it down firmly on the glue and let it set. Later, suggest they reinforce the border inside and out, using strong tape and attach a piece of cardboard over the window of the box to create a cover flap that can be easily removed for root viewing.

3. Have the groups fill their root view box 3/4 full with potting soil. Have them plug the bottom opening of their flowerpot with a piece of clay. Ask them to test the seal by pouring water into the flower pot while holding it over a sink or collecting basin. Once the seal lets little to no water through, have them bury their flowerpot at one end of the the root view box with the opening at soil level. Direct them to place it as close as they can to the Plexiglas or acetate without it showing.

4. Beginning closest to the flowerpot, have them plant their bean seeds at one to two inch intervals along the front of the box, touching the Plexiglas or acetate. Have the students number the seeds, using a grease pencil on the Plexiglas or acetate, beginning with the seed closest to the flowerpot.

5. Have them close the front flap and set their box in a permanent spot. Ask them to fill the flowerpot with water. Explain that this is the only way they will water their seeds.

Extensions: (continued)

stone or block of wood in the soil touching the Plexiglas or acetate. Ask them to plant a seed above it also touching the Plexiglas or acetate. What do they think will happen to the root as it grows? Have them make predictions, monitor the experiment and compare results.

ROOT HAIR-DO

*Would you believe that plants have the longest hair in the world? Well, it's true. A healthy winter rye plant can have 6600 miles of roots made up of over 14 billion root hairs. Now that is a lot of hair. So just what is root hair and why so many? Root hairs are single cells which form just beyond the root tip in response to water. Root hairs grow rapidly as they search out and absorb the microscopic films of water hidden in the soil. A root will actually turn in the direction of the water supply. This selective root growth in response to water is called **hydrotropism**, and it helps the plant find water even in times of drought. Roots are also sensitive to hard things and can usually find the path of least resistance through the soil. When that fails, they can exert tremendous pressure to force their way through, similar to the action of driving a wedge into wood. This determination, combined with a spiraling corkscrew motion, helps roots wriggle their way along to the source of water!*

Directions: (continued)

Explain that the clay is porous and water seeps through the flowerpot into the soil. As a demonstration, set a similar clay flowerpot which has be plugged with clay on a plate in a central location in the classroom and fill it with water. Have the students observe the outside of the pot and the plate throughout the next few days.

6. Ask the groups to observe their root view boxes daily to see which seeds have germinated. Record the seed number and date. Which one germinated first? Last? At the end of the week, compare and discuss class results.

7. At five to seven day intervals, ask the groups to observe the root growth of their plants. In what direction are they growing? After three or four weeks, what do they observe around the flowerpot? Again compare and discuss results. What conclusions can be drawn about plant roots and water?

Plant Pipes

Objective:
Students will learn about the the transport of water by the vascular system in plant stems.

Grade Level: 2-6

Groupings: Small groups

Materials: Slightly wilted house plant; clear plastic cups; red or blue food coloring; selection of plant stems in water such as woody twigs with and without leaves, herbaceous stems with and without leaves, celery with and without leaves, white carnations, white daisies, or stem of succulent plant or cactus. (Provide at least one of each selection for all the groups.)

Time Allotment: 15 minutes to set up experiment, 5-10 minutes at 2-3 hour intervals for observation and 15 minutes on following day for conclusion.

Directions:
1. Show the students a plant that is beginning to wilt. Ask the class to describe the plant. What does it need? (Water.) What will happen to the plant after the water is added? (It will perk up and become firm and upright again.) How did the plant absorb the water? How did it travel to the rest of the plant? (Through the roots and then up through the 'plumbing' or vascular system in the stem.) Explain that one of the main functions of the stem is to transport water and minerals. Tell the class they will set up several experiments that will let them see the plumbing system in several plants.

2. Divide the students into small groups. Give each group several clear plastic cups and red or blue food coloring. Direct them to fill their cups with a few inches of water and add enough food coloring to make a brightly colored solution. Food coloring can stain, so have the students handle colored water carefully.

3. Show them a selection of plants you have cut and put in vases of water. Ask them to choose one of each plant stem to place in their cups of colored water. For older students, let them choose and cut a few plant stems on their own.

4. Ask the groups to make predictions on whether or not the colored water will travel up all stems. Will it travel at equal rates in all stems? If not, which will be the fastest? Which will be the slowest? Will the leaves effect the rate of travel in the different plant stems?

5. Have them check their plants at two to three hour intervals. Ask them to hold the plant stem up to a bright light to see whether they can determine and measure the height of the colored water. Record measurements for each plant. Ask the students to guess how long it will take for the color to reach the top of the plant. Leave the plants overnight.

Extensions:

a. *Challenge the students to make multi-colored flowers. Provide them with white carnations, food coloring, plastic cups and water. They will need to split the stem at the base into two or more sections and place the different sections into different colored cups of water. Encourage the students experiment with combinations of food coloring to create new colors.*

b. *Try coloring the plumbing systems in other plant parts. Use roots like carrots, preferably with the leaves still attached, fruits like zucchini, and other unusual stems such as onions.*

c. *Show the students a log which has been cut in half and has a piece sliced off the rounded edge. Explain to them that the lines and patterns they see in the wood are the plumbing system of the tree. Divide the students into small groups and pass out several pieces of wood and lumber to them. Have the students carefully observe the grain of wood in their piece. If necessary, have them quickly sand and oil the pieces to get a better look. Have them guess where in the tree this piece of wood came from. Have the groups compare their pieces of wood and guesses as to the original orientation.*

Directions: (continued)

6. To conclude, have the students cut thin cross sections of the various stems and observe the plant pipe patterns with a hand lens or microscope. Have them cut the stem lengthwise to view the plant pipes. Have them make drawings of the cross section and lengthwise section. How did their results compare to their predictions? Can they make any conclusions about the transport of water through plant stems?

PLANT PLUMBING

*Ever crunch into a stem of celery and get some strands stuck between your teeth? Don't worry, it's just plant pipes! There's no need to call a plumber or even the dentist, just pull them out and take a look at part of the amazing plumbing system of plants. All plants have pipes running through their stems. They run from the roots to the leaves and into the flowers and fruits, connecting the whole plant. This complicated network is called the **vascular system**. Water and minerals move through these pipes to all parts of the plant. This movement is helped along by the leaves. As the leaves make food through the process of photosynthesis, they give off or transpire a lot of water. This water loss creates a tension or pull on the rest of the water inside the plant, similar to sipping soda through a straw. So water keeps moving up, up, and away in plant stems, exiting through the leaves while the roots constantly seek out a new supply.*

Letting Off Steam

Objective:
Students will learn about transpiration or water loss in plants.

Grade Level: 3-6

Groupings: Small groups

Materials: *(per group)* Small plastic mirror; three pieces of flexible plastic tubing (18-24 inches long and 1/4 inch diameter); two plant stems, one with leaves and one without leaves; clay; clear plastic bags; rubber bands; heavy duty tape; permanent marker.

Time Allotment: 20 minutes for initial set up, 15 minutes at the end of the day for observation and conclusions

Extension:
a. *Have the students conduct the same experiment in the dark. Do they think the transpiration rate will differ? Have them record their predictions. Have them vary the experiment again, this time with the plastic bags removed and a fan blowing on their plants. What do they think will happen? How do they explain the results? Ask the students to think of other variables that might alter transpiration rates and set up new experiments to test their ideas.*

Directions:
This experiment works best if set up on a bright, sunny morning..

1. Ask the class whether they have ever seen their breath. Divide the class into small groups and pass each group a small plastic mirror. Explain that one of the students in each group will hold the mirror in front of his or her face for several seconds. What do they see on the mirror? (Condensed water vapor.) Where does it come from? Explain that people constantly give off water vapor, along with carbon dioxide, as they breathe. This process called **respiration** is the necessary exchange of gases of an oxygen breathing organism with the environment.

2. Show the class the collection of leafy plant stems. Do they think plants also 'breathe' or exchange gases with the environment? Explain that they will set up some experiments to see whether plants give off water vapor as part of this exchange.

3. Give each group three pieces of clear plastic tubing. Have them fill the tubes with water, making certain air bubbles are removed. Ask them to place a plant stem with leaves in one end of the first tube, and seal any opening in that end with clay. Have them cover the plant with a plastic bag and secure the bag to the tubing with a rubber band. Have them bend this tubing into a U-shape and securely tape it to a sunny window, marking the present water level at the open end with a permanent marker.

4. Ask them to place a plant stem without leaves in a second piece of tubing, seal the opening with clay, cover it with a plastic bag, and secure it with a rubber band. They then bend and attach the tubing to the window in a similar fashion to the first, marking the present water level. What do they think will happen to the inside of these plastic bags? What will happen to the water level in the tubes? Ask them to record their predictions.

5. Explain that a **control**, or a standard for comparing, is needed for this experiment to prove that any changes that occur inside the plastic bags or tubing are related to the plants. Ask for their ideas on how they could set up the third tube as a control. Using their ideas, direct them to fill the

UP, UP, and AWAY!

On a cold day you have probably seen your own breath as small clouds of water vapor given off when you breathe. Through a process called **transpiration**, *plants give off water vapor too — more than 17 times the amount we do! In fact, an acre of pasture grass may lose more than 1500 gallons of water during one hot midsummer day! Ninety percent of all the water taken up by plant roots is recycled back into the atmosphere as plants transpire. Transpiration is the principle force that lifts water to the tops of tall trees. As water is lost through the leaves, more is absorbed by the roots to replace it. The* **stomata** *control the amount of water lost through transpiration. Stomata are small openings on the underside of the leaves which are surrounded by two guard cells. These cells change in size and shape, thus changing the size of the opening and regulating the gas and water exchange. Various factors affect the guard cells and hence control transpiration rates, including temperature and humidity, water availability, carbon dioxide concentrations and light. So despite sun, wind, and rain, the perfect balance is always maintained.*

Directions: (continued)

tube with water, seal one end with clay, cover this end with a plastic bag and attach the tubing to the window in a similar manner, marking the present water level.

6. Ask the groups to monitor their experiments at one to two hour intervals and note and record changes. What, if anything, happens to the inside of the plastic bags? (The bags are covered with condensed water vapor.) Are there any differences in the bags of the plants with leaves and the one without leaves? (There will be more water in the bags of the plants with leaves.) Where is the water coming from? (Most of the water is given off by the leaves, ultimately coming from the water the plants absorb.) Explain to the students that **transpiration** is the process of giving off water vapor through the leaves. (See *Up, Up and Away!*, left, for further details.)

7. Have the groups measure the amount of water given off through transpiration by comparing the water level in their tubes at the end of the day to the initial levels. Do they notice a change in all three tubes? How do they explain the differences?

Table for Tulips
• EXHIBIT •

Materials:

Table with two chairs; table-cloth; two place settings including paper plates, bowl, cups, and plastic utensils; a selection of covered serving dishes and pitchers filled with plant food items (see below); two milk crates stacked on top of one another labelled as the pantry and filled with storage containers containing additional plant food items; materials to make menu booklets; extra paper plates bowls and cups; crayons, markers, glue and other art supplies; another table or shelf to serve as the 'buffet table' to display the students' meals and menus; two potted tulips plants (or other real or artificial plants).

Suggested plant food items include:

many small yellow paper **sun** cut outs; potting **soil**; **water**; many paper squares with the word **air** written on them; liquid plant fertilizer; water colored brown with food coloring or ice tea mix to represent manure tea; fish emulsion; seaweed; bonemeal; composted cow manure; dead leaves; straw; grass clippings; peat moss; sand; pine needles. (Have all the **bold** items in the serving dishes on the table, the others are optional and can be on the table or shelf. Label the inside lid of the containers to help the students identify the substances.)

Design:

1. Arrange a table with two chairs, a tablecloth and two complete place settings . In the center of the table, have a selection of several covered dishes and pitchers filled with plant food items. Place the tulip or other plants, elevated, on the chairs or on the table.

2. Set two milk crates nearby to represent the kitchen or pantry cupboards and stock the shelves with containers filled with additional plant food items. Make a kitchen or pantry sign to identify this area.

3. Set up an art supply area. Display a sample menu for students to use as a guideline for the information they will need to include in their menus (you may wish to have an appetizer, soup or salad, entree, side dish, dessert and beverage). Provide menu-making supplies and extra paper plates, cups and bowls for the students' meal creations.

Extension:

a. *Explain to the students that plants have four basic needs. What four plant food items are necessary for plant growth? (Sun, soil, water, and air.) Have the class set up several experiments to prove that these four things are necessary.*

SUN: *Have the students try growing plants in the sunlight versus in compete darkness. Compare plant growth and color over time.*

SOIL: *Have the students germinate and grow seeds in potting soil versus sawdust or wet crumbled paper towels. What happens to the plants over time?*

WATER: *Have the students give water to some plants and not others. What happens?*

AIR: *Have the students cover the bottoms of some leaves with Vaseline and not others. What happens to the leaves that can not 'breathe'?*

Directions: (continued)

4. Set up a 'buffet table' for the students to display their meals and menus.

5. Write the following directions near the exhibit:

Here's a table for two — two tulips, that is. What would you serve them for dinner? Look in the serving dishes and in the kitchen cupboard for some serving ideas and ingredients. Then create your own plant menu. Use the art supplies provided to make and decorate your menu, listing your special meal inside. Check the sample menu for guidelines. Then dish up your meal by gluing the actual plant food items to the extra paper plates and cups provided in the art supplies area. Display your meal and menu on the nearby buffet table.

Activity:

1. Have the students work in pairs. Explain that they are to create a meal for two tulips. Ask them to look over the contents of the serving dishes and those in the cupboard. Explain that they will need to select at least six items to serve for dinner. They may choose from the plant food items on display or add some of their own.

2. Using the art supplies provided, have them make their own menu booklet. Remind them to refer to the sample menu as a guideline for information to include in their menus.

3. Then have them prepare their meal by gluing the items from the containers on to the extra paper plates, bowls and cups provided. Ask them to display their finished products on the 'buffet table' with their menu. (Be sure to post rules for clean-up.)

Posy Poetry

Objective:
Students will sharpen their observation, listening and identification skills through a poetry exercise.

Grade Level: 2-6

Groupings: Pairs and small groups

Materials: Assortment of at least six different flowers in separate numbered vases; paper lunch bags; slips of paper.

Time Allotment: 20 minutes

Directions:

1. Place the vases of each type of flower in different locations throughout the room. Assign a number to each vase and place a paper lunch bag next to it along with several slips of paper. Write the corresponding vase number on a slip of paper and put this inside the bag.

2. Explain to the class that nature has long inspired artists in their work. Read aloud some poetry about different flowers or plants. Try to choose poems that don't mention the plant by name, or if possible, leave its name out while reading. Ask the students to guess the identity of the plant or flower.

3. Explain to the class that they will visit each of the flowers around the room in pairs and record their first impressions of the flower. Ask each pair to write a single word or short phrase on a slip of paper and place it in the adjacent paper bag. Encourage them to record whatever stands out about that flower — perhaps something it reminds them of or its color, shape, or smell.

4. When everyone has had a chance to visit and write about each flower, divide the students into small working groups. Give each group a bag. Explain that they will be using the words and phrases inside the bag to create a poem about their flower. From their writing, the rest of the class must guess which flower they are describing. Explain that inside each bag, there is a slip of paper with a number on it that corresponds to the numbers on the vases and identifies their

Extensions:

a. *Do a similar activity with different insects, various soil samples, or local birds. Instead of poetry, have the students write riddles. As a class, try to solve the riddles.*

b. *Have the students create drawings or paintings based on their impressions of the different flowers. Then make an anthology, including their art work and poems.*

Directions: (continued)

flower. Ask them to keep its identity a secret. Explain they must use all the words in the bag to write their poem, adding words if necessary. Modify any rules depending on your group and purpose.

5. Place all of the flowers in a central location. Explain that every group will first read their poem to the class. Then, after a second reading, the class can match up each poem to a flower.

Flower Power

Objective:
Students will learn the parts of a flower and their function.

Grade Level: 2-6

Groupings: Pairs or small groups

Materials: Flowers; magnifying glasses or hand lenses; index cards; *Flower Power Parts* (see page 229).

Time Allotment: 20 minutes

Extensions:
a. *Have the students mix up the parts from different flowers to create completely new flowers. Challenge them to create new names by using parts of the original names in combination.*

b. *Have a snack of flowers. Serve broccoli, cauliflower, and artichokes with dip; add nasturtiums, calendula petals and Johnny-jump-ups to a salad; or decorate cupcakes with purple violets.*

c. *Go on a wild flower scavenger hunt. Copy pictures of common wild flowers from a field guide and mount them on index cards. Go on a walk in a nearby woods in spring. Pass out the cards to pairs of students and ask them to find the pictured flower. Ask the students not to pick any flowers but to share their discovery with the class. You can also create general scavenger hunt cards, directing the students to find small white flowers, flowers with only three petals, flowers with lots of stamens and pollen, etc.*

Directions:
1. Discuss the fact that although each person in the class is a unique individual with his or her own special combination of characteristics, we all have certain features in common. Ask the students to name a few. Explain that each flower is also unique, but, like the students, all flowers share some common features. Explain that they will look carefully at different flowers to discover the parts they share in common.

2. Divide the students into pairs and give them a flower, a few index cards, and a hand lens. (It is easiest to use large simple flowers. See page 228 for suggestions.) For younger students, it works best if all the groups have the same type of flower. For older students, it is more interesting if they have different types of flowers.

3. Explain that they will carefully take their flower apart and group the similar parts together. Suggest that they begin by looking the flower over carefully to see how many different kinds of parts they can readily see. Caution them that towards the center of the flower the parts are smaller and harder to distinguish. Remind them to use their hand lenses to check for slight differences.

4. Ask them hold the flower upside down and carefully remove the parts, one at a time, working from the outside toward the inside. Have them place all the like parts together on one index card then count and record the number on the card.

Directions: (continued)

5. Have them line these cards up in order from the outermost parts of the flower to the innermost parts. Have available several of the same type of flowers that are not to be dissected so students can refer to the original configuration of the parts.

6. Have students compare their results by observing the order, groupings of parts, and the numbers of parts with other groups. Do they see any similarities? Do they see any differences? Do they notice any relationship between the numbers of parts?

7. Explain to the students that the different parts of the flower have names and specific functions in the plant. Give each student a copy of *Flower Power Parts* (Page 229) with labelled parts. Review the sheet and have the students label the parts of their flower and discuss their functions.

8. Set out some other flowers and wild flowers and have the students identify the parts. If you have enough, let each group dissect and sort the parts of a different flower. Then have them put the similar parts of these different flowers together for comparisons. For example, ask them to make one group for all the petals, another group for the stamens, and yet another for the pistils.

9. For additional review, pass out *Flower Power Worksheet* (page 230) and have students label the flower parts and list their function.

Flower Power Parts

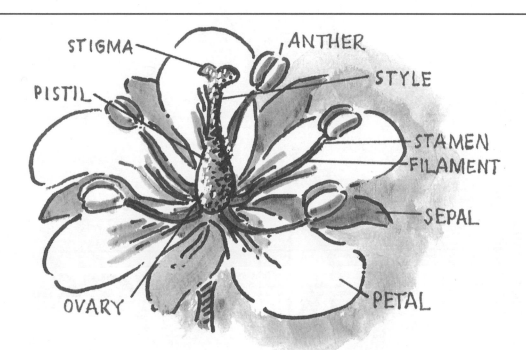

How would you like a bunch of weird, contorted leaves for your birthday? Not especially, you say. Well, that is just what a bouquet of roses is! Flowers are actually a cluster of four kinds of modified leaves arranged in separate groups around a short stem. Look closely at that rose and you can see them.

Turn it over and you will see a little skirt of green leaves around the base. This lower or outermost layer is composed of **SEPALS**. The whole group of them is called the **CALYX**. While in bud, the sepals protect the more delicate flower parts inside. Sepals are usually green, but in lilies and tulips they are colorful and look just like showy petals.

The **PETALS** stand out in a flower because their major function is to attract specific animals to the flower for the purpose of pollination. Petals are variously adapted, colored, shaped and perfumed to insure frequent visits by these specially invited guests, leading to pollination and ultimately the production of seeds.

Look closely inside the petals and you'll see a group of yellow, fuzzy containers on thin stalks. Don't look too closely or you may end up with yellow dust on your nose. That's **POLLEN** from the **STAMENS**. The stamens are composed of a thin **FILAMENT** which holds up an enlarged structure, the **ANTHER**. The anthers are full of pollen and when open, they release the dusty pollen to be picked up by various pollinators (or your nose) and transferred from flower to flower.

Last but not least, hidden among the stamens is the **PISTIL**. There can be just one or many depending upon the flower type. It is always in the right place at the right time, for it can't help but be dusted with pollen in this central location. The pistil is often divided into the three parts. The enlarged base is the **OVARY**, where the seeds develop, and its long thin neck-like **STYLE** ends in a variously divided,branched or lobed **STIGMA**. A sticky stigma no less, all the better to catch pollen, my dear. And pollen on a stigma leads to seed in a fruit!

Flower Power Worksheet

Where are the **SEPALS, PETALS, STYLE, STAMEN, ANTHER, FILAMENT, PISTIL, OVARY** and **STIGMA**? Label this flower and indicate the funtion of each part.

Flower Fashions

Objective:
Students will review the parts of a flower

Grade Level: K-6

Groupings: Individuals

Materials: Paper plates; crayons or magic markers; paper bowls; tissue or crepe paper; glue; stapler; Styrofoam balls with the bottoms trimmed off to make a flat surface; plastic drinking straws; tape; sugar cubes; pipe cleaners; Styrofoam packing peanuts; cinnamon; scissors; an insect or bee puppet made from an old sock.

Time Allotment: 30 minutes

Directions:
*This activity works best if students have done **Flower Power** (page 227) or studied flowers and their parts beforehand.*

1. Copy the **Flower Power Worksheet** (page 229). Pass it out to the class and review the various flower parts and their function. Explain to the students that they will construct their own three dimensional flowers.

2. Pass out paper plates to the students. Explain that this will represent the **sepals**, the outermost layer on their flower. Have them color the plate green and cut the edge of the plate into three, four or five lobes. Punch two holes in opposite ends of the plate and have them attach yarn or ribbon to each hole.

3. To represent the petals on a flower, pass out paper bowls. Have them cut and shape their bowl into **petals** (the same number as their sepals). Using crepe or tissue paper and glue, have them decorate the bowl both inside and out. Have them put the bowl (the petals) in the center of the plate (inside the sepals) and attach it with glue or staples.

4. Give everyone a Styrofoam ball. What part of the flower do they think this represents? (It is the **ovary** of the **pistil**, where the seeds are formed.) What parts of the pistil are missing? (The **stigma** and **style**.) Give them plastic drinking straws and have them cut one end into fringes. Ask them to bend the fringes outward and push the opposite end of the straw into the center of the Styrofoam ball. Now the flower has a long style topped by a fringed stigma. Make the stigma sticky so it can catch pollen by attaching a small loop of tape to the top.

5. Explain that **nectar** is usually stored inside the petals. The nectar smells sweet and attracts pollinators looking for food. Have the students glue some sugar cubes to the paper bowl around the base of the pistil.

6. What part of the flower is missing? (The **stamens**.) Provide pipe cleaners and Styrofoam peanuts to construct the stamens. The pipe cleaner is the filament and Styrofoam peanuts are added to the tops as the anthers. Have the students put a little glue on top of the anthers and generously

Extensions:

a. *Read* THE REASON FOR A FLOWER *by Ruth Heller (Grosset and Dunlap, 1983). Discuss how animals help to pollinate plants and make seeds. Where would the seeds grow in their flower?*

b. *Enlarge the **Flower Power Worksheet** (page 229) and mount it on a piece of poster board. Make several small circles from two different colors of construction paper. One color circle will represent pollen grains, the other seeds. Make enough of each so that there is one per student. Review how flowers are pollinated, including where the pollen must land (on the stigma) to fertilize the flowers and where seeds are then produced (in the ovary of the pistil). Give half of the class pollen grains and the other half seeds, all with tape attached to the back. Blindfold one of the students who has a pollen grain and have them 'pin the pollen on the stigma.' Give several students with pollen a turn, and after a few have successfully placed the pollen on the stigma, explain that seeds are beginning to develop. Have the students with seeds try to 'pin seeds in the ovary' of the pistil.*

Directions: (continued)

sprinkle cinnamon, representing **pollen**, on top. The stamens are then inserted in a ring around the base of the Styrofoam ball. (The number of stamen should equal that of the sepals and petals.)

7. Once their flowers are dry, have the students wear them as hats, using the yarn or ribbon attached to the sepals as ties under their chins. Then demonstrate with a simple sock puppet how an insect pollinates flowers. Have the insect fly from flower to flower looking for nectar and show how pollen accidentally sticks to the insect and is then transferred from one flower to another.

Pollination Parade

Objective:
Students will explore the relationship between flowers and their pollinators.

Grade Level: 4-6

Groupings: Pairs or small groups

Materials: Several different flowers; *Flower Description Cards* and *Pollinator Profile Cards* (see pages 235 - 36); collection of miscellaneous materials for constructing flowers such as paper plates, drinking straws, toilet paper tubes, crepe paper, assorted scents and flavored extracts, toothpicks, play dough, pipe cleaners, cotton balls, scraps of felt, wire floral stems, and string.

Time Allotment: 30 minutes

Extension:
a. *Have the students conduct a pollination survey. Have them observe a flower over time, noting the different types and behavior of pollinators that visit it.*

Directions:
This activity works best if the students are familiar with the material presented in **Flower Power** *(page 227).*

1. Bring in several flowers of different shapes and colors. Ask the students to vote for their favorite flower. When the votes are in, explain that not everyone voted for the same flower as different people have different preferences. Different insects and other plant visitors have flower preferences, too.

2. Explain to the class that the purpose of a flower in the life of a plant is to reproduce the plant. In order to do that, pollen from one flower must be carried to other flowers and vice versa. The pollen fertilizes the pistil of the plant, producing fertile seeds. These seeds can then grow into new plants. Introduce the class to the idea that different flowers are pollinated in different ways. Explain that flowers have evolved specialized parts, shapes, colors, scents, and other characteristics expressly to attract **pollinators** — animals, birds, and insects that spread pollen from flower to flower. The class will construct their own flowers that are adapted in different ways to attract pollinators. Later they will play the role of the various pollinators.

3. Divide the students into pairs or groups. Give each group a **Flower Description Card**. Using the materials provided, have the students make a three-dimensional flower that meets the requirements detailed on their card. Stress that the flower should have all the basic flower parts unless the description states otherwise.

4. Place the finished flowers with their description cards in a central location in the classroom. Provide time for all the students to observe the flowers.

POLLINATION PARTNERS

Flowers have been 'courting' pollinators for a long time. They have evolved specific colors, shapes, nectars and perfumes to attract them. The most efficient pollinators have been rewarded with a flower designed just for them. Petals have evolved into flat landing platform shapes for bees; foul odors are emitted to lure carrion beetles and flies; and nectar is hidden deep inside long flower tubes where only hummingbirds, moths, or butterflies can reach it. Certain orchids go as far as resembling the females of certain species of bees and wasps, even producing a scent that mimics the mating pheromone. Male bees and wasps are attracted and attempt to mate with the flower, pollinating it in the process. One of the most amazing examples of this coevolution of flowers and pollinators is the yucca plant and yucca moth. The female moth only visits yucca flowers, and at each one she rolls up a large ball of pollen. She carries this pollen ball to another yucca flower and deposits it on the stigma, thereby insuring pollination and seed production. She then lays her eggs in the ovary of this flower, insuring a food source for her hatching larvae which emerge just as the seeds are ripening! It is estimated the larvae only eat about 20% of the seeds before they chew their way out of the ovary and are on their own.

Directions: (continued)

5. Pass *Pollinator Profile Cards* to the groups. Have the students read over their card carefully. Explain that each group will now take on the role of the pollinator described on their card. Review the flower descriptions, and ask the pollinators to choose the one flower that best suits their needs. When you say "Go," the pollinators in each group fly, buzz, or crawl to the flower that is best adapted for pollination by them. Review their choices.

6. Show the students examples or pictures of flowers that are pollinated by the various pollinators and compare them to the flowers they made.

POLLINATORS *and their* FLOWERS

Bat: Organ Pipe Cactus (*Stenocereus*), Kapok tree (*Ceiba*), Sausage tree (*Kegelia*), Calabash tree (*Crescentia*).

Bee: Marsh Marigold (*Caltha palustris*), Blue Flag (*Iris*), Foxglove (*Digitalis*).

Butterfly: Wild Blue Phlox (*Phlox*), Daylily (*Hemerocallis*), Wild Geranium (*Geranium*).

Carrion fly: Stinking Benjamin (*Trillium*), Skunk cabbage (*Symplocarpus foetidus*), Carrion flower (*Scapelia*).

Hummingbird: Cardinal flower (*Lobelia cardinalis*), Red columbine (*Aquilega canadensis*), Fuschia, Banana.

Mosquito: Small flowered orchid (*Habenaria elegans*).

Moth: Spanish Bayonet or Yucca (*Yucca*), Tobacco (*Nicotiana*), Evening Primrose (*Oenthera*).

Wind: Paper Birch (*Betula*), Cottonwood (*Populus*), Oak (*Quercus*), and many other temperate trees, also grasses and sedges.

Note: Each pollinator has a specific flower type that it prefers, but it may visit and pollinate many different types of flowers.

Flower Description Cards

1. I am a bright red flower shaped like a long tube fringed with tiny petals. Hidden deep in the tube is lots of nectar. I am very showy and stand out in a crowd, but I have no scent.

2. I am a bright blue, sweet smelling flower. I am tubular in shape with five flat petals on the top. Peek inside: I am full of nectar.

3. I am a white flower. I look like a bell with five zigzag petals on top and nectar hidden inside. I have a very strong, pleasant odor that I emit after sunset. Ahhhh!

4. We are a cluster of tiny white star-shaped flowers with nectar and a little pollen.

5. I am a dark maroon flower with three petals. My color has been compared to red meat. Don't get too close because I smell bad, as if I were rotting. Yuck!

6. I am a bright yellow flower with petals spread open wide. They make a nice landing platform so it is easy to drop in for a visit. Follow the racing stripes on my petals to my nectar supply. Watch out for my anthers, they might dust you with pollen.

7. I am a huge, white, funnel-shaped flower on a thick, strong stalk. I smell very sweet and spicy and have lots and lots of nectar and nutritious pollen.

8. We are small green flowers. Nothing fancy, no petals, no sepals, no scent, just anthers full of pollen. We hang around on long stems and dangle in the breeze.

Answers: **1.** *Cardinal flower, hummingbird pollinator.* **2.** *Wild blue phlox, butterfly pollinator.* **3.** *Yucca, moth pollinator.* **4.** *Small flowered orchid, mosquito pollinator.* **5.** *Stinking Benjamin, carrion fly pollinator.* **6.** *Marsh marigold, bee pollinator.* **7.** *Organ pipe cactus, bat pollinator.* **8.** *Paper birch tree flowers, wind pollinator.*

Pollinator Profile Cards

I am a honeybee. I can't see red, but how I love those bright flashy flowers with distinctive patterns on the petals! People often miss the pattern because they can't see like a bee. Just shine an ultraviolet light on that flower and you'll see it as I do. A tisket a tasket, I love to gather lots of pollen in the 'baskets' on my legs.

I am a hummingbird. Red is my favorite color. Give me a flower with a long tube full of nectar. Don't bother with fancy perfume, because I can't smell a thing.

I am the wind. I don't care much about how a flower looks or smells. I just like to blow pollen about. Whooosh!

I am a carrion fly. I love smelly things, like dead fish or rotting meat. Yum!

I am a little male mosquito. I look for tiny light-colored flowers about my size when gathering nectar.

I am a bat. I have a big appetite, so give me a flower with plenty of nectar and pollen. I am on the lookout for light-colored flowers with strong, sweet and spicy smells, as those flowers are easy to find at night

I am a butterfly. Give me a bright-colored flower that stands out in a crowd. I just unroll my long drinking-straw tongue and sip nectar.

I am a moth. I like flowers that are light in color and have a strong, sweet smell as they are easier to find if you fly by night. My long tongue can find and drink up the hidden nectar.

Bee An Insect

Objective:
Students will learn insect anatomy.

Grade Level: K-3

Groupings: Entire class

Materials: Cardboard; markers or paint; ribbon or yarn; old stockings; batting; poster board; elastic or Velcro; pipe cleaners; Styrofoam balls; headband; egg cartons or old sunglasses; sticky paper dots; kitchen sponge; drinking straw; clean syringe (no needle); clothes pin; old bottle of cologne; *Critter Cards* (see below).

Time Allotment: 30 minutes preparation, 15 minutes with the class

---

CRITTER CARDS

Insects: *monarch butterfly, luna moth, mosquito, honey bee, wasp, praying mantis, ladybug, ant, termite, cricket, grasshopper, walking stick, housefly, Japanese beetle, firefly.*

Other Unrelated Animals:
mouse (mammal), snake (reptile), frog (amphibian), worm (annelid), robin (bird), spider (arachnid), clam (mollusk), lobster (crustacean), kangaroo (marsupial).

Directions:

1. In advance, create an insect costume using the following list as a guideline.

Thorax and Abdomen: *large piece of cardboard, shaped into two sections and decorated as a smaller black thorax on top and a larger yellow and black striped abdomen below. Attach ribbon or yarn to tie the body around a student's neck. Cut three holes on either side of the thorax to attach the legs.*

Six legs: *old stockings or socks stuffed with batting and tied to the holes in the cardboard thorax.*

Wings: *two pieces of poster board cut to shape with two straps of elastic or adjustable Velcro bands on each to attach over the student's arms.*

Antennae: *two pipe cleaners with Styrofoam balls at the end, attached to a head band.*

Compound eyes: *old sunglasses divided into facets with a marker. Or, make special bug eyes using two of the faceted sections of an egg carton. Cut a eye holes in the center of each and use pipe cleaners to attach over the student's ears.*

Simple eyes: *three sticky paper dots.*

Specialized mouth parts: *a new kitchen sponge for the housefly; a plastic drinking straw for the butterfly or moth; a clean syringe (no needle) for a mosquito; a clothes pin for chewing beetles.*

Pheromones: *spray bottle of cologne labeled "Eau de Insect #5".*

Extensions:

a. *To review the characteristics of insects, teach the class the following song, sung to the tune of "Head, Shoulders, Knees and Toes:"*

> *Head, thorax, abdomen, abdomen*
> *Head, thorax, abdomen, abdomen*
> *Two antennae, six wiggly legs*
> *Head, thorax, abdomen, abdomen*

b. *Have the students make their own insect model using miscellaneous classroom items, recycled materials and found objects.*

COLLECTING INSECTS

Your students can collect all kinds of flying, crawling and wiggling insects with a variety of nets, traps and tricks. Here's a few for them to try at school or at home.

HIDE AND SEEK *Play a simple game of hide and seek and look for insects hiding beneath fallen logs and rocks. A host of critters live in these damp moist places. Try to sort the insects from the others types of critters living there. And be sure to close the 'door' gently and replace the 'roof' when you leave.*

Directions: (continued)

2. Explain to the class that as humans, we belong to a class of animals called mammals. What are some characteristic we all have in common? Have them name some other mammals.

3. Explain that different animals belong to different groups and can be distinguished by certain common physical characteristics. Explain that you will pass out some *Critter Cards*. Everyone will have a different critter on their card. The students will need to sort the animals on the cards into two groups. Many students in the class will be in a group of related critters and the others are unrelated animals.

4. Pass out the critter cards and have the students hang their card around their neck with the picture facing out. When you say "Go," have all the students who are related to one another stand in a designated area. What group do they belong to? (Insects.) Have all the other unrelated animals return to their seats. Review the diversity of insects pictured, then collect the critter cards and have everyone, except one student volunteer, return to their seats.

5. Ask the class what makes an insect an insect? What characteristics do they have in common? Explain that this volunteer will help illustrate the common characteristics and amazing adaptations of insects. As the class makes suggestions, you will dress up the volunteer to look like an insect. Be sure to ask leading questions to cover all the important characteristics.

6. What does an insect look like? How many sections are there to its body? All insects all have three main body parts: head, thorax, and abdomen (in order from the top down). To represent the thorax and abdomen, slip the large cardboard cut out over the students neck. Point out that on a real insect, to determine which part is which, they need to look for certain clues. The mouth, eyes, and antennae are located on head, just like you (well, almost). The legs are attached to the thorax and everything else is their abdomen.

DROP IN FOR DINNER

This is a great way to lure all kinds of crawling insects. Bury empty tin cans in the soil with the opening at ground level. Add various bait to the these can traps: pieces of fruit, raw meat, molasses, honey, peanut butter and jelly. Try putting several cans in one location and varying the bait from can to can. Which bait attracts the most insects. Were different insects attracted to different baits? Try this in several locations and make comparisons.

SHAKE, RATTLE & ROLL

Many of the insects that climb in the grass and bushes are not easily seen. Lay a white sheet underneath some promising vegetation then shake nearby bushes, or rattle the grasses and weeds with a stick and watch the hidden insects roll into view on the sheet. Many of them will "play dead" and lie still. This is a great time to put them into a magnifying bug box or insect cage for closer observation.

HOW SWEET IT IS *Kids aren't the only ones said to have a sweet tooth. Many insects love sweet treats, too. Make a sweet solution using molasses or sugar, fruit juice and a mashed banana. Then using an old brush, paint some of this sticky goo on a tree, fence post, or log. Leave it for at least 30 minutes then come back to see who has discovered it.*

(continued on page 240)

Directions: (continued)

7. Speaking of legs, how many does an insect have? (Insects have six legs.) Attach the six stocking legs to the thorax. They are often variously adapted, depending on where the insect lives or what it eats. In addition to locomotion, what else are they used for? (Smell and taste.)

8. What else do most insects use to get around? (Wings.) Attach the wings to arms. Explain that most insects have four wings, but some, like our friend the housefly, have only two. Other insects don't have any at all. Can they name a common wingless insect? One that might join them on their next picnic? (An ant.)

9. What stands out on an insects head? Attach the headband with two antennae. Most insects have a pair on their heads and they use these to smell, feel and even hear!

10. Looking at their heads you can't help noticing their eyes, which sometimes cover a large portion of their head. Attach the compound eye glasses. These large compound eyes are made up of thousands of tiny lenses. They are great for detecting movement, but the picture is not very clear or detailed. In addition to compound eyes, many insects have three simple eyes located between the compound eyes. Attach the three sticky dots to student's forehead. No one is sure how the insect uses these, but they seem to be important in detecting light and dark.

11. You've heard the expression you are what you eat, well you can tell lots about an insect from its mouth. Challenge students to guess the identity of the following insects based on the following sample of different mouth parts and food (hold each prop up as you describe it): a sponge-like mouth to lap up food spilled here and there (a housefly); a plastic drinking straw to sip nectar (moths and butterflies); a syringe to get a meal fit for a vampire (a mosquito); a clothes pin to chew up rose bushes (Japanese beetles and other leaf eating beetles).

12. You can't see this last characteristic, but if you were an insect you could smell it, sometimes over a mile away. Hand the student the bottle of cologne. It is pheromones, a chemical scent produced by insects to help them communicate.

(continued from page 239)

Try it in the daytime, at dusk or during the night to see how the number and variety of visitors changes.

SWEPT AWAY *Make a sweep net with a coat hanger, an old pillowcase and a broom handle. Cut a slit in the inside of the hem on the pillowcase. Unwind and straighten the coat hanger (you might need an adult's help). Slip the end of the hanger through the slit in the pillowcase hem. Push the hanger through the hem and out the slit, bending it into a circle as you go along. Refine your circle so that the opening of the pillowcase is like a net. If you want a smaller net, cut the bottom of the pillowcase to the desired size and sew it closed. Using duct or electrical tape, securely attach the ends of the hanger to a broom handle. Now head out to the closest field and see whether you can sweep some insects off their feet.*

TAKE A DIP *Use wire mesh kitchen strainers to collect aquatic insects. Use the strainer to sample critters swimming through the water and to dredge up those living in the muck at the bottom of the pond. Have two buckets nearby, one for your initial collections from the pond and a second, cleaner one for transferring individual insects from the first bucket.*

Directions: (continued)

13. Review the basic characteristics and thank your volunteer insect. (You might even want to record the event with a photograph!) Then go outdoors with equipment, set up collecting stations, and observe real insects (see *Collecting Insects,* page 238).

Make Scents of Insects

Objective:
Students will learn how insects communicate using scents.

Grade Level: K-6

Groupings: Entire class

Materials: Film canisters *(one per student)*; cotton balls; collection of strong diverse scents such as cut or crushed garlic clove, Vicks Vapo-Rub, root beer extract, almond extract, or scented bubble bath.

Time Allotment: 15 minutes

Directions:

In preparation for the activity, divide the film canisters into two groups. Label the bottoms of one group with numbers and the other group with letters. Put a scent on two cotton balls and place one in a canister from the numbered group and one in a cannister from the lettered group. Record the scent and the matching number and letter on an answer key. Sniff each canister to be certain the scent is strong enough. Place a second cotton ball on top of the first to cover any telltale signs or clues.

1. Discuss with the class how they use their senses to get information about the world. Which senses do they use most often? How do they use their sense of smell? What can different smells tell them? Ask the students to describe their good smells and bad smells. Do certain smells evoke any memories, reminding them of certain things, places, or events?

2. Explain that in other animals, the sense of smell is very well developed and plays a more important role in their lives. Discuss insect **pheromones** and how they are used (see *Insect Perfume*, page 242, for details). Explain to the students that they will pretend to be insects and will communicate using pheromones. Pass out the prepared film canisters. Ask them to open their film canister and smell their pheromone.

3. Explain that at least one other insect (person) in the room has the same pheromone. They will need to quietly walk around the room, smelling each others' pheromone canisters until they have found their match. When they have found their partner(s), have them sit down and try to determine the identity of their pheromone scent. Have they ever smelled it before?

Extension:

a. *Create a maze by spreading large index cards around the hallway or some nearby separate space. Have several spots where the trail forks in two or more directions. At the end of each trail place a paper grocery bag. Pick a pathway through the maze and on top of each card in the path place a film canister with a particular scent. Put a snack in the grocery bag at the end of this scent trail. On all the other cards, place canisters with no scent. Explain to the students that they are all ants. One of the ants from their ant hill has just left a scent trail leading to some food. One at a time, have the ants (students) smell their way through the maze of canisters to the goodies at the end.*

Directions: (continued)

4. Review their answers and confirm their scent and match.

INSECT PERFUME

Do you ever wonder how a whole troop of tiny ants are able to find your picnic blanket in a vast meadow? The answer lies in their ability to produce **pheromones**, *a chemical scent secreted from their body. Think of pheromones as a kind of insect perfume. Some insects produce pheromones that are so strong they can be detected over a mile away! Now that is strong perfume. So the ant who just happened upon your picnic heads home with some goodies leaving a scent trail as she goes. The other ants simply follow her trail back to your blanket and join the picnic. Pheromones are used by insects not only to mark trails, but to signal danger, call together large groups of insects, regulate numbers and types within a colony of social insects, and attract mates. People have taken advantage of this type of chemical communication, especially with insects that are harmful to crops. Scientists have produced chemicals similar to these insects' attracting pheromone. Farmers use the chemical pheromone to confuse the insects or lure them into traps. It is one of the methods used in Integrated Pest Management (IPM), a modern, ecologically sound insecticidal method.*

Water Wizard Learning Stations

Objective:
Students will discover the physical properties of water through experimentation.

Grade Level: 2-6

Groupings: Pairs

Time Allotment: 5 - 15 minutes per station

Introduction:

Water is an excellent material for hands-on science discovery. It is easy to obtain, inexpensive, provides a multitude of learning opportunities, and the very idea of 'messing around' in water captures the interest of students of all ages.

Begin by asking your students to share their knowledge and observations of the properties of water. What makes this liquid unique? How does this remarkable liquid behave while they are swimming, splashing, boating, fishing, skating, or participating in other water related activities? Record their observations and ideas.

Following is a collection of experiments that may be done in any order. They can all be set up as separate learning stations through which the students rotate, or they can be conducted one at a time over a day, week or month. They are designed to let the students discover for themselves, using methods employed by 'real' scientists, some of the physical properties of water.

The directions in these experiments are written on worksheets for the students. Duplicate the sheets provided or create your own. They explain how the students should conduct the experiments. Student pairs will need to work independently to follow directions, then predict, test, observe and record their results and thoughts on why certain things happened. A separate section for the teacher includes objectives, times needed, materials, teacher notes, extensions and background information for each experiment.

As a class, review the students' worksheets for each learning station. Ask them to group together those experiments that demonstrate a similar principle or physical property. Have students share their results and theories. Encourage them to design their own experiments to test various theories. Suggest some of the experiments listed in the extensions for each activity to help clarify their thoughts. Then have the students determine and list the amazing properties of water revealed in these experiments.

Regarding the individual experiments, stress careful experimentation, logical thinking and accurate record keeping. Encourage the students to make honest predictions and not to change these once they see the actual results. Often times a result that is surprising teaches us more than one that is expected, as it challenges us to think more about why something happened.

Be sure to stress to the students to leave each station as they found it and clean up after themselves.

Drip Drop

WATER WIZARD LEARNING STATION

 Student Directions for
Drip Drop

1. Lay a sheet of waxed paper flat on a sheet of newspaper. Using an eyedropper, place a drop of water on the waxed paper. View the drop from the side, at eye level. Draw its shape. How do the letters in the newspaper look through the drop?

2. Place one of the design cards under the waxed paper. Using a toothpick or pencil, try to pull the water drop along the line of the design. Can you do it? Any ideas why or why not?

3. Dip a toothpick into a container of detergent. Let a drop of detergent fall into the water drop. Watch what happens to the drop? Draw a picture of the drop after the detergent has been added. Can you pull the water droplet with a toothpick after the detergent has been added? Any ideas on why or why not?

Objective:
Students will be introduced to the property of cohesion in water.

Materials: Waxed paper; cup of water; eye dropper; newspaper; toothpicks; index cards illustrated with simple line designs; liquid detergent.

Time Allotment: 5-10 minutes

Teacher Notes:
Step #1: The water on waxed paper pulls itself tightly together forming a drop. Its shape is similar to that of a convex lens, so like the lens, it magnifies the newspaper print beneath it.

Step #2: The water's strong attraction to itself also allows it to hold together as it is pulled along the entire length of the design.

Step #3: Adding detergent to water breaks the attraction among the water molecules. The water can no longer hold itself together and it spreads out randomly.

Extensions:

a. *Have the students create mazes by scratching lines with a pen or pencil on a sheet of waxed paper, supported by a piece of cardboard, to form the track. Have them place a drop at the starting gate. They will need to pick up the waxed paper and wiggle it gently to help the drop roll along the track to the finish. Have them keep track of their time, then challenge someone to a better racing time. On your mark, get set, roll!*

b. *Have the students test a water drop's attractiveness to different surfaces. Have the students gather an assortment of small paper samples to test: paper towels, waxed paper, aluminum foil, writing paper, newspaper, and boxboard. Have them work in pairs and predict the shape their water drop will take when placed on each of their samples. Then using an eyedropper, have them test their prediction. Ask them to use a magnifying glass to view the drops at eye level and record the shape of each drop. Have them compare the drops and put them, in order from smallest to biggest. What are their explanations for differing shapes?*

Water is attracted or adheres to different surfaces in varying degrees. This attraction is called adhesion. The more attractive a surface is to water, the more it causes the water droplet to flatten or spread out.

STICKING TOGETHER

*Everyone has seen a drop of water. But why does water form droplets and not just go with the flow? It's because water has the ability to stick to itself and pull itself tightly together. Water has strong molecular bonds that cause it to form tiny drops instead of spreading out randomly. This property is called **cohesion**. Through thick and thin, water will stick together in this drop-like form unless something interferes with or breaks its strong molecular bonds.*

Believe It or Not

Student Directions for *Believe it or Not*

1. Fill a cup with water. Try to float a paper clip or sewing needle on the surface of the water. Use a fork to help place it gently. Why can the paper clip and needle float in the water, if placed correctly?

2. Once the paper clip or needle is floating, observe the water beneath it with a magnifying glass. What does the surface of the water look like?

Objective:
Students will learn about the concept of surface tension on water.

Materials: Several quarts of water; clear plastic cups; several plastic forks; paper clips; sewing needles; magnifying glass.

Time Allotment: 5-15 minutes (This can vary greatly with the initial success and determination of the students.)

Teacher Notes:
Step #1: The paper clip and needle are able to float because of the surface tension of the water. The water molecules at the surface are strongly attracted to one another and they form an elastic skin over the surface. If you can place these items horizontally on the surface, without breaking through this elastic skin, they will float.

Step #2: If you look closely at the water surface around and beneath the paper clip or needle, it appears dimpled. The water's skin appears to stretch and can suspend these light objects.

Extension:

a. *Once they have a paper clip or needle floating, have the students drip a drop of liquid detergent down the side of the cup into the water. Ask them to predict what will happen. Remind them to watch closely and record the results. Ask them to formulate a theory on the detergent's action. (If you include this extension as part of the original activity, each group will need to use a separate cup as traces of the detergent in the cup will make it impossible for future groups to be successful in their floating attempts.)*

The detergent interferes with the attraction between the water molecules. The soap molecules actually get between the water molecules and form a loose bond. The surface tension is weakened and the water can no longer hold up the paper clip or needle so they sink.

WALKING *on* WATER

*You've probably heard of the phrase smooth as glass to refer to the surface of still pond. The strong attraction of water molecules for one another on the pond's surface creates what appears to be a shiny film or skin on the water. These molecular bonds are tight, elastic and hard to break. This property of water is called **surface tension**. This elastic skin can suspend very light objects without collapsing. If you look closely at the water surface beneath a floating object, it appears stretched and dimpled. Visit a pond on a sunny summer day and look for water striders and other insects that use the water's surface tension to walk on water.*

To the Brim

WATER WIZARD LEARNING STATION

Student Directions for
To the Brim

1. Fill a cup to the top or brim with water. Kneel down to get a side view of the cup. Draw a picture of the water in the cup.

2. How many pennies do you think you can add to the cup before the first drop of water spills out? Record your prediction.

3. Add pennies, one at a time, to the cup until the water starts to overflow. How many pennies did you add?

4. Draw a picture of the water in the cup after you added pennies. How can you explain the new shape of the water in the cup?

Objective:
Students will learn about the concept of surface tension on water.

Materials: Several quarts of water; plastic cups; at least 50 pennies.

Time Allotment: 5-10 minutes

Teacher Notes:
As the pennies are added, small amounts of water are displaced. The water's surface tension allows it to expand and keeps this displaced water from spilling over. The water bulges outward, like a convex lens, at the top of the cup. When the bulge reaches a certain height, the force of gravity is greater than the surface tension holding the water molecules together, and the water spills over. The water's skin can not expand anymore to accommodate the water displaced by the pennies.

Extensions:

a. *Have the students make guesses as to how many drops of water will fit on the head of a penny, then use eyedroppers and count the actual number that fit.*

Many drops (15-25+ depending on their size) can be placed on the head of a penny. The water will pile up on the top of the penny forming a convex bulge until gravity finally pulls a drop over the edge.

b. *Have the students fill their glasses to the brim again. Remind them to to be sure that the cups are absolutely full. Ask them to predict how many drops can be added before the water overflows. Using eyedroppers, have them add water a drop at a time and count the number of drops that fit in the glass before overflowing.*

Even after doing To the Brim, students still underestimate the water's strong surface tension and just how full a glass can be. Usually several drops can be added before one spills over.

WATER BULGE

*How full is full? With water it's a lot more than you would think. Because of water's strong surface tension, it can pile up over the top of a glass in a convex bulge without spilling over. This bulge is called a **meniscus**. When you fill a glass only part way, the water clings to the sides of the glass, and you can see the meniscus as a concave curve. So a glass isn't really full until the first drop spills out. That's when the force of gravity is stronger than the bonds holding the water molecules together — splash!*

Rising to the Top

WATER WIZARD LEARNING STATION

Student Directions for
Rising to the Top

1. Gather a collection of four different kinds of paper to test in this activity. Using a ruler, pencil and scissors cut the paper into strips 1 inch wide by 5 inches long. Put a line across each of the strips at the four inch mark. Number the strips 1 to 4 above this line. These are your "racing strips."

2. Fill two identical cups with one inch of water. You will place these racing strips into the cups at the same time, and the water will race to the finish line. Now it's time to place your bets. On which sheet will the water cross the line first? Second? Third? Last? How long do you think it will take? Make your predictions. Then, on your mark, get set, flow!

3. What were the results? Can you explain how and why the water moves faster on some paper and slower on others? Use a magnifying glass to look for clues.

Objective: Students will learn about adhesive and cohesive properties of water by observing the behavior of water and different kinds of paper.

Materials: Several quarts of water; plastic cups; variety of paper samples such as stationary, newsprint, sketch paper and paper towel; scissors; ruler; pencil; magnifying glass.

Time Allotment: 10-15 minutes

Teacher Notes:
If you look closely at the paper, you will see that it is made up of fibers. In between the fibers are air spaces. The water is attracted to these spaces and pulls itself into them, moving up the strip. The paper with the largest air spaces should provide the most surface area for the water. It is the most porous and the water should move through it fastest.

Extension:

a. *Challenge the class to bring in their favorite paper contestant for the "Great Paper Race." Ask them to use a magnifying glass to choose their contestant. Students entering the same type of paper should form a team and enter only one contestant. Ask them to cut the paper as directed in the original experiment and give it a name. Have them fill a glass with one inch of water for their strip. When you say "Go," tell them to place their strip in and let the race begin. Assign other students the role of timers for each cup. If there are more than six entries, run several time trials with a few contestants in each. Congratulate the champion!*

TREE CLIMBERS

*Do you want to see water climb the walls, to heights of 60 feet or more? Just go out and look at some trees. Where's the water you ask? It's climbing the cell walls, inside the tree! All the adjacent cells make up a complex circulatory system within the tree. Water is attracted to the large surface area of these cells, and because of its property of **adhesion** (the tendency to adhere to different surfaces), it readily sticks and pulls itself up. Because water is also **cohesive** (the tendency to stick together in drops rather then spreading out randomly), the drops will follow the leaders of the pack wherever they go. If you could look inside the wood, you'd see columns of water sticking to and climbing the cell walls from the roots to the tips of the branches, right into the leaves. Water's ability to rise to the top is called **capillary action**.*

Sink or Float?

WATER WIZARD LEARNING STATION

 Student Directions for
Sink or Float?

1. Begin by guessing which of the items on the following list will sink and which will float. Record your guess in the proper column.

2. Now test your guess by experimenting with each item in the basin of water. Record the actual result.

3. Look around the room and find at least two more objects to guess, test and record your results. Why do some objects sink and some float?

OBJECT	SINK or FLOAT?	RESULTS
Wooden block		
Crayon		
Lemon		
Walnut in the shell		
Metal jar lid		
Pencil		
Golf ball		
Plastic comb		
Cotton ball		
Twist tie		

Objective: Students will learn about the concept of buoyancy.

Materials: Dish basin full of water; a collection of objects to use in the experiment (see list above for possible ideas).

Time Allotment: 5-10 minutes

Teacher Notes:
The wooden block, crayon, lemon, walnut in the shell, pencil, and twist tie, all float because they weigh less than the water that is pushing upwards beneath them. The metal jar lid may or may not float depending on how it is placed in the water. The cotton ball floats then sinks as it absorbs water. The plastic comb may sink or float, depending on what kind of plastic it is made of. The golf ball sinks.

Extensions:

a. *Have the students bring in an assortment of objects to perform buoyancy tests on. Ask them to try to surprise their classmates.*

b. *Ask the students to predict whether a raw egg will sink or float in a cup of water. Then have them test their prediction. Now have them add salt to the water, one teaspoonful at a time. What happens to the egg? Why?*

The egg will sink to the bottom of the cup. As the salt is added, the weight of the water increases, as does the upward pressure of the water, or its buoyancy. As more salt is added, the egg rises and floats because objects in salt water are more buoyant than objects in freshwater.

c. *One gallon of ocean water has 1/4 pound of salt in it. Have the students make a batch of salt water of similar concentration. Then have them test some of the objects that sink in freshwater. Any changes?*

BUOY OH BUOY!

Boats float on the ocean, you float in a swimming pool and a rubber duck floats in the bathtub. But did you ever wonder why? The ability to stay afloat is caused by the balancing of forces — the water pressure pushing up and the weight of an object pushing down. An object floats when the buoyant force of the water directly beneath it is greater than its own weight. It sinks when its own weight is greater than the water's buoyant force.

Ship Shapes

WATER WIZARD LEARNING STATION

Student Directions for
Ship Shapes

1. Can you make play dough sink? How? Try it.

2. Can you make the same ball float? How? How many ways can you mold this ball to keep it floating? Describe or draw your different play dough shapes.

3. The weight of the play dough did not change. What did you change about the play dough? Can you explain why things float?

4. Now try using beans as cargo in a play dough boat. Which shape do you think can hold the most beans? How many? Make predictions then test your boat designs.

Objective: Students will learn how shape, size and weight affect an object's buoyancy.

Materials: Play dough (see recipe, page 256); dried beans; dish basin full of water.

Time Allotment: 10-15 minutes

Teachers Notes:

Step #1: A ball or lump of play dough will sink.

Step #2: Any boat-like shape will float, from flat square barges to canoes to deeply keeled boats.

Step #3: The boat shape increases the volume of the play dough. The weight of the play dough boat plus the air inside can be supported by the buoyant force of the water underneath.

Extension:

a. *Ask the students to try floating a collection of jar lids and empty tin cans of various heights. Ask them to predict how they will float in the water. Will they ride high or low? Will they tip to one side? Have them draw their predictions for the different lids and cans and then test them. Ask them what will happen to each of the cans if they are loaded with cargo. Will there be a difference in the way they float as they are loaded? How much cargo will sink the boat? Have them make predictions then test them using marbles as cargo.*

Short can and lids float upright. Empty tall cans float at an angle. As tall cans are loaded with cargo, they begin to float upright. The more cargo in a can the deeper in the water it floats. An unbalanced load can make a can sink. If the cargo floats the can low enough to take on water, it will sink.

SINKING BALLS *and* FLOATING BOATS

It's hard to believe huge steel boats float. Long ago, people would have doubted that such boats could. But way back in 200 B.C., a Greek mathematician named Archimedes would have said "I told you so." According to the Archimedes principle, the key to floating is the amount of water displaced. He discovered that the weight of water displaced by a floating object was exactly equal to the weight of that object. Even though a ball of metal sinks, if that same ball could be spread out in a boat shape, it would float. As the volume increases, the object displaces more water. Air fills the space inside the boat shape, and air is lighter than water. When the weight of water displaced equals the weight of the metal and air inside the boat, the buoyant force of the water takes over, supporting and floating the metal boat. Empty boats float higher in the water, heavy boats full of cargo float lower in the water. The differing amount of water displaced affects how they float but not whether they float. But if compressed back into a ball again, the amount of water displaced is far less than the weight of the metal, and down it sinks. Kerplunk.

PLAY DOUGH RECIPE
3/4 c. flour
1/2 c. salt
1 1/2 tsp. powdered alum*
1 1/2 tsp. vegetable oil
1/2 c. boiling water
food coloring (optional)

Mix the dry ingredients. Combine the wet ingredients then add to the dry mixture. If desired, add several drops of food coloring to the wet ingredients. This makes 1 - 2 batches.

available from a pharmacy/drugstore

Liquids in Suspense
WATER WIZARD LEARNING STATION

Student Directions for
Liquids in Suspense

1. Look at the three cups. Gently shake each cup from side to side, being careful not to spill any liquid.

2. Note the consistency and thickness of the liquids and record your observations. Can you guess the identity of the liquids?

3. What do you think will happen if you combine a few drops of each liquid in a test tube? Will they mix? Or remain separate? If they form separate layers, which will be on top, in the middle and on the bottom? Record your prediction.

4. Using an eyedropper, add one liquid at a time to the test tube. Tilt the tube and let it run down along the side of the tube. Wait until each settles before adding another. Observe and record the results.

5. Which liquid is the most dense? Which is the least? Why?

Objective:
Students will learn how liquids of different densities interact with one another.

Materials: A clear plastic cup filled with water and labelled #1; a clear plastic cup filled with the same amount of corn syrup, labelled #2; a clear plastic cup filled with the same amount of oil, labelled #3; three eye droppers; test tubes.

Time Allotment: 5-10 minutes

Teacher Notes:
Step #5: When oil, water and corn syrup are combined, they will separate out in three layers. Oil is the least dense of the three liquids and will float on top. Corn syrup is the most dense and will sink to the bottom. Water will form the middle layer.

Extensions:

a. *Provide a scale and let the students weigh equal volumes of these three liquids. Ask the students if they think the weights will be the same or different. Can they make a correlation between weight and density?*

If you weighed equal volumes of these three liquids, oil would be the lightest and corn syrup the heaviest.

b. *Bring in a variety of other common liquids (milk, juice, rubbing alcohol, liquid soap, honey, syrup, soda, chocolate syrup, vinegar). Randomly label them. Have the students make predictions and then test the density of these liquids compared to the original three liquids tested (oil, water, corn syrup). Be sure to discuss **miscibility** of liquids, or the ability of liquids to dissolve or mix together. For liquids that are miscible, how can they test their density?*

Many liquids are miscible in water so they will mix instead of forming layers. Often they can be compared with cooking oil to get layering Equal volumes of the liquids can be weighed to reveal their density.

THROUGH THICK *and* THIN

Thick as a milk shake or thin as water, all liquids have their own specific density. In other words, a similar volume of one liquid is heavier or denser than another. Denser liquids have more buoyancy and lighter, less dense liquids will float on them. That's why it is necessary to shake up salad dressing before pouring it on your salad. The oil and vinegar don't mix because they have different densities, forming distinct liquid layers in the jar. Shaking the jar temporarily mixes them and blends the flavors.

Motion Potion

WATER WIZARD LEARNING STATION

 Student Directions for
Motion Potion

1. Fill one cup with ice water, one cup with tap water and one cup with hot water. Allow the cups to sit a moment until the water appears still.

2. What do you think will happen to a drop of food coloring when it is added to each of the three cups of water? Record your predictions.

3. Now carefully add the food coloring to each cup. Food coloring will stain, so handle with care. In which cup does the food coloring move the fastest? The slowest? Describe the movement of the food coloring in each of the cups.

4. Can you guess why? What happens to the food coloring in the three cups after one minute?

Objective:
Students will learn about the molecular properties of water at different temperatures.

Materials: Three clear cups; food coloring; a container of ice water; a container of tap water; a container of hot water.

Time Allotment: 5-10 minutes

Teacher Notes:
Step #3: The food coloring disperses very quickly throughout the cup of hot water. It moves very slowly in the cold water.

Extension:

a. *Working in pairs, have the students fill two cups half full of ice water and two cups 1/3 full of hot tap water. Ask them to color the cups of hot water with one drop of food coloring. Have them gently shake these to quickly disperse the coloring. Ask the students what will happen when they pour the first cup of colored hot water into the first cup of ice water, and the second cup of ice water into the second cup of colored hot water. Have them record their predictions and experiment to find the results.*

Hot and cold water have different densities — hot water is less dense than cold water. When hot water is poured on cold water, it will remain in a distinct layer on top of the cold water. Eventually the temperatures will equalize and the food coloring will disperse throughout the cup. When the cold water is poured on hot water, it will sink to the bottom and mix with the hot colored water. Using this information, ask the students to discuss the implications of cold spring runoff into relatively warmer lakes and ponds.

GOOD VIBRATIONS

*Don't look now but the molecules in your glass of water are moving! It's true. Just imagine a complex game of pinball, with many balls whizzing about, this way and that, bumping into each another and flying off in different directions. The hotter the water, the farther apart the molecules are and the faster they move. In fact, the molecular collisions in boiling water can be so strong that they send some molecules flying off as steam or water vapor. As water cools, the molecular motion slows. In ice water, the molecules are vibrating very slowly and are packed together. When frozen solid as ice, the molecules join to form nearly immobile six-sided crystalline structures. By adding a drop of dye to water you can visualize this molecular motion. The dye gets mixed throughout the glass by the action of the molecules, without any stirring from you. This molecular mixing is called **diffusion**.*

Ice Capers

WATER WIZARD LEARNING STATION

Student Directions for
Ice Capers

1. Observe the ice and water in the two cups. Do you think they will weigh the same? If not, which one will be heavier? Record your predictions.

2. Weigh each cup and record the weight of each. How can you explain the results?

3. Mark where you think the water level will be when the cup of ice melts.

4. What happens when the ice melts and why?

Objective:
Students will be introduced to the properties of frozen water.

Materials: Cup of frozen water; cup of the same amount of liquid water; scale.

Time Allotment: 5-10 minutes

Teacher Notes:
Step #2: An equal volume of ice will weigh less than the same amount of water. When water freezes, it expands.

Step #3: When the ice cubes melt the water level will be lower.

Step #4: Ice floats on water as it weighs less or is less dense than liquid water. When the ice melts, the volume of water is less than the previous volume of ice.

Extension:

a. *Have the students add three or four ice cubes to an empty cup. Ask them to predict what will happen to the ice cubes when water is added. Have them fill the cup 3/4 full with water and compare the results to their predictions. Have them mark the present water level in their cups. Ask them if the water level will stay the same, be lower or higher when the ice melts. Record their predictions, then compare and discuss the actual results.*

A SINKING FEELING

Most liquids expand when heated and contract when cooled. When heated, water expands, following this rule, but as it cools it does something unique. Initially, its molecules contract, moving closer and closer together. At 39° Fahrenheit (4°C) the molecules can't move any closer together and liquid water is at its greatest density. As the temperature continues to drop, the molecules now begin to expand! At 32° Fahrenheit (0°C), they freeze into ice, a solid crystalline structure. This expansion to a solid makes ice less dense than very cold water. It accounts for the unique ability of solid ice to float on liquid water! In winter water expands and freezes forming ice that can cover the whole surface of a lake. The cold water beneath it is protected from the freezing air and kept at a stable temperature. A whole lake never freezes from the top to bottom, only the top several inches. Spring warms the surface and melts the ice. As it melts, it becomes more dense and sinks, mixing with the water below. This is spring turnover. During the summer months, the warm sun heats the upper layers of the lake without affecting the lower layers. Warm water is less dense, and it floats on top of the cooler water below it. The cooler, denser water remains trapped below. That is until the fall winds blow. These winds cool the surface of the water, separating the lake into upper and lower layers. As the surface water cools, it becomes more dense and slowly sinks, mixing with the water below. This is fall turnover. Seasonal turnover is an important process that mixes the water in the lake twice a year, keeping it from becoming stagnant.

Disappearing Act

Student Directions for
Disappearing Act

1. In the labelled cups, put in one teaspoon of the appropriate powder. Which ones will dissolve in water? Which ones will merely float throughout the water forming a suspension? Mark your predictions.

2. Fill the cups with water and stir with a spoon. Wait a moment until the mixtures settle. Using an eyedropper, draw off some of the mixture. Hold it up to the light and examine it. Which mixtures dissolved? Which ones formed a suspension? Record your results.

3. What will happen to these solutions if they are left for an hour? Overnight? Until they evaporate? Make your predictions and test them.

POWDER	GUESS	RESULT
Powdered sugar		
Cornstarch		
Baking soda		
Cocoa		
Flour		
Salt		

Objective:
Students will learn about solutions and suspensions.

Materials: Container of water; plastic spoons; plastic cups labelled with permanent marker on masking tape; selection of powders to be tested (see chart above for possible ideas); eyedropper.

Time Allotment: 10-15 minutes

Teacher Notes:
Step #2: The powdered sugar and baking soda dissolve in water; the salt partially dissolves, forming a cloudy solution; cocoa does not dissolve and forms a suspension; flour and cornstarch mix with water to form a thick paste.

Extensions:

a. *Have the students predict how many teaspoons of sugar can be dissolved in a cup of water. Then have them test their guess by adding a teaspoon at a time to a glass of water.*

Several teaspoons of sugar can be added. When no more sugar can be dissolved it is called a saturated solution.

b. *Have the students make "òobleck." Have them mix one part cornstarch with four parts water. Ask them to describe the mixture. Does it form a thick paste or a runny liquid? Have them scoop up a handful of the mixture. Any surprises? Can they explain them?*

The cornstarch-water mixture appears to be a thick paste but when picked up it becomes thin and runny. Why it works the way it does remains a mystery. Oòbleck belongs to a class of substances called colloids, which can exhibit two states of matter at one time. In this case, oòbleck acts as both a liquid and a solid. Other common colloids we encounter everyday are: smoke, mayonnaise, Styrofoam, whipped cream, pudding, paint, jelly and butter.

PRESTO CHANGO!

*There is a bit of magic in science. You can be a magician and make sugar disappear. Just stir a teaspoon full into a glass of water and presto! But did it really disappear? If you taste the water you will see that it is sweet. The sugar is actually broken down or **dissolved** by the water. The water molecules break apart the molecules in sugar and surround them, forming a uniformly colored mixture called a **solution**. When given enough time, water is said to have the ability to dissolve almost anything. Because of this property, water has been called the **universal solvent**. Some substances can not be dissolved immediately and form a cloudy mixture scientists call a **suspension**. Particles float throughout the suspensions. If left to sit for a period of time, the particles will sink to the bottom. They need the action of water over a long period of time to disappear.*

The Pressure is On

WATER WIZARD LEARNING STATION

Student Directions for
The Pressure is On

1. Cover the three holes of the milk carton securely with masking tape. Place the milk carton in the dish basin and fill the carton with water.

2. What do you think will happen if you remove the tape covering the holes? What do you think the water will look like when it comes out of each of the holes? Draw a picture of what you imagine the three streams of water will look like.

3. Now, holding the carton up over the dish basin, remove the masking tape. Observe the path of water coming from each hole. Draw a picture of the three streams.

4. Why do you think the water comes out of each hole differently?

Objective:
Students will learn about the relationship between water pressure and depth.

Materials: Dish basin; empty plastic milk carton punctured with three holes in a vertical line; tape; gallon jug of water; funnel.

Time Allotment: 5-10 minutes

Teacher Notes:
Step #4: The water shoots out the farthest from the bottom hole because it has the greatest amount of pressure on it. This water has the pressure of all the water and air above it. The top hole has the least amount of water and air above it, therefore less pressure, so it just dribbles out.

Extension:

a. *Give the students milk jugs which have three holes in a horizontal line. What will the water look like as it comes out of these holes if they perform the same experiment? Compare the results to their predictions and discuss their explanations. For an added dimension to this extension, have the students try pinching the streams of water together to form one thick stream. Be sure the holes are at least 1/4 inch apart. Do they think it is possible? Why or why not?*

The water streams will be the same out of all the holes because the pressure at any given depth is equal. The cohesive properties of the water will cause the streams to stick together.

DOWN DEEP

"A pint's a pound the world around." Have you ever heard that farming expression? Dairy farmers use it to describe the weight of a pint of milk. A pint of water weighs about the same. Since liquids have weight, they exert pressure which increases with depth. Imagine holding a gallon of water on your head. How much does it weigh? (8 lbs!) Now stack another one on top that, then another, and another? You can feel the pressure can't you? The pressure at the bottom of the ocean is tremendous. That's why deep sea diving tanks and suits, submarines, and other underwater vehicles are designed to withstand and protect those inside from very great pressures.

Mystery Man

WATER WIZARD LEARNING STATION

 Student Directions for
Mystery Man

1. This is Waldo, the Cartesian diver! Gently squeeze the sides of the bottle and observe Waldo. What happens? What happens when you let go?

2. Try to make your own Cartesian diver using the extra materials. (Work over the dish basin to avoid spilling on the floor.)

3. Can you explain how and why Waldo works?

Objective:

Students will learn what happens to air and water when pressure is applied.

Materials:

Two clear plastic soda containers with lids; two eye droppers; jug of water; dish basin. (Fill one eye dropper with water until it floats vertically in one of the soda bottles. Be sure to leave some air space in the bottle. Close the lid securely and test to see if the eye dropper sinks by squeezing the sides of the bottle. Adjust the water level in the bottle accordingly.)

Time Allotment: 5-10 minutes

Teacher Notes:

Step #3: Waldo floats because the combination of air and water within him is equal to the buoyant force of the surrounding water. When you squeeze the closed bottle, you increase the pressure on both the water and the air in the bottle. Air is compressible but water is not. More water enters into Waldo as the air compresses, and his density and weight increase. It is now greater than the buoyant force of the water and he sinks. When you release the bottle, you take the pressure off the air, and the air returns to its original volume. The extra water is forced out of Waldo. He returns to his original density and weight and floats again.

Extensions

a. *Have the students experience the stored energy in compressed air. Divide the class into pairs and give each pair a plastic liter soda bottle without a lid, a drinking straw and some clay. Ask them to fill the bottle two thirds full of water and mark the level. Direct them to pack the clay around the drinking straw and insert this into the bottle opening to create an air tight seal. With the straw beneath the surface of the water, have one student blow as much air as he or she can into the bottle. When the student cannot blow any more air into the bottle, direct them to quickly seal the opening with their finger. What happened to the water level? (It remains the same.) What happened to the air added to the bottle? (It was compressed in the original space.) What will happen when the student removes his or her finger? Record predictions then try it. The water comes spurting out of the top of the straw like a fountain! The compressed air has stored energy. When the pressure is released it pushes down on the water, forcing it out through the opening in the straw.*

SUBMARINE SECRETS

Everyone loves a good mystery, and water science is full of them. For instance, how can a submarine both float and sink? And how can fish swim at different depths, sinking lower and floating higher at will? Are they defying the scientific properties of water or obeying them? A good aquatic detective can unravel these mysteries and more. Here are some clues. Air is lighter than water. Air is also compressible, but water is not. That means air can be squeezed or compressed to take up less space. When the pressure is released, the air rushes back to its original volume. If you try to squeeze water into a smaller space it resists and pushes everything out of its way until it has enough room. So if air and water are within an en-closed space together, the water will compress the air when pressure is put upon them. But when the pressure is released, the air will force the water back where it came from. Case closed.

A submarine has special chambers that allow it to both float and sink. There are special ballast tanks that take in water. As water fills these tanks, the sub becomes heavier and sinks. It also has special tanks where compressed air is stored. When the sub is ready to surface, the compressed air from these tanks is forced into the ballast tanks. It shoots the water out making the sub lighter. As its weight changes, it rises and floats to the surface

As for fish, they have special swimming bladders that help them float and sink. These bladders are filled with air and can be expanded or contracted by the muscles surrounding them. As the bladders expand, the volume of the air in the fish increases, decreasing the density of the fish, and it floats higher. When the bladders compress, the fish becomes more dense, and down it sinks.

Water Cycle Relay

Objective:
Students will review the important steps in the water cycle.

Grade Level: 3-6

Groupings: Two teams

Materials: Two trays of ice cubes; two spoons; tape; two sets of vocabulary words on slips of paper (see step #3); large *The Hydrologic Cycle* (page 272); bucket.

Time Allotment: 20 minutes

Directions:

1. Divide the class into two teams. Show them *The Hydrologic Cycle*, pointing out the missing vocabulary words that describe the steps in the cycle. Explain that they will fill in these blanks with the missing words in the course of a water cycle relay race.

2. Pass out a spoon and a tray of ice cubes to each group. As part of the relay, each group will place an ice cube on the spoon and pass both from the back of the line to the front of the line. Let the groups practice passing the spoon with the ice cube on it.

3. Next, give each group a set of the following nine vocabulary words written on slips of paper: **evaporation, condensation, cloud, precipitation, river, infiltration, ground water, evapotranspiration,** and **hydrologic cycle.** Have the groups attach a piece of tape to each slip of paper. Ask the groups to discuss the words, reviewing their meanings and where they fit in the water cycle exhibit.

4. Explain that you will read a matching water cycle riddle for each of the vocabulary words. The students must quietly decide among their group which word best fits the riddle. The last person in line tapes the slip of paper with the matching word to the bottom of the spoon and places the ice cube in the spoon. He or she then passes the entire spoon to the next person and so on down the line. The person at the head

Extensions:

a. *Have the students create a mini water cycle in a plastic sandwich bag. Have them work in small groups. Ask them to place a mark on a small plastic cup one inch up from the bottom. Demonstrate how to hold the plastic bag at an angle so that one corner of the opening edge is at the top and tape a cup to the middle of the inside of the bag. Then have the groups tape their cups to the inside of their bags. Have them fill the cup with water to the line Ask them to seal the bag carefully and securely tape the closed bag to a sunny window. What do they think will happen to the water in the cup over time? What will the inside of the bag look like? Ask them to record their observations at various time intervals for the next several days. Have them measure the amount of water inside the cup and bag at the end of the experiment. Did it change?*

b. *Have your students make a terrarium to view the water cycle. Have the students bring in large size plastic soda bottles with black bases. The black bottom is removed and used as the base of the terrarium. The clear top quarter of each bottle is then cut off and inverted, fitting tightly into the planter base. Divide the class into pairs. Give each pair a base and clear top. Have them line the base with small pebbles and add potting soil until it is 3/4 full. Ask them to collect moss and some small plants to plant in the soil. Have them water the soil lightly and securely put on the clear top of the terrarium. Put the terrariums on a sunny windowsill and observe.*

Directions: (continued)

of the line walks quickly to the exhibit at the front of the room with the spoon and ice cube, places the ice cube in a bucket and tapes the word to the correct spot on the cycle, then, returns to the end of the line and the race begins again with a another riddle.

5. Before beginning the race, review the rules for the relay. No one may touch the ice cube after it has been placed on the spoon until it reaches the head of the line. That means no holding it as it is transferred up the line or while carrying it to the exhibit. If it falls off, it starts from the back of the line again. If the students are having trouble, let them start the ice cube where it fell off.

6. Invite the students to help decide how points should be awarded and record these figures on the blackboard. Ask them to decide the number of points to be given to the team that finishes first, the team that selects the correct vocabulary word and the correct placement of the word in *The Hydrologic Cycle.*

7. Let the races begin! The winner is the team with the most points.

RECYCLED WATER

If water droplets could talk to one another, they might be heard to say, "Hey haven't I seen you some where before?" The drops that drip out of your faucet today, could have fallen as rain during the time of the dinosaurs, been frozen in the glaciers during the ice age or risen as steam from your great-great Grandmother's tea kettle. Water just keeps going around and around. The amount on the Earth today is the same amount that has always been here. It is the ultimate in recycling. So next time you pour yourself a glass of water, think of where it might have been and where it might be going.

c. *As a homework assignment, send the students on a scavenger hunt. Have them look for and record water in its different forms in and around their homes*

THE HYDROLOGIC CYCLE

Below the surface of the Earth
In between particles of dirt
That's where this water is found
Saturating everything deep underground
Groundwater

In between and all around
Through the soil without a sound
Water seeping down down down
Slowly moving underground
Infiltration/Percolation

Heat from the sun makes water rise
Up as vapor to the skies
Evaporation

Cumulus, stratus, cirrus too,
Water vapor visible in skies of blue
Cloud

Down is the direction this water falls
As crystals, drips or even balls
Precipitation

Once a gas but then it's changed
Into a liquid to be seen again
Condensation

From the pores of plants
water vapor escapes
Into the air without a trace
Evapotranspiration

I start as a trickle and then I grow
Picking up speed as down I go
Over the surface from land to the sea
Obeying the laws of gravity
River

Water going round and round
Changing form but not amount
The Hydrologic Cycle

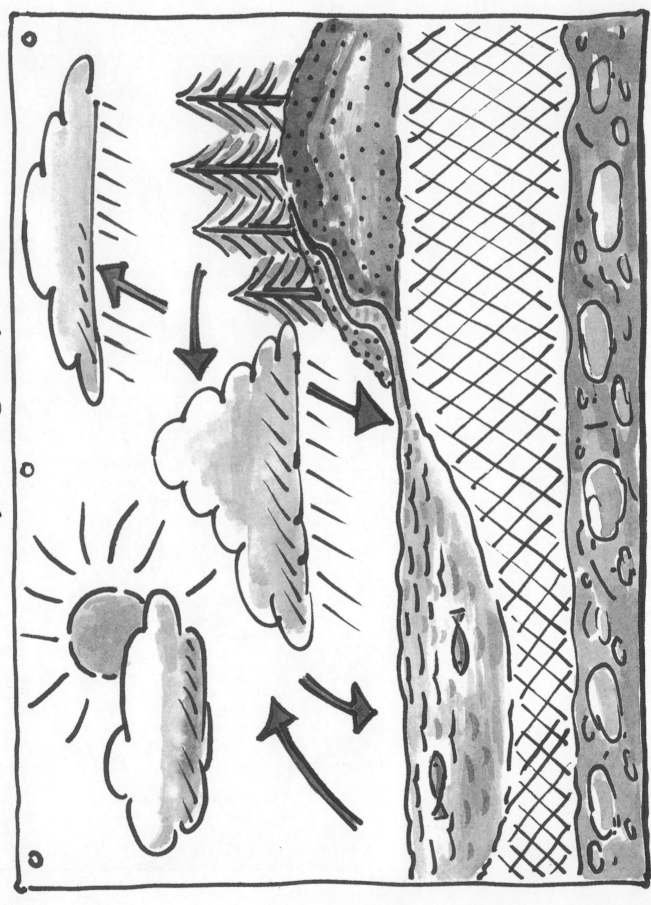

Water Babies

Objective:
Students will learn about the different stages in various water animals' life cycles and will recognize juvenile and adult stages in different animal groups.

Grade Level: 2-6

Groupings: Entire class

Materials: Students' baby pictures; *Animal Cards* (see page 275 - 76) depicting water animals in their juvenile and adult stages.

Time Allotment: 20 minutes

Extension:
a. *Watch and study the life cycles of some common animals such as frogs, salamanders, mealworms, butterflies, or mosquitos that undergo metamorphosis.*

Directions:

1. Ask the students to bring in baby pictures of themselves for homework. Remind them not to show anyone their picture, as the class will be using them for a guessing activity.

2. Collect the pictures and display them together in a central location. Explain to the students that people are mammals and mammal babies look like the adults they become. Ask the students what things change in people's and other mammals' appearances as they get older. What features tend to remain the same?

3. Explain to the students that you will be holding up their baby pictures one at a time. They will need to look at each picture carefully and try to match it to the correct classmate. Remind them to look at the features which tend to remain the same. Continue until you've matched all the pictures.

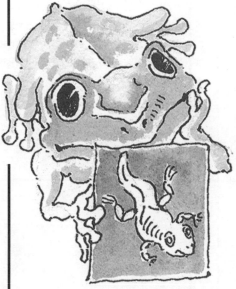

4. Tell the students they will now be doing a matching activity with water animals. Explain that in some groups of animals, the young look very similar to the adults and may only differ in size. In other groups, the young look very different from the adults. These animals are said to undergo **metamorphosis,** or a change in form. Can the children think of any examples? (Caterpillar to butterfly, tadpole to frog, etc.)

5. Pass out cards to the students with pictures of different water animals. Ask the students not to show their cards to each other. Explain that some of the cards are pictures of adult animals and others are pictures of their young. Have

MIRACLE GROWTH

*When you were born, you looked like a much smaller version of the person you are today. The same goes for many other animals, but for some the change from baby to adult is dramatic. Sometimes so dramatic you might not even recognize that they are the same animal! This change in form is called **metamorphosis**. Take the bullfrog sitting on a nearby log. He and other amphibians hatch from gelatinous eggs into gilled tadpoles without legs. Over time they change shape, growing lungs and legs and croaking with the other frogs in the pond. Some insects, like the dragonfly, experience **gradual or incomplete metamorphosis**. They hatch as flightless aquatic nymphs, or naiads, which vaguely resemble their adult counterparts. They gradually increase in size, grow wings and complete the change into flying adults. Those who experience **complete metamorphosis** undergo a truly amazing change. Many insects, including butterflies and mosquitos, hatch from eggs into larvae whose primary purpose is to eat and grow. When they reach a certain size, they form pupae, inside which miraculous transformations occur. Complex changes rearrange their whole body structure, and the creatures that emerge look nothing like their former larval selves! Talk about a short break working wonders!*

the students look at their picture carefully for clues to which stage of the life cycle their card represents. Ask them to divide themselves into two groups according to their card — one for adults, the other for juveniles.

6. Within these groups, have the students show their cards to each other. Have the students who represent the adult animals discuss what they think their animal looked like when it was a juvenile. Did it look similar or did it undergo metamorphosis? Have the students with the pictures of the juveniles do the same. What might their animal look like as an adult?

7. When the students have finished their discussions, bring the two groups together. Explain that each of them has a match in the other group. Have the students stand in two lines facing each other. Have them all hold up their cards simultaneously. Give them time to observe all the cards. When you say, "Go," have each student find his or her match.

8. Review their choices. Which ones were easiest to match? Which ones were more difficult? Which types of animals look similar as juveniles and adults? (Mammals, reptiles, and birds.) Which animals undergo metamorphosis? (Insects and amphibians.)

Baby Animal Cards

TADPOLE

TURTLE

FISH FRY

MALLARD DUCKLING

DRAGONFLY NYMPH

BEAVER KIT

MOSQUITO LARVAE

WATER PENNY

SNAIL

CRAYFISH

CADDISFLY LARVAE

DIVING BEETLE LARVAE

Adult Animal Cards

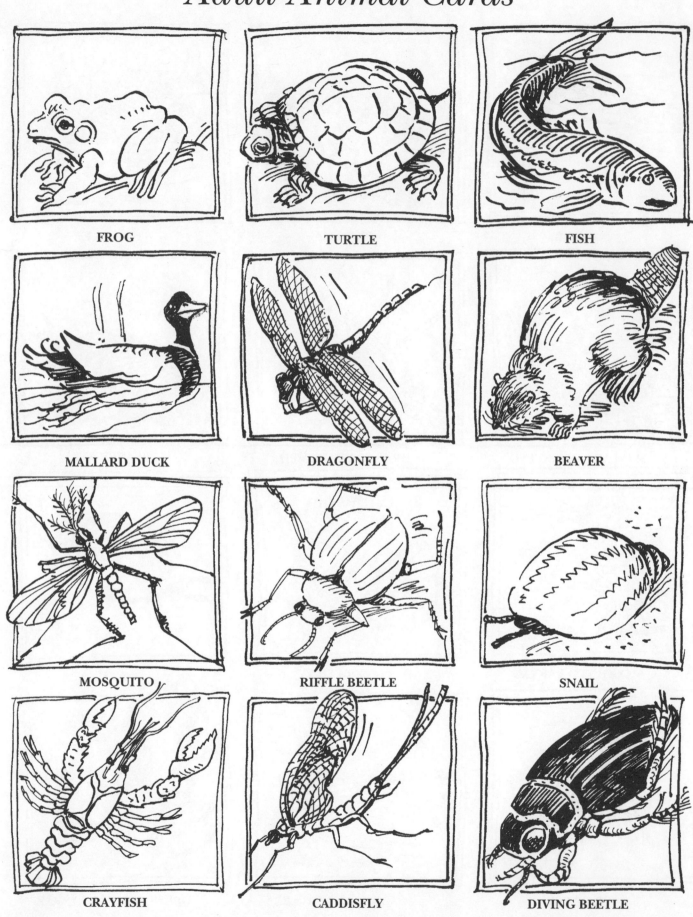

FROG

TURTLE

FISH

MALLARD DUCK

DRAGONFLY

BEAVER

MOSQUITO

RIFFLE BEETLE

SNAIL

CRAYFISH

CADDISFLY

DIVING BEETLE

Critter Clues

Objective:
Students will learn how aquatic organisms can be indicators of water quality.

Grade Level: 3-6

Groupings: Small groups

Materials: Pictures of different bodies of water; *Biotic Index of Water Quality* (page 280); plastic sandwich bags with a selection of macro-invertebrate pictures cut and duplicated from the Biotic Index; water critter costume or mask (optional, see step #2).

Time Allotment: 20 minutes

Directions:
1. Show the students pictures of different bodies of fresh water: lakes, rivers, streams, ponds, puddles. Include some pictures that show pollution. Ask for their impressions of the quality of the water. Would they like to visit there? Would they like to go swimming or boating? Does any of the water look clean enough to drink? What do they think they would find living in these different bodies of water? Record their list of organisms. Would they expect to find the same things living in each of the bodies of water? Why or why not?

2. Explain that good indicators of water quality are the small plants and animals who live there. The organisms scientists look for are **benthic macroinvertebrates.** You may make a costume or mask depicting one of the critters by enlarging their picture from the *Biotic Index of Water Quality* onto poster board. Use this critter to introduce the class to the world of macroinvertebrates and to introduce how and why they are important indicators of water quality. (See *Listen to Lydia*, page 279, for ideas). Use an aquatic field guide to help with the critter's introduction.

3. Divide the children into small groups. Pass out a *Biotic Index of Water Quality* to each group. Ask them to find the organism they were just introduced to. In what quality of water are they typically found? Explain that one organism is not enough to classify the water quality of a body of water. Scientists need to look at many organisms and consider the types and amounts of each. Tell the students they will now get a chance to use the *Biotic Index* to analyze some fictional bodies of water.

Extensions:

a. *Have your students use field guides to write descriptions of other benthic macroinvertebrates. Have them create costumes and introduce their critter to the class.*

b. *Have the class analyze a local body of water. Visit the area and record general impressions of the water and surrounding area. Sample the water using wire mesh kitchen strainers as a dip nets. Look for organisms living in aquatic vegetation and samples of mud. Bring at least two buckets for collecting. Use one for sorting critters from the water and mud, then transfer them to a second bucket filled with clear water. Have the students count and record the number of each type of critter. Using the **Biotic Index,** determine the quality of the water. How could they maintain or improve the water quality?*

FITNESS TEST *for* WATER

Who lives in a body of water depends on the physical features of the water. Several of these features are easy to measure and give important clues to water quality.

Temperature *Most aquatic creatures are cold-blooded, so surrounding water temperature determines and limits their growth and metabolism. Colder water has more oxygen in it, and likewise, warmer water has less oxygen in it. Using*

Directions: (continued)

4. Give each group a plastic sandwich bag containing a selection of pictures of benthic macroinvertebrates (see *Guidelines for Creating Sample Bags,* below). This water sample bag represents the diversity of organisms that were collected from a body of water. Have the students sort these organisms by type and record the amounts of each. Then have the students analyze this information using the *Biotic Index* to determine the water quality.

5. When all groups have rated their body of water, have the groups with similar ratings compare their findings. Have the students discuss variations and similarities. As a class, share the results from all the groups.

GUIDELINES *for* CREATING SAMPLE BAGS

Enlarge the pictures of the various benthic macroinvertebrates from the Biotic Index. Make 10-15 copies of each critter and mount these on index cards and label them. Make up sample bags by adding these cards to plastic sandwich bags based on the following general guidelines.

BODY OF WATER	GROUP 1	GROUP 2	GROUP 3
Good quality	Majority	Several	A few
Wide Ranging Quality	A few	Majority	A few
Poor Quality	None to a few	A few	Majority

Good quality water has a high diversity of critters living in it. A sample bag would contain several different types of critters, possibly from all three groups with the majority in Group 1. There is usually a low diversity of critters in poor quality water. A sample bag would contain only a few different critters.

aquarium thermometers, have students take water temperatures in different areas of a body of water.

pH   Most aquatic animals thrive in water whose pH is in the neutral range (6.5-8.5). Acid rain is the main contributor to aquatic pH changes. Using pH paper, have students test a body of water in several locations, collect and test rain water, and compare readings.

Turbidity   Turbid water is cloudy water. Loose soil, sediments, and pollutants from erosion, runoff and waste water contribute to turbidity, as well as algal growth caused by excess nutrients such as phosphorus and nitrogen. The effect of turbid water on water quality is complex. Less light can enter, inhibiting plant growth, which in turn limits food supply and reduces oxygen levels. Suspended sediments also absorb heat, causing temperatures to rise, further reducing oxygen levels and diverse life forms. Create a Secchi Disk by painting a black "X" on an 8-inch diameter jar lid. Punch a hole in the center and suspend it from a long rope. Have students lower the disk into standing water until it is no longer visible, then direct them to slowly raise it until they can just barely distinguish the "X" mark. Have them grasp the string at the surface and measure the distance between the water surface and the disk. Compare readings in several places.

LISTEN *to* LYDIA

Meet Lydia. Her real name is <u>Plathemis lydia</u>. That's Latin for White-tailed Dragonfly. She is one of the many **benthic macroinvertebrates** who live in water. **Benthic** means bottom dwelling. Look in the sediment and debris at the bottom of a pond to find Lydia or her close relatives. **Macro** means she's big enough to be seen without a microscope, and **invertebrates** describes a whole group of critters without internal backbones unlike you and me. Most benthic macroinvertebrates are insects in one or another stage of their life cycles. Lydia is just a young nymph, but through gradual metamorphosis, she'll become a dragonfly in a few years. Benthic macroinvertebrates are good storytellers, especially when it comes to water quality. Consider Lydia. She's been living in the same neighborhood for a few years, calling the muck at the bottom of Shelburne Pond home sweet home. She can tell you about the history of the pond during her lifetime because she and other benthic macroinvertebrates are sensitive to both physical and chemical changes in the water. Although fast enough to escape predators, even Lydia, with her own special form of jet propulsion, can't swim away from pollution. She tolerates it, but only to a certain point when she gets sick and dies. Some critters are more tolerant and even flourish as the water quality declines, while others die or disappear with the slightest change. The saying "the more the merrier" applies to benthic macroinvertebrates as well. The greater the variety that lives in any body of water, the healthier it is. So next time you scoop up some water critters, listen to their story.

Biotic Index of Water Quality

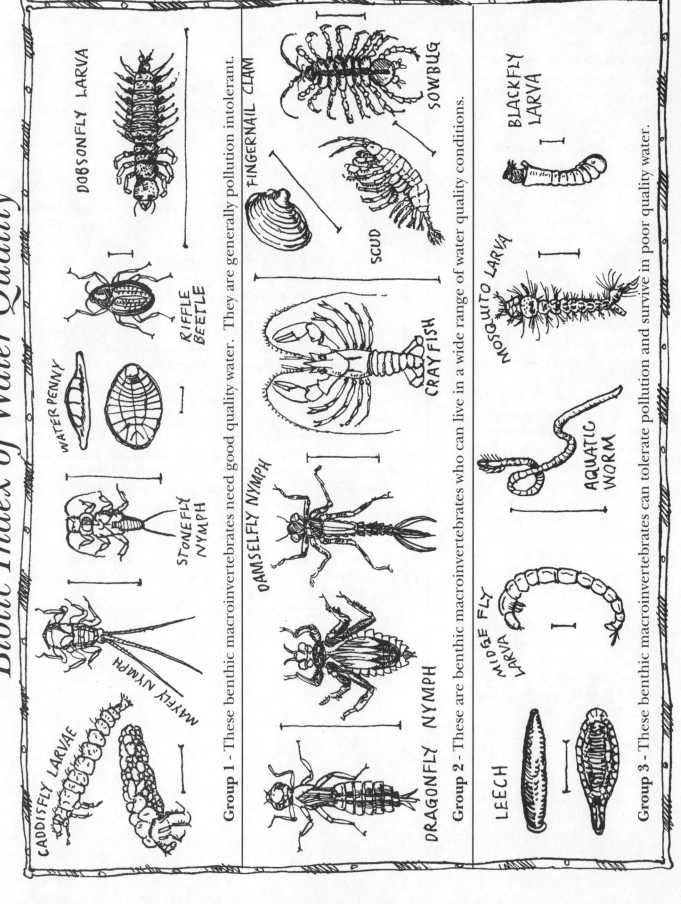

CADDISFLY LARVAE

MAYFLY NYMPH

STONEFLY NYMPH

WATER PENNY

RIFFLE BEETLE

DOBSONFLY LARVA

Group 1 - These benthic macroinvertebrates need good quality water. They are generally pollution intolerant.

DRAGONFLY NYMPH

DAMSELFLY NYMPH

CRAYFISH

FINGERNAIL CLAM

SCUD

SOWBUG

Group 2 - These are benthic macroinvertebrates who can live in a wide range of water quality conditions.

LEECH

MIDGE FLY LARVA

AQUATIC WORM

MOSQUITO LARVA

BLACKFLY LARVA

Group 3 - These benthic macroinvertebrates can tolerate pollution and survive in poor quality water.

I - bar line indicates actual size.

Where Has All the Water Gone?

Objective:
Students will learn about the relationship between world population distribution and global water usage.

Grade Level: 3-6

Groupings: Entire class

Directions:

1. Ask the students to name some important natural resources people use daily. List these on the board. Explain that they will be learning how a very important and scarce resource, water, is used around the globe. Ask the students to list the major continents or land masses. Bring out a globe or map of the world and locate them. Have the students place the paper cut-outs of the land masses on the floor in the proper configuration, leaving large spaces between them.

Materials: Paper cut-outs of the seven major land masses (see charts), cut to scale; index cards with continent names (see *World Population Percentages*, right, for number of each needed); paper cups; ten one-pint jars of lemonade.

Time Allotment: 20 minutes

Extensions:

a. *Brainstorm different methods people across the globe use to obtain their water. Explain that some people work very hard to carry their water from its source, some have to hand pump it from wells, while others simply turn on the tap. Divide the class into two groups. Each group will collect 20 gallons of water for their daily use. The only thing that*

2. Ask the students how they think the world population is distributed among these land masses. Where do they think the most people live? The least? Explain that the class will be divided to represent the population of each land mass based on global population percentages. Have each student draw an index card then stand near the matching land mass. Discuss the actual percentages and uneven distribution of people. Were the students surprised at any of the statistics?

WORLD POPULATION PERCENTAGES		
LAND MASS	**% OF WORLD POPULATION**	**# OF STUDENTS/ INDEX CARDS NEEDED (BASED ON CLASS OF 20)**
Africa	12.5	3
North/ Central America	8.0	1
South America	5.6	1
Asia	59.0	12
Europe	9.1	2
Oceania	0.5	0
Former Soviet Union	5.3	1

Extensions: (continued)

will differ between the groups is how they obtain their water. One group must hike to a spring to get their water. Place the water a distance away in several large containers to be carried back. (You might consider tinging this water brown with a drop of red and green food coloring.) The other group will pump their water from a well located nearby. To simulate the work involved, explain that they will get one gallon of water for every five push-ups done. When both groups have collected their 20 gallons, discuss the amount of work involved for each and the quality of their water. If they obtained their water in this way would it affect how they used water?

b. Do a similar activity based on the food available on different continents. You will need 38 cookies or crackers for your group of 20 students. (If you have more or fewer students, change the numbers/ratios accordingly.) Use the same cards as in the original activity to set the populations for the continents. Then divide the cookies between the continents/populations as follows: Africa receives 1 cookie; North and Central America receive 15; South America receives 10; Asia receives 4 1/2; Europe receives 6; and the former Soviet Union receives 1 1/2. Record the students' reactions to this uneven distribution of food. What if each person must have at least one cookie to survive? Ask the students how they could go about redistributing the food. See Francis Moore Lappé's book, DIET FOR A SMALL PLANET (Ballantine Books, 1984) or contact Food First/The Institute for Food and Development Policy (398 60th St., Oakland, CA, 94618, 510-654-4400) for more information on hunger issues around the world.

Directions: (continued)

3. Have the students now consider the fresh water used on each continent. Do they think fresh water usage is distributed evenly over the globe? Do areas with more people necessarily have more fresh water? Where do they think there is a great fresh water supply? Where would there be little fresh water? Can they name and locate any important large bodies of water on each continent? Or major deserts?

4. Explain that you will be distributing lemonade to each group based on the water usage for their land mass and that the students of each land mass must share the lemonade equally among themselves. Have one student from each land mass get their group's portion of the lemonade and cups. (See *World Water Use Percentages*, below.)

WORLD WATER USE PERCENTAGES

CONTINENT	% OF WORLD WATER USE	AMOUNT OF LEMONDADE
Africa	4.0	1 cup
North/Central America	18.0	2 pints
South America	4.0	1 cup
Asia	43.0	4 pints
Europe	22.0	2 pints
Oceania	0.5	0 pints
Former Soviet Union	9.0	1 pint

Water statistics gathered from World Resources 1992-93 (World Resources Institute, Washington, DC, 1992) and Gaia, Atlas of Planet Management (by Dr. Norman Meyers, Doubleday, London, 1993).

---

5. How do the students feel about the distribution of lemonade? Explain access to water differs from place to place and that on some land masses, some people may have as little as one gallon to use per day, while on other land masses, some people have more than 150 gallons available. Who has the least water? The most? Does the amount of water we use matter? Does it affect the rest of the world? Remind them that the amount of water on Earth never changes — the aquatic dinosaurs could have swum in the water we drink today. What are some threats to our water supply? And how can we protect it?

6. Let the students decide how all the jars of lemonade should be distributed for a class snack.

Water Watchers

Objective:
Students will learn about our dependence on water and the amount of water we use during the day.

Grade Level: 3-6

Groupings: Entire class, in pairs

Materials: Props to demonstrate how we use water such as toilet paper; toothbrush; box of laundry detergent; shampoo; dish drain; etc. and 100 plastic gallon jugs (if storage is a problem, cut out paper jugs instead).

Time Allotment: 30 minutes

Directions:
A few weeks in advance, ask students to bring in milk jugs from home, or visit a recycling center and gather a large quantity of jugs at one time.

1. Explain to the class that water is one of our most valuable resources. Briefly suggest a few of the obvious ways we depend on water: drinking, cooking, and washing. Tell the class they will be doing an exercise that will prove that we use far more water in the course of our daily lives than we realize.

2. Ask the students how much water they think they use in one day. Have them quietly think of ways they use water during the day. Ask them for some examples. Whenever a student mentions a water use, give him or her a prop to represent that use — for example, a toothbrush for brushing teeth, a roll of toilet paper for flushing the toilet, a box of laundry detergent for doing laundry.

3. After all the props have been handed out, pair the remaining students who don't have props with the students who have props. Explain that they should work as a team to decide how many gallons of water are needed to perform their task once during the day.

4. Show the students the collection of empty gallon milk jugs. Explain that once they have decided how many gallons it would take to perform their task, they should gather the appropriate number of jugs.

Extensions:

a. *Send home the:* **Water Usage Inventory** *and* **Average Water Required for Common Activities** *so students and their families can record the amount of water used in their homes for three days. Discuss the results in class. Did the chart help to change their families' behavior patterns? Did water use go up or down over time?*

b. *Calculate the amount of water that could be saved over a year if water saving practices were used. For example, brushing your teeth with the water running uses 2 gallons a day, or 1460 gallons a year. If you don't run the water, brushing your teeth uses 2 cups of water a day, or 46 gallons a year. That's a savings of 1414 gallons.*

Directions: (continued)

5. Designate a large area to display students' guesses. Have the students place their jugs in a line with their prop at the front of the line. For example, if students think brushing their teeth takes two gallons, they should put two jugs in a line with the toothbrush in the front of the line.

6. Give the class time to observe all the guesses, then review each guess. Have the students vote whether or not they agree with each guess. Get opinions as to whether they think each task requires more or less water than was guessed. Reveal the average amount actually used to perform each task once (see chart below).

7. Use the actual figures to tally the amount of water used in one day. Have the students add the figures on the chalkboard. Remind them that some tasks are done more than once a day, and they will need to consider this when calculating total daily usage. For example, if they brush their teeth twice a day, they will need to double the corresponding amount in their tally.

8. Discuss ways to cut down on water use for each task.

AVERAGE WATER REQUIRED
FOR COMMON ACTIVITIES
(in gallons)

Flushing the toilet: 2 - 5
Taking a bubble bath (full level): 30-50
Brushing teeth (tap running): 2
Taking a shower: 5 per minute
Washing clothes (full cycle): 30-60
Washing hands (tap running): 2
Drinking water: 1/2
Indoor sink faucet open: 3 - 4 gallon per minute
Indoor sink 1/2 open: 1 1/2 gallon per minute
Washing the dishes by hand (rinsing with tap running): 10-20
Using an automatic dish washer (full cycle): 12 - 15
Outdoor watering: 10 - 15 per minute
Preparing and cooking meals: 10 gallons
Washing the car: 50 - 100 gallons
Cleaning the house: 10 gallons

Water Usage Inventory

Today's Date: _____

Water Users please sign in: _____

You will be conducting a water use survey in your home, beginning each morning for two days. Each day, post an inventory sheet wherever water is used. Place a check mark in the proper column every time you use water at that location. At the end of each day, tally the amount of water used (refer to the chart provided).

BATHROOM

Flushing the toilet _____

Taking a shower (record time in shower) _____

Taking a tub bath _____

Tooth brushing _____

Face and hand washing/shaving (record time) _____

Other use of bathroom sink (record time) _____

KITCHEN

Hand washing dishes (record time and estimate amounts when using basins) _____

Running the dishwasher _____

Meal preparation (record time) _____

Drinking water (record amount) _____

Other use of sink (record time) _____

LAUNDRY/HOUSEHOLD

Doing the laundry (record water setting—low, medium or high—and number of loads) _____

Household cleaning (estimate amount used in buckets) _____

OUTDOORS

Watering lawn or garden (record time) _____

Car washing (record time and estimate amounts in buckets) _____

Other use of outdoor spigot (record time) _____

How much water was used: _____

As a family, brainstorm how you could conserve water? List your ideas here.

Compare the amounts of water used on the first and second days. Are there any differences? Why or why not?

How Much Water Do You Use?

• EXHIBIT •

Materials:

Poster board; markers; Exacto knife; small piece of fabric; Velcro tabs; ribbon; sponge.

Design:

1. On a large pieces of poster board, outline the main rooms inside a house where water is used — the bathroom, kitchen, and laundry room. Draw a faucet on the outside wall of the house to represent various outdoor uses. In each room, you will create lift-up flaps for each water use, under which is revealed the amount of water that activity uses (see *Average Water Required for Common Activties*, page 284 for these figures). The lift-up flaps, explained in the following steps, can be made using an Exacto knife or other knife good for making detailed cut outs.

Activity:

1. Have students work in pairs or individually. Before they begin, ask them to record how much water they think they use in a day. Then have them go through the house lifting the flaps and removing pieces to see how much water is used for different activities. Have them record the amounts used for each activity and the number of times it is performed per day. Tally the amounts and record their total. Have the students compare their actual results to their predictions.

2. Ask them to brainstorm ways to save water and record these on a suggestion board.

Design: (continued)

2. It is said that almost 75% of our daily water use takes place in the bathroom. Make one large bathroom with the following items: a toilet with a lift-up lid; a shower stall with a fabric curtain that can be pulled back; a bath tub with a large circular drain plug attached with Velcro; and a sink with an overhanging medicine cabinet for toothpaste and a toothbrush. Write the amounts needed for each on heavy paper and attach them underneath so they are readable when the moveable flap or part is opened. Write the amount used in the bath on the underside of the drain plug.

3. In the kitchen, draw a sink with dish drain, a dish washer, and a stove with cooking pots. Cut a slit in the dish drain and have a removeable plate which opens to reveal the amount used when washed by hand. Cut a door in the dishwasher to reveal the gallons used in the dishwasher. Make a lift-up lid on the cooking pot for water used in the preparation of daily meals.

4. In the laundry room, draw a washer and utility sink. Cut a door in the washing machine to reveal the gallons used. Cut a slit in the sink where a bucket can be lifted out revealing the amount used in household cleaning.

5. On one of the outside walls, draw a faucet with a hose for watering the lawn and garden. The hose can be made of ribbon, which is coiled around and hanging from a hook The amount of water used can be written on the ribbon to be revealed when the hose is uncoiled Nearby have a bucket with slit cut in the top, into which is inserted a piece of a sponge for washing the car. Write the number of gallons used to wash the car on the sponge.

6. Write the following directions on or near the exhibit:
Do you leave the water running while brushing your teeth? And for how long do you sing in the shower? Visit each room in the house to discover how much water we use for daily tasks. Lift or remove the moveable piece to learn an average amount. Record these on a tally sheet, being sure to multiply this amount by the number of times you do each task. Add these up to find out how much water you use per day. Are you surprised?

Pollution Solutions

Objectives:
Students will learn some of the ways water is polluted and will simulate the steps in the water-treatment process.

Grade Level: 3-6

Groupings: 3-5 students

Materials:
A large bucket of clean water; two clear plastic cups; green food coloring; mud; labelled film canisters containing pollutant material, one per student (see **Pollutant Materials & Analogues**, page 290). Clean-up Materials Kit: empty quart container for dirty water; dish basin; wire mesh kitchen strainer; funnel; coffee filter; plastic spoon; straw; eyedropper; sponge; quart-size plastic container for waste materials; plastic plant pot with holes in the bottom; clear quart container of clean water; two bottles of pickling alum (available at drugstores). Each group gets one Clean-up kit.

Time Allotment: 1 hour

Directions:

1. Have the whole class sit in a circle around a large bucket of water. Dip a clear plastic cup into this water and then pour the water back and forth between the two clear cups. Ask the students to observe, listen and think about their favorite body of water. Have them close their eyes and continue to listen and imagine this special place. What are they doing there? Who else is there? What does it smell like? While the students have their eyes closed, add green food coloring and mud to the cup of water and continue pouring. Ask the students to open their eyes. Discuss their reactions to the changes in the water. Tell them they will learn how water becomes polluted and how it is cleaned up again.

2. Explain that the bucket of water represents a lake that has slowly been polluted over the years by various sources. Explain that each student will represent someone who lives or works near the lake. Give each student a labelled film canister containing pollutant material. Tell the students that you are going to describe the lake and the pollutants that affect it. As each source of pollution is mentioned, have the student holding the corresponding pollutant dump the contents of his or her canister into the water jug.

3. Describe the lake to the class. Recount the lake's history. For example, back in 1960 only a dairy farm and apple orchard bordered the lake. Later a small fishing access and parking lot were built to allow for public boating. A campground with a store and laundromat followed and attracted many summer visitors. Then in the 1980's, summer houses

Extensions:

a. *Read the book* THE MAGIC SCHOOL BUS AT THE WATERWORKS, *by Joanna Cole (Scholastic, 1983). Compare methods used by the class to those encountered by Mrs. Frizzle and her class.*

b. *Let the students experiment with additional steps to try to improve the quality of their water.*

c. *Go on a field trip to the local water-treatment facility.*

d. *Have the students design their own watershed. Place two or three plastic cups upside-down on a lunch tray. Have the students mold tin foil over the cups to create mountains, valleys and rivers. When the watershed is finished, invite the students to develop and discuss the types of land use that take place in their watershed: agriculture, homes, industry, highways, malls, and ski resorts, to name a few! Do these land-use activities have any effect on the water quality? Have the students sprinkle water tinted with unsweetened Kool-Aid over the land-use areas of their watershed that they think will cause pollution to the water. What will happen when it rains? Use a watering can to simulate a rain shower in their watershed. Where did the water travel? What happened to the color of the water after traveling through the land-use areas?*

Directions: (continued)

were built along the shore, and several are now under construction. The water quality in the lake has slowly changed over the years. Mention the *farmer*, whose fertilizers and manure are washed into the lake by the rain; the *orchard*, whose pesticides are washed into the lake by rain; the *motorboat driver/fishermen*, whose fuel and engine exhaust enter the water; the *campers*, whose litter gets into the water; the *campground laundromat*, whose washing machines' leaky underground drainpipe adds soapy water to the lake; the *homeowner*, whose household waste water drains into the lake; the *new building sites*, where erosion and runoff add sediments to the lake; the careless *house painter*, whose unused paint and turpentine seeps into the lake; and the *motorists*, whose cars parked near the lake contribute polluting oil drips, antifreeze, and windshield wiper fluid. By the end of your description of the lake, the water in the jar should be dirty.

POLLUTANT MATERIALS *and* ANALOGUES

POLLUTER & POLLUTANT MATERIALS	ANALOGUE
Farmer's fertilizers and manure	Corn starch and soil
Orchard's pesticides	Baking soda
Motorboat driver's fuel and oil	Vegetable oil
Campers' litter	Paper, pieces of tin foil and Styrofoam scraps
Laundromat's soapy water	Dish detergent
Homeowner's waste water	Molasses
New construction site's runoff	Soil
House painter's unused paint and turpentine	Food coloring
Motorist's leaks	Vinegar

---

4. Ask the students who polluted the lake. Who is going to clean the lake up? How? Discuss what actions the students might take if they lived around the lake to prevent the pollution from continuing.

5. Divide the class into small groups. Give each group a quart container of dirty water from the bucket and a cleanup kit. Explain that they will play the role of managers of the water-treatment plant that has been built to clean

SPARKLING CLEAN

Water treatment is the process of cleaning water to make it safe to drink. Water treatment plants throughout the United States have set standards for clean drinking water. The water is regularly tested to make sure it is as clean or cleaner than required before it leaves the facility. There are several steps in the treatment process.

First, the water is drawn from various sources, and large objects are screened out. Chemicals are added (chlorine, alum, lime), and the water is mixed to distribute them evenly. These chemicals kill germs and help improve the taste and odor of the water. The alum coagulates small particulate matter into larger heavier particles called floc. When the water and floc enter the sedimentation basin, the floc sinks to the bottom and the water flows off. The water then passes into a filtration tank. Filters of sand and gravel remove fine impurities. The water is disinfected again with chlorine to kill remaining germs and stored in closed tanks. It then enters the water distribution system, flowing through large water mains into smaller and smaller pipes, and finally out the faucet in your home or school.

Directions: (continued)

up this lake. They will work to clean the lake, represented by the water in the jar. Show them the materials they have to use for this task. Explain that pickling alum will be available for any group that wants to use it. A 1/2 teaspoon full will coagulate small particles, causing them to stick together and sink to the bottom where they can be removed.

6. Set a time limit and ask the students to produce the cleanest water possible, using any or all of the materials in their kits. They should try to lose as little water as possible. Have them designate one person in each group as a recorder to write down cleanup steps as they are performed. Have each group keep its cleaned water in a clear quart jar.

7. When the allotted time is up, have all the groups set their jars of treated water side-by-side. Compare the results and vote which group produced the cleanest water. Have these students list their treatment steps and compare cleaning processes with other groups to decide which steps were most effective.

Watery World Worksheet

On Earth there are two types of water available to us:
salt water and *freshwater*.

Salt water is found in oceans.

Freshwater exists in three different states.
It may be *solid* (frozen) in the form of ice in the glaciers and polar ice caps;
liquid in lakes, rivers, and as groundwater;
or a *gas* in clouds and water vapor.

Can you guess how much of each type of water there is on Earth? The jugs below represent 100%, or all of the water on Earth.

Use your **BLUE** crayon to color in the amount you think is *salt water.*
Use your **YELLOW** crayon to color in the amount you think is *solid,* or *frozen, freshwater.*
Use your **GREEN** crayon to color in the amount you think is *liquid freshwater.*
Use your **RED** crayon to color in the amount you think is *freshwater gas* or *vapor.*

Make your guess.

Now with your teacher, color in and compare the actual amounts of each type of water.

Watery World

Objectives:

Students will learn about the two main kinds of water — salt water and freshwater — and the three states of freshwater: solid (frozen), liquid, and gas. They will also learn how much of each there is in the world.

Grade Level: 3-6

Groupings: Pairs

Materials: Water cards (cards with words or pictures describing the different places where water occurs in the world: oceans, seas, rivers, streams, lakes, ponds, polar ice caps, glaciers, groundwater, clouds, rain, snow, puddles, swimming pools, etc.); *Watery World Worksheet* (page 292), one for each pair; blue, green, yellow, and red crayons; ten plastic one-gallon jugs filled with water; a plastic 1/2 gallon jug and a one-cup measure; a small cup; blue, green, yellow and red food coloring.

Time Allotment: 30 minutes

Directions:

1. Earth is called the water planet. Ask the class how much of the Earth is covered by water (75%). Show the students a world map or a globe to help them guess. Explain that water exists on the Earth in many different places. Have the students name examples. (Oceans, seas, rivers, lakes, etc.) When a student gives an example, pass him or her a water card, with the name and/or picture of that example. Have some blank cards available for student examples that are not in your original set of water cards. (You might want to have larger cards for each of the oceans to emphasize their large size.)

2. Once you have passed out all the water cards, explain to the class that there are two main kinds of water on Earth: salt water and freshwater. Have the students form two groups based on the cards they are holding, a freshwater group and a salt water group. Explain that freshwater can exist in three states: solid, liquid and gas. Have the freshwater group subdivide into three groups for these three states.

3. Pair the students in the groups and send them back to their desks with a *Watery World Worksheet* to make predictions about how much of each type of water there is on Earth.

4. Explain that you will be using ten plastic one-gallon jugs and food coloring to show the students the actual percentages of salt water and freshwater in various forms. Ask the students to make believe that the ten jugs represent 100%, or all of the water on Earth. With a show of hands, ask how many of them think that at least 10% of the water in the world is salt? Add a drop of blue food coloring to the first jug. The food coloring matches the crayon color the students used for salt water on their worksheets.

5. Continue to ask the students for their guesses: how many think at least 20% of the Earth's water is salt? 30%? 40%? Continue up to 90% salt water, adding blue food coloring as you go. Do any of the students think the percentage of salt water is higher than 90? Pour off five cups from the tenth jug into the plastic 1/2 gallon jug. Explain that 97% of all the water on Earth is salt, and add food coloring to the water remaining in the tenth jug.

Extensions:

a. *Go on a "water form scavenger hunt" around your school and home to find examples of the three different states of water.*

b. *Have your students use maps to identify the major sources of fresh water in your area. What is the condition of the nearby lakes, rivers, ponds and streams? What is the source of their drinking water?*

c. *Ocean water is 3% salt. How does this compare to the salt concentration of the Great Salt Lake (15%) or of the Dead Sea (30%)? Have your students make up batches of water with representative salt concentrations and compare them by taste, the ability to float a variety of objects, and/or the effect the salt water has on plants.*

d. *The salinity of the Great Salt Lake fluctuates depending on various environmental conditions. Have students look into changes over the past 20 years. How do these effect those that live in and around the lake?*

e. *In the Middle East, salt water is desalinated for drinking water. Have the students research the process and related costs and problems. Is this a solution to the water crisis?*

Directions: (continued)

6. Ask the students what percentage is left as freshwater? (3%) How do they think this is broken down between the three states: solid, liquid, and gas? Ask for their opinions. Reveal that 2% of the Earth's freshwater is frozen in the glaciers and polar ice caps. Pour off one cup and add a drop of yellow food coloring for frozen water to the remaining water in the 1/2 gallon jug.

7. Of this last cup, or 1% of the Earth's freshwater, how much do the students think is in a liquid state as opposed to water vapor or gas? Approximately 0.9% percent is liquid freshwater. Remove five drops from the cup and add to the small cup. Add a drop of green food coloring to the cup. The remaining five drops represent the water that exists as gas, less than 0.1%. This can be colored with red food coloring.

8. Have the students complete this activity by coloring their *Watery World Worksheets* with the actual percentages of salt water and freshwater in different states.

9. Discuss that although water is plentiful, freshwater is relatively scarce and is therefore a most valuable resource. Is all the liquid freshwater on Earth drinkable? If not, why? (Some of it is polluted.)

One in a Million

Objective:
Students will perform a dilution experiment demonstrating how a substance in solution can have differing concentrations.

Grade Level: 5-6

Groupings: Pairs

Materials: (per pair) Seven small cups; tablespoon measure; a cup of mouthwash (choose one that is strongly colored and flavored); quart of tap water; cup for rinse water.

Time Allotment: 20 minutes

Maximum Allowable Levels of Some Common Minerals in Drinking Water in parts per million (ppm)

Chloride	250.00
Sodium	250.00
Iron	.30
Manganese	.05
Flouride	4.00

Source: Environmental Protection Rules, Chapter 21: Vermont Water Supply Rule, September 1992.

Directions:

*This activity is best done after **Pollution Solutions** (page 289) to help clarify the concept of a pollutant's having a certain concentration in parts per million of treated water.*

1. Explain to the class that tap water can contain various substances besides the water itself. For example, certain minerals, including iron, chloride and sodium, may be in tap water in different concentrations. Water is often tested to see what minerals it contains. In these tests, scientists look closely at the concentrations of substances in the water. They determine whether the concentrations of certain substances are at safe levels or are too high. The amount of any mineral or other substance in water is often expressed in *parts per million* or *ppm*. Tell the class that they will be doing a series of dilutions to see just how small a concentration of a few parts per million is.

2. Divide the class into pairs and give each pair a set of materials. Have each pair label their cups (1 through 7) and line them up in a row. Have each pair place ten tablespoons of mouthwash in cup 1. They then remove one tablespoon of the mouthwash from cup 1 and add it to cup 2. Have them rinse the measuring spoon with tap water, then add nine tablespoons of water to cup 2. Mix thoroughly.

3. Have the students use their measuring spoons to remove one tablespoon of dilute liquid from cup 2 and add it to cup 3. Rinse the measuring spoon thoroughly with tap water and add nine tablespoons of clean water to cup 3. Mix thoroughly. Have the students observe what is happening to the color of the solution as the mouthwash is diluted. Ask them when they think the solution will appear clear. Have them record their predictions.

4. Repeat the dilution procedure for cups 4-7. Each cup receives one tablespoon of liquid from the preceding cup and nine tablespoons of clean water.

5. Have the students look carefully at the seven cups. What do they notice about the colors of the solutions? Record observations on the ***Dilution Chart*** (page 296). How did the observations compare with the predictions?

Extension:

a. *Have the class collect tap water samples from school to send to a laboratory for analysis. Contact your local water utility or health department for information and assistance on the available tests and their cost.*

CRYSTAL CLEAR

*Ever smell water with an odor resembling rotten eggs? Or see a sink with reddish brown stains under the spout? Or find tan deposits coating the inside of your tea kettle or a grimy ring around the tub when you finish your bath? Even though it looks crystal clear, water may contain a whole variety of minerals which can cause these problems and more. Water with a high percentage of such dissolved mineral salts is called **hard water**. Hard water has a pH greater than 7 and is easily tested with an inexpensive pH kit available from pet stores. Or try the soap suds test on your water. Using a bit of soap, try to work up a good lather. The harder the water, the harder it will be to get good sudsing action.*

Directions: (continued)

6. Ask the students if the undiluted mouthwash has a strong odor and/or flavor. Can they detect any scent in cup 2? In cup 3? In which cups are they unable to detect any odor?

7. Have the class work together to determine the concentrations of the various cups in parts per million. Explain that cup 1 is 100% mouthwash (a million parts per million). In cup 2, one of the ten tablespoons are mouthwash; it is a 1/10 concentration (100,000 parts per million). Cup 3 is one tenth the concentration of the preceding cup. Can they figure out the concentration of cup 3? (1/100 or 10,000 parts per million.) Have the students continue until they have figured the concentrations of all seven cups.

8. Relate this dilution experiment to the actual concentration of substances in tap water. Find out some acceptable concentration levels for common minerals and other substances (see **Maximum Allowable Levels** chart page 295).

DILUTION CHART		
Cup Number	Color & Odor	Concentration (ppm)

FALL

Harvest

Children's Story Books

Asch, Frank. **Oats and Wild Apples**. *New York: Holiday House, 1988.*

Carle, Eric. **The Tiny Seed**. *Natick, MA: Picture Book Studio, 1987.*

dePaola, Tomie. **The Popcorn Book**. *New York: Holiday House, 1978.*

Ehlert, Lois. **Growing Vegetable Soup**. *San Diego: Harcourt Brace Jovanovich, 1987.*

Gibbons, Gail. **The Seasons of Arnold's Apple Tree**. *San Diego: Harcourt Brace Jovanovich, 1984.*

Hutchins, Amy and Richard. **Picking Apples and Pumpkins**. *New York: Scholastic, 1994.*

Kroll, Steven. **The Biggest Pumpkin Ever**. *New York: Holiday House, 1984.*

Lindbergh, Reeve. **Johnny Appleseed (A Poem)**. *Boston: Joy Street Books, 1990.*

Miller, Edna. **Mousekin's Golden House**. *New York: Simon & Schuster, 1964.*

Parnall, Peter. **Apple Tree**. *New York: Macmillan, 1987.*

Titherington, Jeanne. **Pumpkin Pumpkin**. *New York: Greenwillow Books, 1986.*

Children's Information/Activity Books

Aliki. **Corn is Maize**. *New York: Harper & Row, 1976.*

Bourgeois, Paulette. **The Amazing Apple Book**. *Reading, MA: Addison-Wesley, 1987.*

Gillis, Jennifer Storey. **In a Pumpkin Shell**. *Pownal, VT: Storey Communications, 1992.*

Johnson, Sylvia. **Apple Trees**. *Minneapolis: Lerner Publications, 1983.*

Johnson, Sylvia. **How Leaves Change**. *Minneapolis: Lerner Publications, 1986.*

Lauber, Patricia. **Seeds: Pop, Stick, Glide**. *New York: Crown Publishers, 1981.*

Maestro, Betsy. **How Do Apples Grow?** *New York: Harper Collins, 1992.*

Overbeck, Cynthia. **How Seeds Travel**. *Minneapolis: Lerner Publications, 1982.*

Patent, Dorothy Hinshaw. **An Apple A Day: From Orchard to You**. *New York: Cobblehill/Dutton, 1990.*

Schnieper, Claudia. **An Apple Tree Through the Year**. *Minneapolis: Carolrhoda Books, 1987.*

Webster, David. **Exploring Nature Around the Year: Fall**. *Englewood Cliffs, NJ: Julian Messner, 1989.*

Wexler, Jerome. **Flowers, Fruits and Seeds**. *New York: Prentice-Hall Books for Young Readers, 1987.*

Teacher's Resource/Activity Books

Goodwin, Mary and Gerry Pollen. **Creative Food Experiences for Children.** *Washington, D.C.: CSPI, 1980.*

Farm Life and History

Children's Story Books

Brown, Margaret Wise. **Big Red Barn**. *New York: Harper & Row, 1989.*

Carrick, Donald. **Milk**. *New York: Greenwillow Books, 1985.*

Cross, Verda and Owens, Gail. **Great Grandma Tells of Threshing Day**. *Morton Grove, IL: Albert Whitman and Co., 1992.*

Ericsson, Jennifer. **No Milk!**. *New York: William Morrow, 1993.*

Fowler, Allan. **Thanks to Cows**. *Chicago: Children's Press, 1992.*

Goodall, John S. **The Story of a Farm**. *New York: McElderry Books, 1989.*

Greeley, Valerie. **Farm Animals**. *New York: Harper & Row, 1984.*

Hall, Donald. **Ox Cart Man**. *New York: Viking Press, 1979.*

Heller, Ruth. **Chicken's Aren't the Only Ones**. *New York: Grosset and Dunlap, 1981.*

Henderson, Kathy. **I Can Be a Farmer**. *Chicago: Children's Press, 1989.*

Lewison, Wendy Cheyette. **Going to Sleep on the Farm**. *New York: Dial Books for Young Readers, 1992.*

Lindbergh, Reeve. **The Midnight Farm**. *New York: Dial Books for Young Readers, 1987.*

Locker, Thomas. **Family Farm**. *New York: Dial Books, 1988.*

McFarland, Cynthia. **Cows in the Parlor.** *New York: Atheneum, 1990.*

McPhail, David. **Farm Boy's Year**. *New York: Atheneum, 1992.*

McPhail, David. **Farm Morning**. *San Diego: Harcourt Brace Jovanovich, 1985.*

Miller, Jane. **Farm Noises**. *New York: Simon and Schuster Books for Young Readers, 1988.*

Morris, Ann. **700 Kids on Grandpa's Farm**. *New York: Dutton's Children's Books, 1994.*

Peterson, Cris. **Extra Cheese, Please!**. *Honesdale, PA: Boyds Mill Press, 1994.*

Priceman, Marjorie. **How to Make an Apple Pie and See the World**. *New York: Knopf, 1994.*

Provensen, Alice and Martin. **Our Animal Friends at Maple Hill Farm**. *New York: Macmillan, 1978.*

Provensen, Alice and Martin. **The Year at Maple Hill Farm**. *New York: Macmillan, 1988.*

Ryder, Joanne. **My Father's Hands**. *New York: Morrow Junior Books, 1994.*

Sanderst, Scott. **Warm as Wool**. *New York: Bradbury Press, 1992.*

Siebert, Diane. **Heartland**. *New York: Crowell, 1989.*

Smith, E. Boyd. **The Farm Book**. *Boston: Houghton Mifflin, 1982.*

Tafuri, Nancy. **Early Morning in the Barn**. *New York: Greenwillow Books, 1983.*

Whybrow, Ian. **Quacky, Quack, Quack**. *New York: Four Winds Press, 1991.*

Ziefert, Harriet. **A New Coat for Anna**. *New York: Knopf, 1986.*

Children's Information/Activity Books

Aliki. **Milk from Cow to Carton**. *New York: Harper Collins, 1992.*

Bellville, Cheryl Walsh. **Farming Today, Yesterday's Way**. *Minneapolis: Carolrhoda Books, 1984.*

Bushey, Jerry. **Farming the Land: Modern Farmers and Their Machines**. *Minneapolis: Carolrhoda Books, 1987.*

Cook, Brenda. **All About Farm Animals**. *New York: Doubleday, 1989.*

de Bourgoing, Pascale and Gallimard Jeunesse. **The Egg**. *New York: Scholastic, 1992.*

Duffy, Deedee. **Barnyard Tracks**. *Honesdale, PA: Bellbooks, 1992.*

Gibbons, Gail. **Farming**. *New York: Holiday House, 1988.*

Gibbons, Gail. **The Milk Makers**. *New York: Macmillan, 1985.*

Gunby, Lise. **Early Farm Life**. *New York: Crabtree Publishing, 1983.*

Graff, Nancy P. **The Strength of the Hills.** *Boston: Little, Brown & Co., 1989.*

Griffin, Margaret and Deborah Seed. **The Amazing Egg Book**. *Reading, MA: Addison Wesley, 1989.*

Isenbart, Hans-Heinrich. **Baby Animals of the Farm**. *New York: Putnam, 1981.*

Jobin, Claire. **All About Wool**. *Ossining, NY: Young Discovery Library, 1988.*

Mitgutsch, Ali. **From Grass to Butter**. *Minneapolis: Carolrhoda Books, 1981.*

Mitgutsch, Ali. **From Milk to Ice Cream**. *Minneapolis: Carolrhoda Books, 1981.*

Paladino, Catherine. **Spring Fleece: A Day of Sheep Shearing**. *Boston: Little, Brown & Co., 1990.*

Paladino, Catherine. **Our Vanishing Farm Animals**. *Boston: Little, Brown & Co., 1991.*

Patterson, Geoffrey. **Dairy Farming**. *London: Andre Deutsch, 1983.*

Riquier, Aline. **The Cotton in Your T-Shirt**. *Ossining, NY: Young Discovery Library, 1993.*

Ross, Catherine and Wallace, Susan. **The Amazing Milk Book**. *Reading, MA: Addison-Wesley, 1991.*

Selsam, Millicent. **Egg to Chick**. *New York: Harper & Row, 1970.*

Young, Caroline. **The Usborne Book of Tractors**. *London: Usborne Publishing, Ltd., 1992.*

Teacher Resource/Activity Books

Belanger, Jerry. **Raising Milk Goats the Modern Way**. *Pownal, VT: Storey Communications, 1990.*

Jorgensen, Eric and Trout Black and Mary Hellesy. **Manure to Meadow to Milkshake.** *Los Altos Hills, CA: Trust for Hiden Villa, 1991*

Mercia, Leonard S. **Raising Poultry the Modern Way**. *Pownal, VT: Storey Communications, 1990.*

Rubin, Laurie. **Food First Curriculum**. *San Francisco: Institute for Food and Development Policy, 1984.*

Simmons, Paula. **Raising Sheep the Modern Way**. *Pownal, VT: Storey Communications, 1989.*

Tourtillott, Leeann. **Food For Thought**. *Novato, CA: Marin Agricultural Literacy Project, 1992.*

Wright, Merideth. **Put on Thy Beautiful Garments: Rural New England Clothing 1783-1800**. *East Montpelier, VT: The Clothes Press, 1990.*

Soil and Worms

Children's Story Books

Dunrea, Olivier. **Deep Down Underground**. *New York: Macmillian, 1989.*

Lewy, Constance. **I'm Going to Pet a Worm Today**. *New York: M. K. McElderry Books, 1991.*

Ryder, Joanne. **Under Your Feet**. *New York: Four Winds Press, 1990.*

Ziefert, Harriet. **Worm Day**. *New York: Bantam, 1987.*

Children's Information Books

Anderson, Lucia. **The Smallest Life Around Us**. *New York: Crown Publishers, 1978.*

Atkinson, Kathie. **Life in a Rotten Log**. *St. Leonards, Australia:Little Ark Book, 1993.*

Bourgeois, Paulette. **The Amazing Dirt Book**. *Reading, MA: Addison-Wesley, 1990.*

Darling, Lois and Louis. **Worms**. *New York: William Morrow, 1972.*

Glaser, Linder. **Wonderful Worms**. *Brookfield, CT: Millbrook Press, 1992.*

Henwood, Chris. **Earthworms.** *New York: Franklin Watts, 1988.*

Lavies, Bianca. **Compost Critters**. *New York: Duttons Children's Books, 1993.*

Mayes, Susan. **What's Under the Ground?**. *London: Usborne Publishing Ltd., 1989.*

Ruffault, Charlotte. **Animals Underground**. *Ossining, NY: Young Discovery Library, 1987.*

McLaughlin, Molly. **Earthworms, Dirt, and Rotten Leaves**. *New York: Atheneum, 1986.*

Teacher Resource/Activity Book

Appelhof, Mary. **Worms Eat My Garbage**. *Kalamazoo, MI: Flower Press, 1993.*

Trees
Children's Story Books

Arnold, Caroline. **A Walk in the Woods**. *Englewood Cliffs, NJ: Silver Press, 1990.*

Arnosky, Jim. **Crinkleroot's Guide to Knowing the Trees**. *New York: Bradbury Press, 1992.*

Arnosky, Jim. **Crinkleroot's Guide to Walking in Wild Places**. *New York: Bradbury Press, 1990.*

Arnosky, Jim. **I Was Born in a Tree and Raised by Bees**. *New York: Bradbury Press, 1988.*

Cherry, Lynne. **The Great Kapok Tree**. *New York: Harcourt Brace Jovanovich, 1990.*

Ehlert, Lois. **Red Leaf, Yellow Leaf**. *San Diego: Harcourt Brace Jovanovich, 1991.*

Gile, John. **The First Forest**. *Stevens Point, WI: Worzalla, 1989.*

Hiscock, Bruce. **The Big Tree**. *New York: Atheneum, 1991.*

Jaspersohn, William. **How the Forest Grew**. *New York: Greenwillow Books, 1992.*

Karpin, Florence Baker. **Tree Spirits**. *Woodstock, VT: Countryman Press, 1992.*

Myers, Christopher. **McCrephy's Field**. *Boston: Houghton Mifflin, 1991.*

Miller, Edna. **Mousekin's Lost Woodland**. *New York: Simon & Schuster, 1992.*

Romanova, Natalia. **Once There Was a Tree**. *New York: Dial Books, 1985.*

Ryder, Joanne. **Hello Tree!**. *New York: Lodestar Books, 1991.*

Seuss, Dr. **The Lorax**. *New York: Random House, 1971.*

Silverstein, Shel. **The Giving Tree**. *New York: Harper & Row, 1964.*

Thornhill, Jan. **A Tree in a Forest**. *New York: Simon & Schuster, 1992.*

Tresselt, Alvin. **The Gift of the Tree**. *New York: Lothrop, Lee & Shepard, 1992.*

Children's Information Books

Arnosky, Jim. **In the Forest**. *New York: Lothrop, Lee & Shepard, 1989.*

Bourgeois, Paulette. **The Amazing Paper Book**. *Reading, MA: Addison-Wesley, 1989.*

Burnie, David. **Tree Eyewitness Book**. *New York: Knopf, 1988.*

de Bourgoing, Pascale and Gallimard Jeunesse. **Tree**. *New York: Cartwheel Books, 1992.*

Ingoglia, Gina. **Look Inside a Tree**. *New York: Grosset and Dunlop, 1989.*

Johnson, Sylvia. **How Leaves Change**. *Minneapolis: Lerner Publications, 1986.*

Lauber, Patricia. **Be a Friend to Trees**. *New York: Harper Collins, 1994.*

Thomson, Ruth. **Usborne First Nature Trees**. *Tulsa, OK: EDC Publishing, 1980.*

Teacher Resources/Activity Books

Adirondack Teacher Center. **Spruce Up America**. *Paul Smiths, NY: Adirondack Teacher Center, 1991.*

The American Forest Council. **Project Learning Tree**. *Washington, DC: The American Forest Council, 1993.*

Rockwell, Robert, Elizabeth Sherwood, and Robert Williams. **Hug A Tree: And Other Things To Do Outdoors With Young Children**. *Mt. Rainer, MD: Gryphon House, 1983.*

Spurgeon, Richard. **Ecology: Usborne Science and Experiments**. *Tulsa, OK: EDC Publishing, 1988.*

Snow, Animals and Tracks

Children's Story Books

Arnosky, Jim. **Crinkleroot's Book of Animal Tracking**. *New York: Bradbury Press, 1989.*

Brett, Jan. **The Mitten**. *New York: Putnam, 1989.*

Coxe, Molly. **Whose Footprints?**. *New York: Crowell, 1990.*

de Sairigno, Catherine. **Animals in Winter**. *Ossining, NY: Young Discovery Library, 1988.*

Keats, Ezra Jack. **The Snowy Day**. *New York: Viking Press, 1962.*

Low, Josephine. **Mice Twice**. *New York: MacMillan, 1980.*

Miller, Edna. **Mousekin's Woodland Sleepers**. *New York: Prentice Hall, 1990.* OUT OF PRINT.

Ryder, Joanne. **Chipmunk Song**. *New York: Dutton, 1987.*

Ryder, Joanne. **Step Into the Night**. *New York: Four Winds Press, 1988.*

San Souci, Daniel. **North Country Night**. *New York: Doubleday, 1990.*

Selsam, Millicent and Joyce Hunt. **Keep Looking**. *New York: Macmillan, 1989.*

Steig, William. **Dr. Desoto**. *New York: Farrar, Strauss & Giroux, 1982.*

Williams, Terry Tempest and Ted Major. **The Secret Language of Snow**. *San Francisco: Sierra Club/ Pantheon Books, 1984.*

Yolen, Jane. **Owl Moon**. *New York: Philomel Books, 1987.*

Children's Information/Activity Books

Bash, Barbara. **Shadows of Night**. *San Francisco: Sierra Club Books for Children, 1993.*

Docekal, Eileen M. **Nature Detective: How to Solve Outdoor Mysteries**. *New York: Sterling Publishing Co., 1989.*

Facklam, Margery. **Do Not Disturb: The Mysteries of Hibernation and Sleep**. *Boston: Little, Brown & Co., 1989.*

Kalman, Bobbie. **Forest Mammals**. *Toronto: Crabtree Publishing, 1987.*

Markle, Sandra. **Exploring Winter**. *New York: Atheneum, 1984.*

Nail, Jim. **Whose Tracks are These**. *Niwot, CO: Robert Rinehart, 1994.*

Schweninger, Ann. **Let's Look at the Seasons: Wintertime**. *New York: Viking Press, 1990.*

Selsam, Millicent. **Where Do They Go? Insects in Winter**. *New York: Scholastic Book Services, 1981.*

Simon, Seymour. **Animal Fact/Animal Fable**. *New York: Crown Publishers, 1979.*

Simon, Seymour. **Winter Across America**. *New York: Hyperion Books for Children, 1994.*

Webster, David. **Exploring Nature Around the Year: Winter**. *Englewood, NJ: Julian Messner, 1989.*

Teacher Resource/Activity Books

Bentley, W. A. and W. J. Humphreys. **Snow Crystals**. *New York: Dover, 1962.*

Bianchi, John and Frank B. Edwards. **Snow: Learning for the Fun of It**. *Newburgh, Ontario: Bungalo Books, 1992.*

Caduto, Michael and Joseph Bruchac. **Keepers of the Animals**. *Goldon, CO: Fulcrum, 1991.*

Kappel-Smith, Diana. **Wintering**. *Boston: Little, Brown & Co., 1984.*

Nestor, William. **Into Winter: Discovering a Season**. *Boston: Houghton Mifflin, 1982.*

Osgood, William and Leslie J. Hurley. **The Snowshoe Book**. *Brattleboro, VT: The Stephen Greene Press 1983.*

Stall, Chris. **Animal Tracks of New England**. *Seattle: The Mountaineers, 1989.*

Stoddard, Gloria May. **Snowflake Bently: Man of Science Man of God**. *Shelburne, VT: New England Press, 1985.*

Stokes, Donald W. **A Guide to Nature in Winter: Northeast and North Central North America**. *Boston: Little, Brown & Co., 1976.*

Stokes, Donald and Lillian. **A Guide to Animal Tracking and Behavior**. *Boston: Little, Brown & Co., 1986.*

Birds

Children's Story Books

Arnosky, Jim. **Crinkleroot's Guide to Knowing the Birds**. *New York: Bradbury Press, 1992.*

Wolff, Ashley. **A Year of Birds**. *New York: Puffin Books, 1988.*

Children's Information/Activity Books

Arnosky, Jim. **A Kettle of Hawks and Other Wildlife Groups**. *New York: Lothrop, Lee & Shepard Books, 1990.*

Bash, Barbara. **Urban Roosts**. *Boston: Little, Brown & Co., 1990.*

Burnie, David. **Bird Eyewitness Book**. *New York: Knopf, 1988.*

Esbensen, Barbara J. **Great Northern Diver: The Loon**. *Boston: Little, Brown & Co., 1990.*

Hickman, Pamela. **Birdwise**. *Reading, MA: Addison-Wesley, 1989.*

Pallotta, Jerry. **The Bird Alphabet Book**. *Watertown, MA: Charlesbridge Publishing, 1986.*

Weidensaul, Scott. **A Kid's First Book of Birdwatching and Audio Cassette**. *Philadelphia, PA: Running Press, 1990.*

SPRING

Maple Sugaring

Children's Story Books

Gerstein, Mordicai. **Anytime Mapleson and the Hungry Bears**. *New York: Harper & Row, 1990.*

Gibbons, Gail. **The Missing Maple Syrup Sap Mystery**. *New York: Frederick Warne, 1979.*

Hiscock, Bruce. **The Big Tree**. *New York: Atheneum, 1991.*

Sloane, Eric. **Diary of an Early American Boy**. *New York: Promontory Press, 1986.*

Watson, Aldren A. **A Maple Tree Begins**. *New York: Viking Press, 1970.*

Watson, Nancy Dingman. **Sugar on Snow**. *Viking Press, 1964.*

Wilder, Laura Ingalls. **Farmer Boy**. *New York: Harper & Row, 1971.*

Wilder, Laura Ingalls. **Little House in the Big Woods**. *New York: Harper & Row, 1971.*

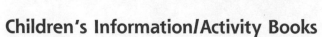

Children's Information/Activity Books

Burns, Diane. **Sugaring Season: Making Maple Syrup**. *Minneapolis: Carolrhoda Books, 1990.*

Gemming, Elizabeth. **Maple Harvest**. *New York: Coward, McCann & Geoghegan, 1976.*

Lasky, Kathryn. **Sugaring Time**. *New York: Macmillan Publishing, 1983.*

Linton, Marilyn. **The Maple Syrup Book**. *Toronto: Kids Can Press, 1983.*

Teacher Resource/Activity Books

Lawrence, James and Rux Martin. **Sweet Maple**. *Shelburne, VT: Chapters Publishing and Vermont Life, 1993.*

Lockhart, Betty Ann C. **The Maple Sugaring Story: A Guide for Teaching and Learning about the Maple Industry**. *Charlotte, VT: Vermont Maple Promotion Board, 1990.*

Nearing, Helen and Scott. **The Maple Sugar Book**. *New York: Schocken Books, 1973.*

Green Plants

Children's Story Books

Cooney, Barbara. **Miss Rumphius**. *New York: Viking Press, 1982.*

Heller, Ruth. **Plants that Never Ever Bloom**. *New York: Grosset & Dunlap, 1984.*

Heller, Ruth. **The Reason for a Flower**. *New York: Grosset & Dunlap, 1983.*

Lobel, Arnold. **The Rose in My Garden**. *New York: Greenwillow Books, 1984.*

Children's Information/Activity Books

Cox, Rosamund Kidman and Barbara Cork. **Usborne First Nature Flowers**. *London: Usborne Publishing Ltd., 1990.*

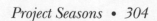

Hirschi, Ron. **Spring**. *New York: Cobblehill/Dutton, 1990.*

Mayes, Susan. **What Makes a Flower Grow?.** *London: Usborne Publishing, 1989.*

Pallotta, Jerry. **The Flower Alphabet Book**. *Boston: Quinlan Press, 1988.*

Pallotta, Jerry and Bob Thomson. **The Victory Garden Alphabet Book**. *Watertown, MA: Charlesbridge Publishing, 1992.*

Perenyi, Constance. **Growing Wild: Inviting Wildlife into Your Yard**. *Hillsboro, OR: Beyond Words Publishing, 1991.*

Raftery, Kevin and Kim. **Kids Gardening**. *Palo Alto, CA: Klutz Press, 1989.*

Rahn, Joan E. **Grocery Store Botany**. *New York: Atheneum, 1978.*

Ring, Elizabeth. **Tiger Lilies and Other Beastley Plants**. *New York: Walker and Co., 1984.*

Seymour, Peter S. **How Things Grow**. *New York: Dutton, 1988.*

Suzuki, David and Barbara Hehner. **Looking at Plants**. *New York: Warner Books, 1985.*

Waters, Marjorie. **The Victory Garden Kid's Book**. *Boston: Houghton Mifflin, 1988.*

Webster, David. **Exploring Nature Around the Year: Spring**. *Englewood Cliffs, NJ: Julian Messner, 1989.*

Teacher Resource/Activity Books

Appel, Gary and Roberta Jaffe. **The Growing Classroom**. *Reading, MA: Addison-Wesley, 1990.*

Ocone, Lynn. **The Youth Gardening Book**. *Burlington, VT: Gardens For All, 1983.*

Pranis, Eve and Joy Cohen. **Grow Lab: Activities for Growing Minds**. *Burlington, VT: National Gardening Association, 1990.*

Water

Children's Story Books

Cherry, Lynne. **A River Ran Wild**. *San Diego: Harcourt Brace Jovanovich, 1992.*

Cole, Joanna. **The Magic School Bus At The Waterworks**. *New York: Scholastic, 1986.*

George, William T. and Lindsay Barrett George. **Beaver at Long Pond**. *New York: Greenwillow Books, 1988.*

Rockwell, Anne. **Ducklings and Pollywogs**. *New York: Macmillan, 1994.*

Yolen, Jane. **Letting Swift River Go**. *Boston: Little, Brown & Co., 1992.*

Children's Information/Activity Books

Dewey, Jennifer. **At the Edge of the Pond**. *Boston: Little, Brown & Co., 1987.*

Fowler, Allan. **Frogs, Toads and Tadpoles, Too**. *Chicago: Children's Press, 1992.*

Graham-Barber, Lynda. **Toad or Frog, Swamp or Bog?**. *New York: Four Winds Press, 1994.*

Holmer, Marilyn. **Beaver Stream**. *Norwalk, CT: Soundprints, 1994.*

Lewis, James. **Learn While You Scrub: Science in the Tub**. *New York: Simon & Schuster, 1989.*

Parker, Steve. **The Pond and River Eyewitness Book**. *New York: Knopf, 1988.*

Pfeffer, Wendy. **From Tadpole to Frog**. *New York: Harper Collins, 1994.*

Seed, Deborah. **Water Science**. *Reading, MA: Addison-Wesley, 1992.*

Taylor, Barbara. **Sink or Swim**. *New York: Random House, 1991.*

Wyler, Rose. **Puddles and Ponds: An Outdoor Science Book**. *Englewood Cliffs, NJ: Julian Messner, 1990.*

Teacher Resource/Activity Books

AIMS Education Foundation. **Water, Precious, Water**. *Fresno, CA: AIMS Education Foundation, 1988.*

Gartrell, Jack E. Jr., Jane Crowder, and Jeffrey C. Callister. **Earth the Water Planet**. *Washington, DC: National Science Teachers Association, 1989.*

Massachusetts Water Resources Authority. **Water Wizards**. *Boston: Massachusetts Water Resources Authority, 1987.*

Massachusetts Water Resources Authority. **Water Watchers**. *Boston: Massachusetts Water Resources Authority, 1987.*

Perdue, Peggy K. **Diving into Science: Hands-on Water Related Experiments**. *Glenview, IL: Harper Collins/Good Year Books, 1989.*

Stangl, Jean. **H₂O Science**. *New York: Simon & Schuster, 1990.*

Stille, Darlene. **Water Pollution**. *Chicago: Children's Press, 1990.*

Western Regional Environmental Education Council. **Aquatic Project Wild**. *Boulder, CO: Western Regional Environmental Education Council, 1987.*

Insects and More

Children's Story Books

Carle, Eric. **The Very Quiet Cricket**. *New York: Philomel Books, 1990.*

Clyne, Densey. **Flutter By, Butterfly**. *Chicago: Allen & Unwin, 1994.*

Heller, Ruth. **How to Hide a Butterfly and Other Insects**. *New York: Grosset and Dunlap, 1985.*

Karle, Eric. **The Very Busy Spider**. *New York: Philomel Books, 1984.*

McNulty, Faith. **The Lady and the Spider**. *New York: Harper & Row, 1986.*

Ryder, Joanne. **The Snail's Spell**. *New York: F. Warne, 1982.*

Children's Information/Activity Books

Charman, Andy and Sarah Erskine. **Be a Bug Detective**. *New York: Derrydale Books, 1992.*

Gibbons, Gail. **Monarch Butterfly**. *New York: Holiday House, 1989.*

Heiderose, and Andreas Fischer-Nagel. **Life of the Honeybee**. *Minneapolis: Carolrhoda Books, 1986.*

Henwood, Chris. **Snails and Slugs**. *New York: Franklin Watts, 1988.*

Hickman, Pamela. **Bugwise**. *New York: Addison Wesley, 1990.*

Katz, Bobbi. **The Creepy, Crawly Book**. *New York: Random House, 1989.*

Kilpatrick, Cathy. **Usborne First Nature Guides: Creepy Crawlies**. *London: Usborne Publishing Ltd., 1982.*

Lecht, Jane. **Honeybees**. *Washington: National Geographic Society, 1973.*

Mitgutsch, Ali. **From Blossom to Honey**. *Minneapolis: Carolrhoda Books, 1981.*

Owen, Jennifer. **Mysteries and Marvels of Insect Life**. *London: Usborne Publishing Ltd., 1984.*

Pallotta, Jerry. **The Icky Bug Alphabet Book**. *Chicago: Children's Press, 1991.*

Pallotta, Jerry. **The Icky Bug Counting Book**. *Watertown, MA: Charlesbridge Publishing, 1992.*

Parker, Nancy W and Joan Wright. **Bugs**. *New York: Greenwillow Books, 1987.*

Peterson, Roger Tory and Robert M. Pyle. **A Field Guide to Butterflies Coloring Book**. *Boston: Houghton Mifflin, 1983.*

Seymour, Peter. **Insects: A Close Up Book**. *New York: Macmillan Publishing, 1984.*

Sowler, Sandie. **Amazing Animal Disguises**. *New York: Knopf, 1992.*

Starosta, Paul. **The Bee: Friend of the Flowers**. *Watertown, MA: Charlesbridge Publishing, 1991.*

Suzuki, David, and Barbara Hehner. **Looking at Insects**. *New York: Warner Books, 1986.*

Teacher Resource/Activity Books

Echols, Jean C. **Buzzing a Hive: Teacher's Guide**. *Berkeley, CA: The Regents of the University of California, 1989.*

GENERAL SCIENCE and ENVIRONMENT

Children's Story Books

Hirschi, Ron. **Discover My World: Mountain**. *New York: Bantam, 1992.*

Singer, Marilyn. **Turtle in July.** *New York: MacMillan, 1989*

Children's Information/Activity Books

Allison, Linda. **The Reasons for Seasons**. *Boston: Little Brown & Co., 1975.*

Allison, Linda and David Katz. **Gee Wiz!**. *Boston: Little Brown & Co., 1983.*

Gillespie, C., et.al. **Smithsonian Science Activity Book**. *New York: Galison Books, 1987.*

McKean, Barbara. **Wild Animals: Land and Sea Mammals**. *Milwaukee, WI: Penworthy Publishing, 1986.*

Milord, Susan. **The Kids' Nature Book**. *Charlotte, VT: Williamson Publishing, 1989.*

Ontario Science Center. **Scienceworks: 65 Experiments that Introduce the Fun and Wonder of Science**. *Reading, MA: Addison-Wesley, 1984.*

Ontario Science Center. **Foodworks: Over 100 Science Activities and Fascinating Facts that Explore the Science of Food**. *Reading, MA: Addison-Wesley, 1987.*

Shedd, Warner. **The Kids' Wildlife Book**. *Charlotte, VT: Williamson, 1994.*

Suzuki, David. **Looking at Senses**. *Toronto: Stoddart Publishing, 1987.*

Suzuki, David, and Barbara Hehner. **Looking at Weather**. *New York: Wiley, 1991.*

Svedberg, Ulf and Ingrid Selberg. **Nicky the Nature Detective**. *New York: R & S Books, 1983.*

Taylor, Barbara. **Weather and Climate**. *Las Vegas, NV: Kingfisher, 1993.*

Whayne, Susan Santaro. **Night Creatures**. *New York: Simon and Schuster, 1993.*

Teacher Resource/Activity Books

Brown, Sam. **Bubbles, Rainbows & Worms: Science Experiments for Preschool Children**. *Mt. Rainer, MD: Gryphon House, Inc., 1981.*

Caduto, Michael and Joseph Bruchac. **Keepers of the Earth**. *Goldon, CO: Fulcrum, 1989.*

Cornell, Joseph. **Sharing the Joy of Nature**. *Nevada City, CA: Dawn Publications, 1989.*

Fiarotta, Phyllis. **Snips & Snales & Walnut Whales: Nature Crafts for Children**. *New York: Workman Publishing Co., 1975.*

Harlow, Rosie and Gareth Morgan. **175 Amazing Nature Experiments**. *New York: Random House, 1992.*

Hart-Davis, Adam. **Scientific Eye: Exploring the Marvels of Science**. *New York: Sterling Publishing, 1989.*

Herman, Marina Lachecki, et. al. **Teaching Kids to Love the Earth**. *Duluth, MN: Pfeifer-Hamilton Pub., 1991.*

Levenson, Elaine. **Teaching Children About Science**. *Englewood Cliffs, NJ: Prentice Hall, 1985.*

Lingelbach, Jenepher. **Hands-On Nature: Information and Activities for Exploring the Environment with Children**. *Woodstock, VT: Vermont Institute of Natural Science, 1986.*

Mitchell, John and The Massachusetts Audubon Society. **The Curious Naturalist**. *Englewood Cliffs, NJ: Prentice-Hall, 1980.*

National Wildlife Federation. **Ranger Rick's NatureScope Series**. *Washington, DC: National Wildlife Federation, 1989.*

Pedicord, Susan. **AVR Teacher's Resource Guide for Solid Waste and Recycling Education**. *Montpelier, VT: Association of Vermont Recyclers, 1989.*

Reynolds, Jane, Phil Gates and Gaden Robinson. **365 Days of Nature and Discovery: Things to Do and Learn for the Whole Family**. *New York: Harry N. Abrams, 1994.*

Sheehan, Kathryn and Mary Waidner. **Earth Child**. *Tulsa, OK: Council Oak Books, 1991.*

Sherwood, Elizabeth, Robert Williams, and Robert Rockwell. **More Mudpies to Magnets: Science for Young Children**. *Mt. Rainer, MD: Gryphon House, 1990.*

Sisson, Edith. **Nature with Children of All Ages**. *Englewood Cliffs, NJ: Prentice-Hall, 1982.*

Tolman, Marvin, and James Morton. **Life Science Activities for Grades 2-8**. *West Nyack, NY: Parker Publishing, 1986.*

Vermont Institute of Natural Science. **Waste Away: A Curriculum on Solid Waste**. *Woodstock, VT: Vermont Institute of Natural Sciences, 1989.*

Walker, Leslie Clare. **Nature All Year Long**. *New York: Greenwillow Books, 1991.*

Western Regional Education Council, Inc. **Project Wild**. *Boulder, CO: Western Regional Environmental Council, 1992.*

Williams, Robert A., Robert E. Rockwell and Elizabeth Sherwood. **Mudpies to Magnets: A Preschool Science Curriculum**. *Mt. Rainer, MD: Gryphon House, 1987.*

Index

Bundle scars, 116
Buoy Oh Buoy!, 254
Buoyancy, 253-54, 255-56, 267
Buried Treasure, 83-85
Butter Cake Song, 51
Butter Making 49-51
Butter, about formation 51
Butterfly, 239; and pollination, 234, 236
Buttermilk, 50

C

C horizon, 75
Caddisfly, 275, 276, 280
Calyx, 229
Cambium, 207, 208, 209
Capillary action, 252
Carbon dioxide, 131, 132
Carbon, in compost 87, 88, 89
Carders, 40
Carnivores, 55, 153
Carrion fly, as pollinator 234, 236
Cashews, 21
Cat, tracks, 160, 161
Catch a Snowflake, 133
Cattle, 36
Cellulose Secret, 110
Cellulose, 110; in paper making 129
Centipede, 76, 82
Central America, 281, 282
Cheese, 52
Chickens, 36, 57, 166, 171
Chipmunks, tracks, 160, 161, 166; in winter, 147, 171
Chloride, 295
Chocolate, 21
Circumference Chart, 192
Clams, fingernail, 280
Classification, of trees, 113-14
Clay, 67, 71-72
Clitellum, 98
Cloth Leaf Poundings, 103
Clouds, 271
Coconut, 21
Coevolution, 234
Coffee, 21
Cohesion, in water 245-46, 251-52, 266
Collecting Insects, 238-41
Colloids, 264
Colonists, and maple sugaring 185, 186
Community Supported Agriculture, 21, 34
Compaction sticks, 63, 66
Composite flowers. 228

Compost Cake, 87-89
Compost Ingredient Cards, 88
Compost, 71, 81, 87-89
Compression, of air, 267
Condensation, 271
Coping with Cold, 145-46
Corn husk dolls, 13
Corn, 11-12
Corny Facts 12
Cottage cheese, recipe, 52
Cotyledons, 211, 212
Cow Relay, 41-42
Cows, activities about, 41-42, 43-44; amount of food and water ingested, 54; by-products, 42; digestive process, 43-48; exhibit about, 53-54; milk and manure produced, 54; products from, 36; and sustainable farming, 54; tracks, 160, 166; in winter, 171
Coyote, tracks, 166, 160, 161; in winter, 148
Cranberries, 21
Crayfish, 275, 276, 280
Crayon Leaf Rubbings, 102
Creature Features, 76
Critter Cards, 237
Critter Clues, 277-79
Crystal Clear, 296
Cycles, air, 131-32; agriculture, 31; hydrologic/water, 269-72

D

Daily Ins and Outs of a Cow, 54
Dairy cows, *see Cows*
Damselfly, 280
Decomposer, 81
Decomposition, 81, 85; activities about 79-81, 83-85, 87-89
Deer, 148, 160, 161; track 166
Deer mouse, 148
Density, of ice 262; of water, 257-58, 260, 262, 267-68
Depth, and water pressure, 265-66
Dichotomous identification key, 113
Diffusion, in water molecules, 260
Dirt Cake Recipe, 60
Dirt on Decomposition, 81
Dirt, 59
Disappearing Act, 263-64
Diving beetle, 275, 276
Do Not Disturb, Exhibit, 172
Dobsonfly, 280
Dog, 160
Dogwood tree, 116

O

O horizon, 74
Oceania, 281, 282
Oil, in bread making, 17
Old Farmer's Taste Test, 64
Omasum, 46
Omnivores, 55, 153
On the Bright Side, 214
One in a Million, 295-96
Opossum, 160
Opposite branching, 115
Organic materials, 67, 71
Organisms, aquatic, stages of life 273-76; and water
    quality, 277-79
Otter, 160
Outer bark, 207, 208
Outside of a Worm, 99
Ovary, 229, 231
Owls, 171, 176
Oxygen, in air cycle 131, 132; in water, 278, 279

P

Pan, preheater, in maple sugaring, 184, 197, 203
Paper Making, 127-29
Paper Making Then & Now, 128-29
Paper Making, history, 128
Paper, use per person per year, 127
Patterns, of animal tracks, 157-61
Peanuts, 21
Pecans, 21
People Key, 113
Percolation, 271
Percolation test, 63, 66, 68
Petal, 229, 231
pH, 63,64; of snow, 138; of water, 296; and water quality, 279
Pheasant, 176
Pheromones, in insects, 239, 241-42
Phloem, 208
Phosphorus, and turbidity, 279
Photodegradable, 81
Photosynthesis, in air cycle, 131, 132; in food chain 55; in
    plants and trees, 208, 212
Phototropism, 214
Pigs, 36, 57
Pineapple, 21
Pipeline, in maple sugaring, 184, 204
Pistil 229, 231
Pitter Patter 157-60
Plant Parts We Eat, Exhibit, 18

Plant Pipes, 219-20
Plant Plumbing, 220
Plants, activities about: effect of gravity on plant
    growth, 215-16; effect of light on plant growth,
    213-14; flower anatomy, 227-28, 231-32; flowers
    and their pollinators, 233-34; root growth and
    water, 217-18; seed anatomy, 211-12; transpira-
    tion in plants, 221-22; transportation of water and
    vascular system in plants, 219-20; writing poetry
    about flowers, 225-26
Plants, exhibits about: basic needs of plants, 223-24;
    herbs, 22; plant parts we eat, 18
Plants, in air cycle, 131, 132; in food chain, 55; parts
    we eat 7, 18; and soil pH, 63, 64
Playdough Recipe, 256
Pollen, 229, 232
Pollination Parade, 233-34
Pollination Partners, 234
Pollinator Profile Cards, 236
Pollinators, 233
Pollinators and Their Flowers, 234
Pollutant Materials and Analogues, 290
Pollution Solutions, 289-91
Pollution, and turbidity 279; and water treatment
    process, 289-91
Population, of the World, 281
Porcupines, and defense, 160; tracks, 160, 161, 166;
    in winter, 148, 171
Possible Salad Ingredients, 18
Possible Soil Ingredients, 70
Posy Poetry, 225-26
Precipitation, 271
Predator-Prey, 153-154
Predators, 153
Pressure, and depth of water, 265-66; applied to air
    and water, 267-68
Pressure is On, 265-66
Presto Chango!, 264
Prey, 153
Primary consumers, 55
Prints, of animals in winter, 161, 165-67
Producers, 55
Products, from farm animals, activities, 35-36, 37-38,
    39-40, 41-42; from trees, activities, 109-10
Pseudoscorpions, 76
Psychrophiles, 88, 89
Pulp, 127

R

Rabbits, products from, 36; cottontail, 148; tracks
    160, 161, 166; in winter, 171

Raccoons, tracks, 160, 161, 166; in winter, 147, 171

Rain, *see Precipitation*

Reading the Rings, 126

Recipes, cottage cheese, 52; *Dirt Cake*, 60; flavored butter, 50; *Indian Corn Pancakes*, 12; *Magic Bread*, 17; *Milk Glue*, 42; playdough, 256

Recycled Paper Beads, 130

Recycled paper, making, 127-29; beads, 130

Recycled Water, 270

Recycling, 81

Refractometer, 194

Renewable resources, 30

Rennet, in cheese making, 52

Reptiles, 274

Respiration, in plants, 221

Reticulum, of cows, 46

Reusable, 81

Reverse osmosis, in maple sugaring, 184

Riffle beetle, 280

Rising to the Top, 251

Rivers, in the water cycle, 271

Rolags, 40

Root Hair-Do, 218

Root with a View 217-18

Roots, 7, 109; hairs, 218; products made from, 110; and relationship to water source, 217-18; in a seed, 212

Rotten Truth, 79-81

Rotting Life, 85

Rumen, of cows, 45

Run for the Sun, 55-58

Run for the Sun Cards, 58

S

Salamanders, 76

Salt water, 293

Salt, in bread, 17

Sand, 67, 71-72

Sap to Syrup Race, 193-94

Sap, 184; function in tree, 207, 208, 209; products made from, 110; rate of flow and temperature, 209; sap to syrup ratio, 193-94

Sapsuckers, 176

Sapwood, 207, 208, 209

Say Cheese Please!, 52

Scud, 280

Seasonal turnover of lakes, 262

Secchi Disk, 279

Secondary consumers, 55

Seeds, activities about: anatomy, 211-12; dispersal, 25-26; effect of gravity on growth, 215-16; effect of light on growth, 213-14; life cycle of, 23-24; shapes and sizes of, 3-4; survival and growth condition, 27-28

Seeds, coat, 212; collecting, 23; examples of, 7; germination, 27; part of tree, 109; production and survival of, 27; products made from, 110; shapes and sizes of, 5-6

Sepal, 229

Sesame, 21

Shake It! Song, 51

Sharp Eyes, 151-52

Sheep, in winter, 171; products from, 36; tracks, 160, 166; and wool production, 39-40

Sheeting, in maple sugaring, 184

Shelburne Farms Worm Rap, 92

Sherlock Holmes Track Detective Card, 170

Sherlock Holmes Tracking Formula, 169

Ship Shapes, 255

Shrews, 140, 160

Silt, 71-72

Simple Flowers to Dissect, 228

Sink or Float?, 253-54

Sinking Balls and Floating Boats, 256

Sinking Feeling, 262

Sinzibuckwud, 184, 203

Skunks, and defense, 160; tracks, 160, 161, 165; in winter, 147, 171

Slugs, 76

Slurry, 127

Small intestine, of cows, 47

Snail 275, 276

Snakes, 171

Sneaky Pete, 173-74

Snow goggles, 142

Snow Melt, 137-38

Snow Seeds, 138

Snow Vocabulary of the Inuits of the Kobuk Valley, Alaska, 142

Snow, activities about: conversion of snow to water, 137-38; insulating effects of snow, 139-40, 143-44; making paper snowflakes, 135; catching and preserving snowflakes, 133-134; words for snow in other cultures, 141-142

Snow, formation of crystals, 138; Inuit words for, 142

Snowflake Bentley, 133, 134

Snowflake Key, 136

Snowflake Snapshots, 134

Snug in the Snow, 140

Sodium, in drinking water, 295

Soil, activities about: compost, 87-89; decomposition, 79-81, 83-85, 87-89; erosion, 77-78; ingredients of soil, 59-60; physical properties of soil, 61-64; soil types, water drainage and retention, 67-69, 71-73

X

Y

Z

SHELBURNE FARMS

A Center for Environmental Education

In 1972 a nonprofit environmental education organization was established at Shelburne Farms with the hope that it would one day make a significant contribution to global environmental conservation. Since then the 1,400 acre historic Shelburne Farms property, with its productive and beautiful farmland, forests, landscape and buildings, has evolved from a private agricultural estate into a resource center for environmental education.

PROJECT SEASONS is an integral part of a larger program being developed at Shelburne Farms to cultivate a conservation ethic in students, teachers and the general public in Vermont and around the world. The mission of Shelburne Farms is to teach the stewardship of natural and agricultural resources and demonstrate rural land use that is environmentally, economically and culturally sustainable.

The goals of the Farms' visitor and education programs are:

- to increase awareness and appreciation of natural and agricultural resources and the working landscape; and
- to inspire active stewardship of our environment.

Teacher training and school programs are offered throughout the year from the J. Warren & Lois McClure Center for School Programs in the Farm Barn. All members of Shelburne Farms receive a calendar of events, newsletter and annual report.

Shelburne Farms is open daily to the public from late May through mid-October. Visitors are invited to enjoy tours of the property, walking trails, a Children's Farmyard and many special events. The Inn at Shelburne Farms welcomes guests by reservation for overnight stays, breakfast and dinner.

Please call or write for education program, membership and visitor information:

SHELBURNE FARMS
Shelburne, VT 05482
General Information: 802-985-8686
Fax: 802-985-8123

PROJECT SEASONS

Hands-on activities for discovering the wonders of the world.

 Link your curriculum to the seasons with exciting multidisciplinary activities designed for the Kindergarten through sixth grade classroom. Students discover through hands-on investigations that science is a way of thinking about the world around them. Project Seasons includes:

 • *Over 147 classroom-tested activities using low cost and easily found materials.*

• *Directions and illustrations for creating hands-on seasonal bulletin boards and learning stations to liven up your classroom.*

 • *Learning objectives, grade level, and time required are clearly outlined for each lesson.*

• *Background information and thematic bibliography.*

PROJECT SEASONS *Order Form*

Yes! I want to enrich my curriculum with **PROJECT SEASONS**.

Quantity: _____

Item: **PROJECT SEASONS**

Unit Price: $24.95

Sub Total: _____

5% Sales Tax
for VT delivery:

(or Tax exempt no.): _____

Shipping & Handling:
Book Rate:
$3.50/1st copy
$1.50/each additional copy : _____

TOTAL: _____

I am interested in learning more about programs at Shelburne Farms. Please send information about:
☐ Teacher Workshops
☐ Programs for Schools

Method of Payment: (check one)
☐ Check
☐ VISA/Mastercard/American Express
(circle one)

Acct # _____

Expiration Date: _____/_____/_____

Purchase Order #: _____

Signature: _____

Name: _____

Address: _____

City: _____

State: _____ **Zip:** _____

School Address: _____

_____

Please ship to: ☐ Home   ☐ School

Complete this form and mail to:
Shelburne Farms, Shelburne, VT 05482
(802)985-8686   FAX: 802-985-8123